A CINEMA WITHOUT WALLS

Movies and Culture After Vietnam

TIMOTHY CORRIGAN

ROUTLEDGE

LONDON

Copyright © 1991 by Timothy Corrigan
All rights reserved
Manufactured in the United States of America
Design by John Romer

First published in the United States in 1991
     by Rutgers University Press
First published in Britain in 1992
     by Routledge, 11 New Fetter Lane,
          London EC4P 4EE
ISBN 0   415   07133   X   (cloth)
       0   415   07134   8   (pbk.)

British Library Cataloguing-in-Publication Data available on request

A CINEMA WITHOUT WALLS

For Marcia, Cecilia, and Graham

CONTENTS

ACKNOWLEDGMENTS

I have been fortunate over the last several years to be able to try out early versions of these chapters on different audiences at conferences and university seminars: at the University of Texas, the University of California at Irvine, the University of Southern California, Ohio University, Rutgers University, the Columbia Seminars on Cinema and Interdisciplinary Interpretation, SUNY Binghamton, Cornell University, and the CUNY Graduate Center. Additionally, I am grateful to the editors of *Film Quarterly, Wide Angle,* and *New German Critique,* where portions of this manuscript originally appeared. The discussions and suggestions that have come out of those various encounters have been enormously helpful.

Temple University provided me with a study leave to do some of the initial research; Lindsay Davies helped me considerably in continuing that research.

Many individuals commented on parts or the whole of the manuscript in the course of its writing, sometimes working with rough drafts or only partly worked-out ideas: Jim Collins, Miriam Hansen, Dana Polan, Hilary Radner, Eric Rentschler, Maureen Turim, Larry Venuti, William Van Wert, and Alan Wilde. Beyond all the good they individually did the manuscript, discovering the generosity of other scholars in this way is always the best part of writing. In this, I wish especially to thank William Galperin not only for our debates but for our distractions.

Leslie Mitchner has been a sensational editor. She encouraged the book many years ago when it was a vague notion, and since then she has prodded and directed it all along the way. I am not certain this book would have been finished without her. I am certain that, without her assistance, it would have been a lesser book.

One of the themes of this study is the pleasure and importance of looking through or away from the daily obsessions of our contemporary private and professional lives. My constant guardians in these pleasures have been Cecilia, Graham, and Marcia. Through them I know that this book is important—but not so important. We know where the best and hardest work is done.

A CINEMA WITHOUT WALLS

INTRODUCTION
Leaving the Cinema

□□

The topic of this study is contemporary movies or, to give it strict boundaries, movies made from 1967 through 1990. More particularly, this book investigates what it has meant to watch movies during this period and how those movies have responded to the changing social and technological conditions that inform their viewings. This is then, in an important sense, a historical study.

I shall attempt to detail how the aesthetic, economic, and technological pressures behind the production and distribution of contemporary movies have massively altered how those movies are received by viewers and, *as a consequence of those new patterns of reception,* how those movies now address their audiences. I am not concerned with an exhaustive formula or a fully representative list of films. I am investigating certain trends in contemporary film culture that have dramatically realigned the relationship between movies and their audiences and which have forced the movies, for sometimes better and sometimes worse, to admit those shifting and multiple audiences as a presence that determines, in critically revised ways, the form and meaning of movies.

Since the beginning of the conglomerate take-overs of the major studios in the sixties and the sweeping arrival of video and cable technologies in the seventies, the center of movie viewing has shifted away from the screen and become dispersed in the hands of audiences with more (real and remote) control than possibly ever before. The shifting and often uncertain identities of those audiences (in age, gender, economics, and race, for instance) have, at the same time, become much more difficult for a single movie to address. The four walls of theatrical viewing, which might have once reflected the way movies were able to "capture" an audience within carefully constructed cultural parameters, are thus no longer, it seems to me, an appropriate metaphor with which to describe who watches movies, how they watch them, and how movies acknowledge this new audience. The growing budgets of movies have required audiences too large to be truly circumscribed; those audiences have increasingly dispersed themselves in terms of their social and cultural neighborhoods; and movies have had to follow those audiences from theatrical settings into homes and onto videocassette recorders and cable screens. Within this contemporary cinema without walls, the stories, styles, and structures of many commercial movies have then (logically and economically) had to discover how to address these audiences who no longer need or care to watch movies as they may once have.

The anxieties and promises that accompany this disappearance of a clear and stable viewer clearly resemble those often associated with postmodernism and its reputed subversions of the traditional human subject. Just as viewers and critics have bemoaned the loss of "good" movies and wonder (while watching) whom movies are now being made for, observers of postmodernism commonly condemn contemporary culture's seeming dehumanizing vacuities and shifting, centerless visions (through its notorious pastiche sensibilities, retro-obsessionisms, and empty simulations of simulations). Conversely, just as many other viewers marvel at the unprecedented artistic and technological splendor of the latest blockbusters or observe how VCRs and cable technologies have become household items that have made available a growing variety of films and videos (both commercial and noncommercial), champions of postmodernism have seen it in the most recent and promising overthrow of antiquated notions about authentic art and the privileges of aesthetic canons (such as those that would qualitatively distinguish the products of high culture from those of popular culture). These two opposing perspectives on movies are, to be sure, both part of an apocalyptic characterization of the times, as the cynical end of cultural value and historical coherence or the utopian liberation from the burden of those restraints. Their energetic opposition has made it sometimes difficult to agree even on what the object of inquiry is, let alone a definition of it.

Trying to resolve these disagreements about what postmodernism is may be in fact a violation of, in Linda Hutcheon's words, "the pluralist, provisional, contradictory nature of the postmodern enterprise" (183). Within the conditions of contemporary culture, there are many kinds of films that seem to have little to do with postmodernism and many other films that engage that postmodern enterprise in distinctively different fashions (their exceptional variety itself being a signal for some of a postmodern culture). I am consequently not arguing here that "postmodern movies" are the only kind of films being made within contemporary cultures or that all viewers watch movies as postmodern spectators. Nor, despite my preference for some films over others, am I making a categorical or even qualitative distinction between the movies in this study that seem more a part of the commercial mainstream (frequently aligned with the "bad" postmodernism) and those films that are more consciously self-reflexive or intellectually rigorous (the "good" products of postmodernism). It is obvious that *Raiders of the Lost Ark* (1981) follows a far different agenda from *The Third Generation* (1979); it is less obvious how artistically and culturally far apart *Blue Velvet* (1986) and *9 1/2 Weeks* (1986) are. For my purposes, these represent only different types of engagements across a postmodern culture that embraces a multitude of contemporary activities, all of these films sharing a vision of a powerfully altered contemporary audience but some of them more lucidly dramatizing the possibilities of those engagements than others. Since I am more exactly talking about the contemporary or postmodern condition through which films are watched, many different kinds of movies enter that purview, from the commercially common to the artistically adventurous.

The organization of this book follows what I consider key issues across this terrain, as these issues differentiate themselves from their classical and modernist predecessors. While the argument regularly returns to central themes about, for instance, cultural narcissism or the strained status of the patriarchal family, it follows a scheme that describes certain salient conditions in contemporary film culture, from the socio-historical and industrial to the textual, and then presents a variety of cultural and textual engagements with those conditions. The first section locates these differences in a historical shift that occurs amidst the media politics of the Vietnam war, the restructuring of the movie industry through conglomerate take-overs, the widespread effect of technologies such as the VCR, and the contemporary fascination with different kinds of nostalgia. Related to these historical shifts, the second section then argues two major changes in the relationship of audiences to movie images: one whereby movies now generate and audiences respond according to patterns of "illegibility" that foresake a traditionally common need to understand viewing a movie as a type of reading; the other whereby audiences replace the securities and authorities of reading a film with a more assertive (and sometimes reckless) disregard for essential meanings or secrets in a movie, viewers now *performing* that film as a kind of cult object that they can both appropriate and relinquish themselves to. The third section examines more specific interpretive strategies through which filmmakers and films address spectators across these altered viewing formations. Here I examine conventional categories and schemes for understanding movies, such as auteurism, genre, and narrative, but demonstrate how contemporary film culture has absorbed and redefined them in a way that changes fully what they mean and how they can be used as critical concepts today. The final section discusses the sticky problem of ideology and a politics of viewing within a contemporary scene in which audiences seem to have more control than movies themselves over how a movie will be politically and socially mobilized. The analysis of specific films in each chapter or the reappearance of certain directors is not intended to be summary or even emblematic but rather to be recognizable to most readers as resonant across the contemporary cultural scene.

This book is about watching movies from within American culture. At the same time, however, films discussed here describe an international menagerie. Without denying the continuing significance of different nationalisms in the cinema today, this merging and overlapping of cultural differences is meant to reflect the growing internationalization of national cinema cultures. Stuart Hall has suggested some of what is behind this cultural internationalism when he observed that, through the globalization of Hollywood, "the world dreams itself to be 'American'" (Bird 45–46). But by "menagerie" I also mean to delineate how watching movies in American culture today involves (or can involve), more widely than ever before, stories, movies, television serials, and filmmakers from other cultures. A condition encouraged surely by the video market, it is, more importantly, a product of an international industrial state that supports a cross-cultural dreaming in a variety of directions. Sony's recent purchase of Columbia Pictures from Coca-Cola in 1989, the Australian News Corporation's (Rupert Murdoch's) acquisition of 20th Century-Fox in 1986, Pathé Communications's (Italian Giancarlo Parretti's) buying of MGM–UA in 1990, and Matsushita's 1990–1991 takeover of MCA and Universal mean only that Hollywood has continued to enlarge and perhaps vary the international weave of its fabric and that, at least for the American audience, international complicity is a better model of the conditions informing their viewing than cultural difference.

This is not to say that the issue of national cinemas is not pertinent today. In certain cases it clearly is. As I try to indicate, the national character of many of these films—such as the broadcast of *The Singing Detective* (1986) on British television—can complicate and support the unusual way they address their audiences. For this study, though, the American viewer is an international viewer, capable, in Charles Jencks's phrase, of "ironic cosmopolitanism" (27). To treat a filmmaker such as Raoul Ruiz as fundamentally a Chilean in exile or a movie such as *My Beautiful Laundrette* (1985) as being primarily about British politics is, I believe, to diminish the complexity of their reach. To speak here of a cinema without walls refers also to the walls of cultural nationalism within an international landscape.

A cinema without walls is thus a contemporary recollection of and a departure from André Malraux's modern museum without walls. Malraux's museum describes a way of collecting art and the details of aesthetic culture not as separate and distinctive objects but as a family of photographs. In this imaginary museum, art objects are transformed into pure instances of aesthetic style, capable of being possessed and shared by a boundless group of viewers: "In our Museum Without Walls, picture, fresco, miniature and stained glass window seem of one and the same family. . . . In the process they have lost their properties as *objects;* but by the same token, they have gained something: the utmost significance as to *style* that they can possibly acquire" (44). In a cinema without walls, however, the development of that reproductive technology and its pervasive spread through culture has meant exhausting any transcendent relationships between viewers and images and allowing audiences to claim their own place and perspective as the essential authority. Since the shifting family of contemporary viewers can now literally possess images as the ubiquitous backgrounds and ornaments of their lives, those images are recast as social objects defined by the conditions and contexts in which they are viewed. Their previous homogeneous lack of particular and concrete meaning in Malraux's museum now transforms them into a heterogeneous collection of object-images. If in Malraux's museum, images removed objects from their authentic cultural place, in the contemporary cinema without walls, audiences remove images from their own authentic and authoritative place within culture and disperse their significance across the heterogeneous activity that now defines them.

The cultural collapse of those authoritative walls has therefore meant endings and beginnings, the growing impossibility of finding those old authorities and audiences for the cinema and the increasing possibility of admitting new ones. In this study, I emphasize how those endings have been reflected at the movies: how they have changed the way movies are understood and how they position audiences outside previous stabilities. But the potential beginnings toward which each chapter moves are at least as important: the endings and evacuations that these chapters describe also represent the groundwork for possible intervention by viewers outside those now-vacated dominant cultural hierarchies, viewers, for example, of genders, races, and classes who have traditionally been asked to check their differences before they enter the cinema. In her discussion of a postmodern or at least contemporary meaning for a "women's cinema," Teresa de Lauretis neatly describes these beginnings that follow from those endings: in the shift "to what may be called an aesthetic of reception, where the spectator is the film's primary concern," the most significant change "is the particular conception of the audience, which now is envisaged in its heterogeneity and otherness from the text," a "heterogeneity of the audience" that also responds to and "entails a heterogeneity of, or in, the individual spectator" (*Technologies of Gender* 141, 142).

Finally, I do not intend to disguise the problem in discussing movies whose primary definition might be to befuddle certain interpretive categories or to muddle any authoritative understanding of them. Characteristic of the uncertainties surrounding a critical position in many other fields of postmodern culture, the problem appears to cut two ways: on the one hand, many of these films (and the majority within contemporary culture) are so transparent that to examine them seems to violate them by making too much out of too little; on the other hand, many movies in this study work rigorously and expressly to attack the traditional avenues by which we might organize and make sense of them. What both the vacancies of the first and the densities of the second call attention to is, I believe, the same thing: that real difficulties and serious questions in viewing movies today lie beyond what we see on the screen. If, therefore, I have responded by making difficult some of these films (theoretically, sometimes conceptually), it is because, however transparent or impenetrable these movies may seem, their address and viewing involve them in extremely complex and difficult issues about how we can or cannot engage them. This book seeks, in short, to release these movies toward a common groping for understanding about not so much the films themselves but the contemporary cultural dynamics that inform them. If contemporary culture has begun to create a cinema without authoritative walls, the advantage may be that we can recognize what is now culturally most important: namely, how we talk long and hard to each other on the outside.

THE NOSTALGIA FOR HISTORY

GLANCING AT THE PAST
From Vietnam to VCRs

□□□

> "The best example must be the Vietnam war. . . . What sense did that war make, if not that its unfolding sealed the end of history in the culminating and decisive event of our age?"
>
> —JEAN BAUDRILLARD

> "What one loves about life are the things that fade."
>
> —PROMOTIONAL POSTER FOR *HEAVEN'S GATE* (1980)

If there is a single movie that, deservedly or not, has come to represent the crisis in contemporary film culture, it is Michael Cimino's *Heaven's Gate*. Whatever one's opinion about that film and however fair or accurate its prominent historical position may be, *Heaven's Gate* was quickly mythologized by film critics and historians as a watershed film that, much like *Breathless* and *The 400 Blows* in 1959 and *The Godfather* (1972) and *Jaws* (1975) in the early seventies, focused dramatic changes in the way movies would be made and viewed. It is certainly going too far to claim, as some have, that this specific movie single-handedly turned the movie industry on its head. Yet its complicated story before and after its release does indeed sum up and foreshadow many of the excesses, breakdowns, and readjustments that define how contemporary movies are made and viewed today and, just as importantly, how those movies have attempted to engage their own cultural history.

Intricately tied up with the take-over of United Artists by Transamerica Corporation in 1967, *Heaven's Gate* was primarily a product of the urgency, especially in Hollywood after 1970, to make blockbuster movies. Far more than traditional epic successes or the occasional predecessor in film history, these contemporary blockbuster movies became the central imperative in an industry that sought the promise of massive profit from large financial investment; the acceptable return on those investments (anywhere from $20 million to $70 million) required, most significantly, that these films would attract not just a large market but *all* markets. In a powerfully resonant transformation of United Artists's history—the studio traditionally associated with independent production and noted for its recent successes like *Last Tango in Paris* (1972)—the new conglomerate leadership at Transamerica decided that the studio should assimilate to its parent company's financial logic and, in keeping with the economic potential that spurred the take-over, urged pursuing the large audiences and profits of blockbuster production. *Heaven's Gate* would, supposedly, be a major step into the financial future of a new conglomerate studio system.

To attract that mythical universal audience, this kind of movie must always be "made" before it is actually made, either through the promise of a particular star or group of stars, rumors of spectacular new technologies, or astonishing production costs. It must always exist, first and foremost, as an advertisement of promises it usually cannot possibly keep; it must create an audience that does not in fact exist. In this particular case as in many other, Transamerica-United Artists recruited Michael Cimino as that promise, as a mixed-up contemporary version of the filmmaker as auteur-artist, part epic genius and part promotional commodity, who would be their new great communicator. Perhaps because he was, paradoxically, a relatively unknown quantity with a background, significantly, in advertising, Cimino became the conglomerate image of the blockbuster auteur: solely on the basis of the massive *potential* of his Vietnam film, *The Deer Hunter* (1978)—which many of the studio executives had not yet seen, United Artists signed Cimino to the *Heaven's Gate* deal for a $7.8 million projected cost and almost unprecedented directorial freedom. As is well known, the budget ultimately exceeded $40 million, and the film became one of the most notorious financial and critical disappointments in movie history. Just as it attempted to produce an auteur without a legitimizing history, the film seemingly appealed to no one because of its attempts to appeal to everyone (which is of course no one). As at least an indirect result, Kirk Kerkorian's MGM would, in the wake of this major financial blow to Transamerica-United Artists, purchase United Artists; this merger would in turn soon founder and the studio would wind up in the Italian-French hands of Pathé Communications. A very significant by-product of these conglomerate quick changes, moreover, would be the formation of a smaller "minimajor" studio, Orion, by a number of United Artist executives who moved out and reorganized in the wake of Transamerica's new agendas.

Whatever Cimino's purported self-indulgences, *Heaven's Gate* became as much a cultural scapegoat as anything else, the unrealistic dream-child of a corporate and financial vision and the compensatory victim of critics' and viewers' outrage at a waste and expense that affronted and overwhelmed them just as it had attracted them. Whatever its real accomplishments as a film narrative (which I think are considerable), the movie could only, in a sense, sacrifice itself to its own impossible definition of its larger-than-life audience. In this sense, the most concrete indication of its predicament—of having to obsessively avoid addressing an audience because that audience could never exist—is its infamous attempt to refuse a final cut:

> Of the 1.5 million feet of film exposed on *Heaven's Gate* (1.3 million of which were printed) and the thousands of rolls of film exposed by still photographers, not one frame, not one color transparency, not one black-and-white glossy found its way back to California or New York before shooting was completed. . . . Any attempt to see the picture *in toto* was regarded not merely as an intrusion into the creative process but as an active threat. (Bach 281–282, 348)

The wild bashings that *Heaven's Gate* provoked after its release might be seen as directed, consequently, as much at the industry that those audiences were a part of as at the stunning emptiness that the film presented. The swiftness with which some reviewers and viewers even returned to and denigrated the once critically acclaimed *Deer Hunter* while others claimed that *Heaven's Gate* was in fact a masterpiece suggests, furthermore, that the excessive disturbance which *Heaven's Gate* put into play between filmmakers and film viewers refers to much more than this particular story. Besides describing a general unease about a stable evaluation and understanding of contemporary movies in general, there was acted out here the disturbing sense that the movies have fundamentally changed and that the way contemporary audiences watch movies is in part responsible for those changes.

Even more so than the topical *Deer Hunter,* the specific history of *Heaven's Gate* is, therefore, as much about the history of contemporary viewing as it is about how the contemporary film culture views its histories. In general, the dynamics within those views and viewings indicate a decidedly contradictory blend of nostalgia for the older rituals of seeing epic movies and a refusal to fully believe in those images and unifying rituals. More specifically, the contradiction in these blockbuster epics today (a contradiction that *Heaven's Gate* seems fully cognizant of) is that to be true to their traditional historical and social scope (as well as their financial imperatives) means making their narrative and visual excesses at heart vacancies, imagining and addressing a spuriously collective audience that is actually a diverse multiplicity, and fashioning their eternal temporal myths as always transitory. While most audiences expected to gaze at overpowering images of heros conquering the land, as audiences might once have remained mesmerized before the mythic union of story and image in *Gone With the Wind* (1939), *Heaven's Gate* reflected a contemporary dissipation across images that simply do not seem to make sense anymore (spread through too many underdeveloped figures of Harvard scholars, prostitutes, and flashes of different social complexities), that seem to lack a singular narrative motivation (undermined by a hero who from the beginning is mostly passive), and that create elaborate visual spectacles which distract from rather than concentrate viewers on the barely visible story which is, likely as not, displaced by stunningly complicated dance-hall numbers and long takes of scintillating landscapes.

Heaven's Gate presents itself as a mythical story of American origins, of how capitalism and the immigrant masses clashed in the Johnson County War of the 1890s in an effort to establish their separate identities as the image of that land. But, just as *The Deer Hunter* captures the way the Vietnam War is often understood today only through the exaggerations, distortions, and incoherencies that im-

Heaven's Gate: The Historical Spectacles of Beginning and Ending (United Artists, 1980)

pede any accurate historical representation of that war, this archetypal Western fails as a ritualistic description of a mythic past because it so accurately reflects the contemporary trouble with representing *any collective history* for an audience that, at least since Vietnam, has only the most temporary sense of itself as a singular historical image among an unprecedented plethora of cultural and historical images.

Attracting an audience nostalgic for those public rituals of the cinema but with a cultural identity too fractured to invest in any totalizing ritual, *Heaven's Gate* thus provides, only too clearly, an historical spectacle that instead temporally distracts the diverse audiences it aims to gather as one. It becomes, in short, a public ritual that simply puts into play a collection of private, fragmented glances. With some justification (despite a shaky distinction between *The Deer Hunter* and *Heaven's Gate*), Vincent Canby derisively remarks: "The grandeur of vision of the Vietnam film has turned pretentious. The feeling for character has vanished and Mr. Cimino's approach to his subject is so predictable that watching the film is like a forced, four-hour walking tour of one's own living room" (Bach 363). The remark unwittingly contains, I think, that larger truth about contemporary ways of seeing perhaps more appropriate to the film, that these films are *invariably* viewings distracted in one sense or another. No matter what one may decide about its so-called textual integrity, viewers such as Robert Sklar are thus correct in one very important sense when they claim that the complete film "has been rescued by home video from the limbo of lost films" ("Homevideo" 29): it has been rescued for and restored to, I would claim, its proper contemporary conditions where it can be watched across the distractions rather than the collective gaze of its audiences. In fact, if *Heaven's Gate* has become a common allegory for contemporary Hollywood and its passion for blockbusters, it is the allegory that its own story recounts: the pervasive tale of a territorial war between contending, barely dominant, powers and an uncontrollable heterogeneity. In the end, the showdowns of this war, much like those of the Vietnam that drift through *The Deer Hunter,* do not become victories or defeats but dissipate anticlimactically like the final battle scene in *Heaven's Gate.* What remains is primarily a history of fragmentation and images of spectacular excess, codified, in that concluding sequence, in the disaffected narrator Jim Averill, as the wistfully empty reflections of distracted nostalgia.

Blockbusters, VCRs, and Viewers

Heaven's Gate and the extremity of the responses to it might be seen, to set my argument here, as symptomatic of the conditions of contemporary film culture and the particular varieties of historical nostalgia that inform it. These conditions are the product of a number of economic, industrial, and social shifts that are hardly peculiar to that one movie, describing in fact the way a majority of movies are now produced, viewed, and understood.[1] Clarifying them and their large, critical differences from previous patterns in film history permits, I think, a better assessment of the complications and significance of numerous contemporary movies. Through this history of contemporary production and viewing, moreover, that recurrent and widespread theme of postmodern nostalgia appears more various and complex (and significantly less reactionary) than is often admitted.

Like many other contemporary commercial films, the expectations and longings that *Heaven's Gate* most immediately elicits and disappoints, as a version of postmodernism's "new classicism," are those of the so-called classical cinema. According to most accounts, that extended classical period occurred from 1915 through much of the 1950s. The prescriptive formulations usually identified with it are more or less agreed upon, even when the specifics are disputed. These formulations include narrative continuities and closures, the centralization of character psychology and depth, a flexible realism, and the standardization of feature-film formats such as running time and distribution paths. The industrial and social conditions that fostered these patterns through the thirties and forties include the domination and independence of the studios, a carefully controlled distribution system (that retained much of the spirit of blockbooking, even when the letter of the law disallowed it), and social conditions that elevated the movies to being one of the central public rituals of the times.

As with other cultural and social movements in the late fifties and much of the sixties, the movies during this next period represent the ambivalent impulses and possibilities for films and their audiences. If classical movie rituals and formulas through the thirties and forties largely supplement, reflect, and support relatively stable social identities and ideologies, film audiences found this relationship basically intact but questioned in the fifties and then directly challenged by the new waves and counter-cinemas of the next generation, who used the cinema to undermine and oppose the dominant cultural myths with alternative visions even in Americanized products such as *Bonnie and Clyde* (1967). Particularly when seen against the changes that would begin to appear in the seventies and eighties, however, these challenges and subversions in classical film form and matter—which go hand-in-hand with the restructuring of the studio system in the fifties, the rise of art cinema, and an increasingly younger audience—disrupted the patterns of production and reception of classical Hollywood much less than is often claimed. Few studios had difficulty assimilating an art-cinema division; old genres adapted to new audiences; and technologies (from Cinemascope to Sensaround) mostly elaborated the basic sound and visual components of classical cinema.

The European and Asian art cinema in the sixties (which so many contemporary directors, from Cimino to David Lynch and Stephen Frears, are oddly and uncomfortably associated with) is indicative of limitations in its radical aspirations: while the films of Akira Kurosawa, Ingmar Bergman, Michelangelo Antonioni, and the early Jean-Luc Godard dramatically counterpoint a classical tradition in production methods, formal strategies, and the activities of its reception, their frequently oppositional stance regarding politics, gender, and aesthetic involve an inevitable complicity with more traditional patterns of address and reception. Most importantly, these films continue to rely on an interpretive exchange that merely complicates and redirects the sender-receiver network of the older tradition. If the movies no longer invisibly and transparently reveal the world, these modernist and "first wave" films do offer a world of images that can be humanistically and politically understood by the supposed universal viewer-subject found (appropriately) at international film festivals. The central activity of "a world viewed" has shifted to the central activity of an "alternative viewer" but each spectator shares the stability of universal centering points and counterpoints. Along these lines, David Bordwell, Kristin Thompson, and Janet Staiger make the right suggestion: the fundamental paths of viewing feature films became, though disturbed, more resilient through the fifties and sixties (369–385).

If the logic that relates the spectator of an art cinema to a classical mainstream is an oppositional one in which the constructions of one become the deconstructions of the other, the meaningful stability of that opposition begins to blur in the seventies and the eighties. The movement from a modernist to a postmodernist film industry remains, of course, part of a historical logic: the relative failure of an art cinema and avant-garde in the United States and to a lesser extent in Europe to create new institutions and audiences encourages the dispersal of that counterculture into the mainstream. The Hollywood fate of the so-called New Australian Cinema of Bruce Beresford and Peter Weir is just one recent instance. Following contemporary culture's fascination with the sixties, alternative cinemas themselves become commercially absorbed—like Jim McBride's 1983 Hollywood remake of Godard's 1959 *Breathless* or George Lucas's bankrolling of Kurosawa in order to make an Asian blockbuster, *Ran* (1985)—as a kind of historical nostalgia for active subject or countercultural positions.[2]

Rather than opposing or counterpointing the dominant social sphere, images in this third generation now literally *invade* cultural spheres both private and public through the abundance of television screens, magazines, and other visual media, making differentiations of spectator positions and films much more difficult to sustain. This is what Jean Baudrillard has termed "the *very abolition of the spectacular*" (*Simulations* 54). With the fading of these distinctions, however, there also arrives a viewer capable of forsaking entirely those previous stable and differentiated positions and of mobilizing historically that self in new and varied ways across an excess of images. Whereas once viewers may have been schematized as having a participating or an oppositional engagement, now viewers may be beyond engagement because they are nowhere and everywhere at once.

The foundation of the cultural and industrial conditions behind these changes began in the late sixties, that transition generation, when the impending birth of the contemporary blockbuster would in turn encourage the invasion of VCRs, satellite dishes, and cable networks. Up to this point, the economics of the international movie industry largely operated, in contrast to more recent formulas, according to a lucid internal logic of profitable investment: most broadly and barely, a successful movie invests efficient and stable resources such as actors, technicians, and sets to meet the desires of predictable and culturally dominant audiences—usually white, often male, adult or at least overseen by adults, and located within the expandable parameters of the middle class. During the period after 1965, however, that logic lost much of its antiquated clarity as the industry moved full force into an age of "inflation and conglomeration" (Cook 635). The most dramatic indicators of this shift are the acquisitions of major studios by multinational corporations attracted by growing movie profits: Universal by MCA (1962), Paramount by Gulf and Western (1966), United Artists by Transamerica Corporation (1967), Warner Brothers by Kinney Services (1969), and MGM by Las Vegas businessman Kirk Kerkorian (1970). These industrial realignments begun in the sixties would lay the foundations for the transformation of the movie business as it progressed through the seventies and eighties, and, while many changes would follow in their wake, the largest of all would be, as *Heaven's Gate* showed, the newly complicated relation of audiences to the screen.

The general consequences of these new production structures follow clearly from their economic attractions. Responding to the inflation of costs such as those caused by the new computer and laser technologies and better organized union labor (a star like Marlon Brando or Jack Nicholson commanding over $5 million for a film), the corporate conglomerates become simply the next necessary step in economic expansion of the studios. Within this structure, however, the movie industry becomes one of many products, albeit one with the special attraction of offering the extremely large and relatively fast turnovers that blockbuster movies like *The Godfather* or *Jaws* or *Batman* (1989) can provide. Despite failures and nods to other kinds of movies, this blockbuster vision—which at earlier stages in film history was something between the exception and the accident that *Birth of a Nation* was in 1915—would decisively guide the American movie industry through and beyond the seventies and spill over into other national cinemas where successful movies, *Gandhi* (1982) or *The Never-Ending Story* (1984), for example, are fundamentally foreign versions of the same economic story. While in the 1960s only five American movies made profits of at least $40 million, four movies would make that much in 1979 alone (*Superman, Every Which Way But Loose, Rocky II,* and *Alien*). According to this revised logic, a movie could attract audiences through the excess of its investment in capital, technology, and any other assets that carry the glow of extremity: laser technology, a sensationally priced novel bought as a script, or a star's million-dollar salary all become investments whose expanding size will be justified and recuperated by an enormous payback. Every conglomerate would pursue the *Star Wars* figures: $27 million invested in 1977 ($11 million in the shooting budget) returning well over $500 million by 1980, for a 1,855 percent profit in three years.

As those investments grow astronomically, they do much more than simply increase the size of the stakes that once were invested in classical film stars of the forties or 3D technology in the fifties. They alter the fundamental nature of the film product by forcing a massive alteration of the conception of an audience, since to return those massive investments means appealing to and aiming at not just the largest possible audience (the more modest strategy of classical films) but *all* audiences. No longer is investment capital directed at differentiating one, albeit dominant, audience from another, as, for example, investment in wide-screen technologies in the fifties hoped to distinguish movie from television audiences. Instead, those investments and technologies must aim to "undifferentiate" the desires of different audiences, usually by emphasizing the importance of that investment *in and of itself* (the presence or use of computer animation or of an expensive star) rather than what they might be able to represent (new spaces or depths, for instance). With blockbusters, what begins as an attempt to win a mass of teenagers quickly becomes an attempt to absorb as many other groups as possible within that mass, the only figure that makes sense of a conglomerate's bottom line. Contemporary movies thus necessarily begin to align themselves with advertising not only to abate their costs by advertising other people's products on the screen but because blockbuster movies can themselves only succeed as an advertisement of a product that, in appealing to everyone, cannot possibly be realized for an audience of individuals.

Not surprisingly, horror, science-fiction, and human epics become the standard forms for a strained attempt at this filmic version of television's Least Objectionable Programming: each allows for the presentation of the psychologically or technologically grandiose and sensational, while remaining within an adolescent and often regressive purview of the imaginary. As part of an economic formula, movies from *Star Wars* (1977) to *Platoon* (1986) offer narratives and pictures that are at once reduced (in moral or historical complexity, for instance) and inflated (with technological or psychological bombast) in order to offer the appearance of abundance while offending the fewest numbers in the market place.

These historical rearrangements of film culture in the seventies and eighties thus produce and reflect terms dramatically different from the classical and modernist precedents for the circulation of films and their meanings. Those older systems of cultural and cinematic representations necessarily reflected and communicated the logic and values of the economic system that produced them, the proliferation of genre films reflecting, for instance, the assembly-

Blockbuster Images Gathering an Empty Mass (*Close Encounters of the Third Kind*, Columbia, 1977. Museum of Modern Art/Film Stills Archive)

line methods of the studio system and the dependable response of a clearly demarcated audience. More recent stages in the movie industry, however, have been unable or unwilling to maintain those productive stabilities, primarily *as a result of* far more incoherent relations with their audiences. Since the mid-seventies, the international film industry has been defined by more economic and productive contention and alteration than coherence. (In 1984, as one small example, three of the seven major studios changed their top management). This, I would argue, follows clearly from the uncertainty and instability about the reception of a product that has too many audiences or too vague an audience: an audience that can only be designated, in the jargon of Hollywood producers today, as "fly-overs," a mass of undifferentiated desires that lives below planes moving between Los Angeles and New York City. In an important sense, that audience and the blurry conception of it will invariably produce contemporary films such as *Ishtar* (1987). Like *Heaven's Gate*, its financial voices (Elaine May, Warren Beatty, Dustin Hoffman) seem largely about the hysteria of production for an audience fragmented beyond any controllable identity.

As a powerful revision of Baudrillards' "mirror of production" model, the fluidity and unpredictability of the international market has made, it would seem, the structures of production less and less determinant, and so force films increasingly to anticipate the volatility of their reception as a textual determinant. With contemporary movies, the fractured mirror of reception has become the more accurate model for textual meaning, as it reflects a viewer who is, singularly or as part of a group, spread in too many geographical and cultural directions and so emptied of any certain subjectivity or clearly identified image of self. Here the uncertain and fragmented audience that blockbuster productions pursue later materializes in the random and fragmented reception of these movies as they are glanced at by the heterogeneous audiences of VCR technology and through ancillary markets such as cable. Not coincidentally, admitting the power of this audience occurs because, as with *Heaven's Gate,* granting viewers this power is often the only chance to balance the astronomical costs of blockbuster production.

The deleterious effects of this conglomerate and blockbuster perspective have all too often been remarked upon. Linking this perspective to the postmodern "high-concept film" as an offshoot of the blockbuster, for example, Justin Wyatt and R. L. Rutsky describe this type of movie—such as *Top Gun* (1986) and *9 1/2 Weeks*—as "one that relies less on a well-developed story and characters than on a big name star, a commercial musical score, and high visual impact." "Shareability" is a way of describing the ability of a high-concept film to recuperate large budgets in advance by being marketable to the audiences of both television and theaters. This accounts, I would add, for the common, easy mobility of actors and directors between television and film (usually bringing television styles with them). High-concept movies, from *Saturday*

Night Fever (1978) to *Rambo III* (1988), become advertisements that can be abstracted to singular, easily assimilable images and re-generated through multiple viewings and the ancillary sales of various tie-ins (records, tee-shirts, and other paraphernalia). "In a postmodern world," this position contends, "high concept is the 'rational' conclusion of those processes of capitalism which tend toward the abstraction and fetishization of the image, and to the increasingly rapid movements of fashion and style" (42). More recently, Mark Crispin Miller has deplored the same tendency as it follows the strategies and pressures of advertising to create de-humanized cartoon-like narratives: "This general drift toward ad technique drastically reduced the movies' narrative potential, for cinematic narrative works through a range of visual conventions or devices, and the recent rise of ad technique has all but wiped out that earlier diversity, coarsening a various and nuanced form into a pounding hypnotic instrument—a mere *stimulus,* and an ugly one at that" (50). Yet, however and wherever one may agree with these assessments of the by-products of the new Hollywood, it should be noted that these complaints are themselves motivated by another variety of nostalgia—this one for humanistic representations and, more importantly, for a filmic and narrative image as the place where meaning is made for the viewer. Even with blockbusters and high-concept films, I would argue in contrast, an undefined and un-regulated audience can be "stimulated" with many different effects.

Indeed, directly related to the impossibly large and undefined audience of the conglomerate blockbuster are the movies produced by the semi-independent companies or minimajors such as Orion and Tri-Star. If the conglomerate blockbuster admitted an audience too large to be defined and actually addressed, these smaller production houses redefined that audience as a plurality of special interests, a proliferation of positions rather than an opposition. An immediate consequence of the corporate studio system that alienated and often cut loose former studio executives (such as Arthur Krim's departure from United Artist to form Orion), these groups represent smaller enterprises than both those systems and, in many cases, the studios that existed prior to the take-overs. Many of these satellites are re-fashioned production houses, "minimajors" that, because of more circumscribed ambitions, have been more able and willing to take risks than the majors (significantly in Tri-Star's case because of a financial arrangement with the HBO cable network). Others such as Robert Redford's Sundance Institute, whose successes include the *Milagro Beanfield Wars* (1988), Vestron Pictures with *Dirty Dancing* (1987), Mirimax Films with *sex, lies, and videotape* (1989), or Avenue Pictures with *Drugstore Cowboy* (1989) have positioned themselves as alternatives to the blockbuster mentality, semi-independent or independent houses offering purportedly more serious, "specialized" films. Often, these companies produce films for well under the average price of a usual studio production (under a $10 million average as opposed to the Hollywood average of nearly $20 million), raise their funds by putting together packages around a variety of investors, and then make deals to have the studios distribute the finished projects.

Where these satellite organizations and minimajors have had the greatest impact is, ideally, in distribution and marketing strategies that have identified and made visible at the box office those multiple audiences who remain the vague specters the blockbusters aim to attract. During the last two decades, a number of distinct small companies, such as Goldwyn, Island Pictures, Skouras Pictures, and Cinecom, have made and distributed specialty films that address their audience's economical and critical presence precisely as a diversity with diverse interests. Films such as *Kiss of the Spider Woman* (nominated for an Oscar as Best Picture in 1985) and *My Life as a Dog* (also nominated for an Oscar in 1986), as well as more offbeat movies like *Choose Me* (1984) and *Stop Making Sense* (1984), have gained more than their share of praise and money (since their production costs are comparatively small) to make the powerfully absent audiences imagined for the blockbusters an actively present one. In fact, after independent or foreign films creatively package their production costs from, for example, television networks or private investors, even the major studios have found it useful to resurrect or create some version of their worn-out classics divisions in order to distribute these films. Truffaut's *The Last Metro* (1980), Rainer Werner Fassbinder's *Lili Marlene* (1980), and Andrzej Wajda's *Man of Iron* (1981) have been some of the more notable beneficiaries of the majors's renewed commitment to the foreign fringe, while *Repo Man* (1984) and *Stranger Than Paradise* (1984) are part of the new wave of the successful distribution of independent productions. In both cases, a more flexible and varied distribution network has responded to contemporary audiences, who now have the need and power to pick and choose among the glut of images in contemporary television and film culture. Within this climate and under these conditions, the different, the more peculiar, the controversial enter the marketplace not as an opposition but as a revision and invasion of an audience market defined as too large and diverse by the dominant blockbusters.[3]

Paralleling these two trends in contemporary movie production, the movie technology behind these pseudo-wars, invasions, and corporate defections has likewise supported audience positions that dissipate and disperse rather than divide audiences. On the one hand, the magic of new technologies, which promote large-scale productions such as *Star Wars* or *Total Recall* (1990), has always been a marker of movie history's ability to change without changing, to say the same thing differently. What laser models and computer graphics offer fits the tried pattern of technological evolution in film history: like the technicolor or widescreen processes, the revolution of recent technological attractions responds fairly predictably to conservative patterns of standardization and differentiation. Even recent practical advancements in film stocks such as Eastman's 5247/7247, ADR sound technologies, and camera movement technologies like Steadicam and Camrail have mostly expanded the field of what can be filmed and how it can be filmed, but rarely attempt to change how films are seen. At most, the production technology of contemporary movies has worked to abstract instead of naturalize itself in the traditional manner. As Wyatt and Rutsky note, the high tech of commercials and music videos—the abstraction of decor, iconography, and other stylized techniques usurping both character and story—follows high concept simply "as a kind of fetishization of technique" (46).

The far more crucial direction in film and video technology—without doubt one of the most significant changes in film history—is the one offered by the reception mechanisms of the VCR and other viewer-oriented distribution technologies such as satellite dishes and cable (the interactive technologies of the near future being the logical extension of this trend). These, I believe, have changed the nature and structure of film audiences as few other technologies have even approximated, reshuffling both classical and modernist positions for viewing films, creating viewer-movie relations as impulsive and contingent as contemporary production processes. By 1990, there were at least sixty million VCRs showing movies in the United States; approximately ten million new units were being sold each year; and more than forty percent of homes now have VCRs. According to *Variety,* there are over twenty thousand video-rental stores, which are rapidly expanding the more than twenty-five thousand "theatrical/entertainment" titles already available. As it continues to permeate all cultures (from the First to the Third Worlds), this spectator-oriented technology, from home-video machines to TV cable distribution, becomes the counterpart and the complement of the theatrical showcasing that serves mainly blockbusters. In fact, it develops as the linchpin that unites the two main trends of corporate and semi-independent production, as well as the many films that might straddle the ground between blockbusters and specialty film. Both small and large movies now figure on the advances or expectations from video sales and rentals; the lag time between a commercial theatrical release and its video reappearance decreases every year, with some movies recently attempting simultaneous releases; and the ability of a movie, even the most marginal, to find an audience or audiences—however large or small, discriminating or not—becomes a demographic and bankable likelihood. "Shareability" becomes a technological and economic imperative, as well as a textual, production, and financial strategy for addressing audiences now outside the walls of cinema and outside its more institutionally regulated viewing situations.

This conflux of inflated corporate economics, the multiplication of "small," specialty movies to complement blockbusters, and the development of the VCR and other viewer technologies thus support two sharply distinctive but culturally bound patterns for seeing and receiving movies: the fragmented domestic performance and the public outing. The first relates clearly to the institution and psychology of television and VCR viewing whereby one watches a movie, in Cocteau's words, "out of the corners of the eyes," whereby watching movies become a combination of, in current jargon, visual "grazing" and domestic "cocooning." When any movie is watched as a television show, that is, the domestic setting of the experience may create a kind of immediacy and complicity between the television image and the viewer, but that imagistic immediacy is very significantly redefined across the fragmentation that is either built into the television text (such as commercial interruptions and the cuttings or reductions of the image) or simply intrude upon and invade it as part of the distractions of a domestic environment (conversations or the ringing of a phone). The television spectator, according to John Ellis, "glances rather than gazes at the screen; attention is sporadic rather than sustained" (24).

When that movie is viewed through a VCR, it is even more so a *selected* experience and subject to the choices and decisions of the spectator—to stop it, to replay parts of it, to speed through sections of it. With the viewing of a VCR film, in short, the spectator gains an unprecedented power to appropriate a movie text that the viewer can then relinquish him- or herself to. Remote control literally or figuratively in hand, this audience positions and performs that movie at least as much as the movie might position and perform its audience. Viewers watch and control its images more extremely than ever before as the narcissistic subject of their own active desires, distractions, and domestic conditions; simultaneously, they are re-

The Multiple and Fragmented Address of the Television Movie (*Network*, United Artists, 1976)

flected in that experience as always *potentially* a discontinuous or fragmented subjectivity without a centered or stable position, a discursively mobile identity. Within a domestic space where family groupings can at least be nostalgically simulated, the new desiring machine of the VCR and the remote-control networking of cable allow the viewer the pleasure of dispersing, rather than fixing, subjectivity through a plethora of image-fragments. Complementing and counterpointing the mass audience of the blockbuster (those faceless figures seemingly without any subjectivity), these viewers become, in Jim Collins's words, the dramatization of multiple identities:

> The complexity of this situation necessitates a notion of the television subject that is likewise both decentered and recentered, neither completely absorbed by all programming, nor entirely detached from all of it, a subject that is a construct acted upon by a number of discursive formations, but who also *acts* in making distinctions within the glut of those formations. The activity of the subject in media-sophisticated cultures is not that of an existential subject whose ability to act is founded upon idealist notions of freedom and being, but a media-glutted subject whose ability to act and distinguish is founded on a profound cynicism that results from being hailed perpetually, by being offered 'you' identities that cannot possibly correlate. ("Watching Ourselves" 265)

What I am calling a public outing, that second direction in contemporary viewing, at first seems to line up with the more traditional ritual of moviegoing, except for its crucial connection to contemporary blockbuster production and to domestic viewing through VCRs. Following this path, viewers do not "go out to the movies," as, one could argue, audiences did in the thirties and forties when the cinema as an institution was a primary social ritual. Nor do audiences primarily go out "to see *a* movie," as many did in the sixties and early seventies in pursuit of the singular film experience. Rather, today's audiences, whose numbers have remained fairly steady and whose age has gone up slowly but steadily since the early eighties (so that there is now a contending audience over twenty-five), frequently "go out" for the sake of the outing.[4] Theatrical movies are

Movies: Rituals as Distraction (author's collection)

now in many ways simply a forum and a backdrop for that departure from domestic space: "People do not go to the cinema, on the whole, because the film has pulled them out of their homes; they go because they want to go out and the film has enough clout to channel this leisure demand in its direction" (Docherty, Morrison, and Tracy 82). Blockbuster films anticipate and respond smoothly to this cultural swerve since, following their own economic imperatives, they often offer an unimaginable audience a minimal amount of textual engagement: they usually either provide an audience with familiar or inoffensive material or with momentary shocks and instant stimulations that rarely interfere with the primary occasion of being "out"—blockbuster sequels from *Star Trek* (1979) to *Die Harder* (1990) being the common combination of the inoffensively banal and instantly stimulating.

The fact that during the last five years (in the United States at least) there has been a recent expansion, rather than the predicted shrinkage of showcase cinemas, is therefore culturally unsurprising. The National Association of Theater Owners reports that theaters have added almost 6,000 movie screens since 1981 (an increase of over 30 percent); United Artists Theaters, which runs 2,700 screens in 650 theaters, is expanding by an average of 230 screens a year; despite the massive competition of VCRs, the number of showcase cinema tickets sold in the United States has remained virtually unchanged since 1981. What has changed, however, is that, as recent research has argued about British cinema, "The *irregular* audience is becoming an increasingly important category for the industry" (Docherty, Morrison, and Tracey 83, my emphasis). Since the total number and variety of movies produced and distributed in showcase cinemas has decidedly decreased over the last several decades, this strongly suggests that the majority of movies shown in theaters are no longer addressing that audience as part of a shared public ritual but that these "irregular" audiences are simply using these movies as a backdrop for their own social activities.

As an "outing" this more public pattern is both a reaction to the claustrophobia and ultimate control of the home viewing experience and a clear parallel with it. Whether these public screens are being scaled down to the multiplex format or are part of a more recent trend to create a new large-screen movie palace, movie technology and viewing reproduces a version of the *glance aesthetics* acted out at home:

> A decade ago, a film-maker could use the edges of the frame as part of compositional graphics—to lead the eye, to counterbalance other visual elements. But now cable and video distribution are the financial heart of the media storytelling business, so film-makers have to keep essential information away from the edges of the screen, and

have to forget about using the graphic potentials of 2.3:1, 1.85:1 or 1.65:1 frame formats. All films must be composed of what the Europeans call "amphibious" life, for viewability on both on theater and television screens. Without control of the shape or edge of the frames, visual control must be done kinetically—especially since TV screens do not carry enough visual information for long-held static shots to retain viewer attention. Glance Esthetics, our contemporary period-style, has almost completely replaced Gaze Esthetics, in which the film-maker left time for the viewer to contemplate the mise-en-scène. (Eidsvik 26)

While the emphasis here is on the technological, I am drawing as much attention to how social and cultural pressures have generated ways of watching theatrical movies as distracting outings.[5] If the first tends to describe a universal, textual spectator, the second seeks to emphasize that these audiences are defined primarily by the various social activities from which they are momentarily distracted. The necessary combination of the two locates my contemporary viewer of the movies.

Surrounded by the fragmented images of a domestic space or before the spectacular backgrounds of public outings, contemporary audiences thus view movies and their histories on the visual fringes of their public or domestic experiences, disengaged from any unilateral bond through which those movies and those experiences might once have reflected each other. Watching movies across the distractions of home viewing or the glances of public outings, the contemporary viewer thus activates an image of self and subjectivity that is fractured and emptied through the possibility of multiple other viewing and social positions. As the vast number of movie-video rentals and the relatively stable box-office revenues indicate, however, movies remain, within these new conditions, more significant than ever: they continue to elicit both general and specific desires and nostalgia for relationships with images that they nonetheless can never provide. At home and in the theater outside traditional cinematic walls, the movies become the necessary attraction for a fragmented glance through which spectators concurrently vacate and reform a continually mobile identity, remembering and forget-

THE HENLEY COLLEGE LIBRARY

ting themselves in a multitude of images and places, just as they easily remember the pleasures and forget the disappointments of the movies they have just seen.

Back to Vietnam: The Songs of War

The allegory of *Heaven's Gate* expands further to reflect not only the complications in the contemporary film industry but how those complications are entwined with a two-fold nostalgia. As a film financially and culturally built on and out of *The Deer Hunter, Heaven's Gate* puts into play the crisis of historical representation and the longing for an historical subjectivity that, in less extreme terms, informs that first major epic about the Vietnam War. As an odd historical account of the Johnson County Wars, *Heaven's Gate* is also about the 1890s when both the American social structure and its film industry were in the process of forming themselves. While the first point suggests that the excesses and difficulties found in the address of *Heaven's Gate* may be those that trouble those earlier (and later) nostalgic representations of Vietnam (as it either directly or indirectly appears in a movie), the second point displaces those troubles, not coincidentally, to the turn of the century, that historical origin when movie spectators could, mythically, inhabit an imaginary world of unregulated ways of seeing.[6] These two fascinations with things past certainly parallel and reflect each other in the same way that *The Deer Hunter* mirrors *Heaven's Gate:* they both dramatize a longing for the possibility of active and unrestricted selves and social relations at different mythical turning points in history, the first the primarily social one of the 1960s and the second the primarily cinematic one of the 1890s. Across this double nostalgia, therefore, spectators may indeed "appropriate" cultural histories such as Vietnam (as critics of postmodernism so often point out). Yet the narcissism of these nostalgic appropriations frequently dramatizes another, equally important, action, one in which that nostalgia historically mobilizes the viewer within the crisis of subjectivity itself.

There are of course many kinds of nostalgia. Of these, one of the most obvious and commonly noted in recent movie and television history has been the fascination with and the nostalgia for various historical periods and decades, differentiated as generations. Versions of this nostalgia have taken many forms, from naively embrac-

Nostalgias for the Future: The Play of Generations (*Back to the Future*, Universal, 1985. Manayunk Pictures)

ing it the way *American Graffiti* (1973) does to virulently confronting
its historical implications as *Nashville* (1975) does; its material has
been a mélange of images, figures, and sounds taken primarily (but
not exclusively) from the forties, fifties, or sixties. Indeed, for many
viewers and critics, this kind of nostalgia has described and encouraged much of what troubles and confuses contemporary culture. As
part of a "blockage of history," its back-to-the-future trajectory becomes identified, as Fredric Jameson argues, with the blur of a postmodern perspective, a sort of advertisement that serves to distract us
from some supposedly more legitimate sense of history:

> Nostalgia gives us the image of various generations of
> the past as fashion-plate images that entertain no deter-
> minable ideological relationship to other moments of
> time: they are not the outcome of anything, nor are they
> the antecedents of our present; they are simply im-
> ages. . . . The increasing number of films about the past
> are no longer historical; they are images, simulacra, and
> pastiches of the past. They are effectively a way of satis-
> fying a craving for historicity, using a product that sub-
> stitutes for and blocks it ("On Magic Realism" 318).

It is possible, in fact, to further refine the place and nostalgic appeal of different periods and generations for the contemporary film
viewer. With more specific distinctions, the fifties often appear as a
lost utopia whose innocence and coherence—*Back to the Future*
(1985)—are all the more meaningful (and exaggerated) because of
their implicit or explicit contrast with World War II, the threat of
nuclear annihilation, and the horrific collapse of traditional human-
ism in images of apocalypse—*Back to the Future II* (1989). The
sixties then become the generational turning point where that historical home shatters along various fronts and individuals find themselves on the outside resisting or, later, disillusioned—*Born on the
Fourth of July* (1989). One way of describing this generational evolution might be from the romance of a public sphere centered on the
family through the oppositional splinterings from that sphere in
the sixties to its more recent dissipations into the multiple private
spheres of the disillusioned "me-generation."

Within this historical scheme, the sixties thus appear to have a richly paradoxical significance: they become the middle of three generations following World War II, located at the end of one era (often associated with "modernism") and at the beginning of the next (frequently discussed as "postmodernism").[7] If that modernist period, even as it struggled through the fifties, promoted the power of the individual within the increasing trouble with the traditional patriarchal structures such as the family, the postmodern celebrates the end of any stability in either the family or the individual. Between the two, the sixties come to represent the radical possibilities for rejecting past definitions of self and new ways of conceiving subjectivity in society, utopian potentials that could and would develop into versions of self-centered emptiness and aggression: the sixties could map, in short, the path of Francis Coppola's Kurtz, François Truffaut's Antoine Doinel, Ingmar Bergman's Elisabeth, and a variety of other filmic heros and antiheroes who live through the sixties into the seventies.

The main public event that marks the climactic point (especially for America and Hollywood) for those utopian aspirations and the disturbing vacancies they are built on is the Vietnam War. During this extended period, sons and daughters broke off from families, fabricated that separation as the dramatic difference of generations, attempted to envision themselves through the unlimited potential of radical and undefined subjectivities and communities, and then, after the war and in the wake of Watergate, settled frequently into the cynicism of social narcissism. Quite logically, therefore, that war and the international events that surrounded it (such as the Paris demonstrations in May of 1968) become, for filmmakers from Jean-Luc Godard to Cimino, the central and short-lived image of the collapse of the family history and its related ideologies and the opening of real potential for new and various subjectivities and social communities.

The continual contemporary return to those images of the Vietnam War and the generation of the sixties describes, consequently, not just the need, as some critics such as Jameson would have it, of viewers to appropriate and empty the meaning of a lost generation. Demonstrated especially in the timing of Hollywood's delayed response to that war, that nostalgia also involves the desire for something lost: it acts out the ability of those viewers to relinquish themselves to potentials and crisis within subjectivity; it is the forgetting as well as the remembering that might release viewers from the binds of contemporary narcissism. In terms of the seemingly troubled positions of postmodernism, this is a nostalgia for an image of a self regressively emptied of traditional symbolic and social definitions (such as the patriarchal family or conventional gender relationships) and thus a self opened to other relationships between history and subjectivity, relationships according to which the individual might be at least *imagined* as an agent of history.

More specific to movie culture, the second movement within contemporary nostalgia reflects the first as the memory of a fully mobile viewing position unburdened of a cinematic history. With this second narrative of nostalgia, the memory acted out is more exactly that of the pre-classical viewer found in film culture somewhere before 1915 when the dynamics of watching movies were still being formulated and when spectators seemed to have unusually undefined and often unusually active relationships with the plethora of images that were beginning to fill their screens. Like the drama of *Cinema Paradiso* (1989), this, too, is a regression fantasy whereby contemporary film culture manages to both exceed and precede its own historical conditions. Yet, as with a return to the sixties, this is also an empowering fantasy of a relationship in which a mobile and fragmented subjectivity might merely glance at images that no longer have the power to fix that viewer, a fantasy urged and bolstered by those specific social, industrial, and technological conditions of contemporary viewing as a distraction played out around the activity of the viewer. As with the vexed response to *Heaven's Gate,* the distractions of the blockbuster and the VCR now might offer viewers, for better or worse, that primary social place of a pre-classical spectator where identity seems defined mainly as potential.

The debates about this pre-classical audience are still themselves unsettled; yet, recent clarifications introduced by these investigations suggest a multitude of contending discourses that anticipate the spectatorial positions formed within the very different conditions of postmodernism. One of these social structures concerns the "democratization" of class positions, according to which movie audiences, which originally came from immigrant and working classes, quickly expanded to include middle and upper classes, women as well as men, and, to a certain extent, racial minorities. This democratization refers, moreover, not only to the fact that people from all social groups go to the movies but to the fact that the institutions and social structures for viewing films remained, for a time, outside of set cultural and ideological norms. The cultural variety of these early audiences has its institutional counterparts, in other words, in nickelodeons and sidewalk theaters, in which the viewing of movie shorts and fragments that rarely look like codified narratives became part of a casual and fluid social landscape. In Russell Merritt's account of these early films and their audiences, "Those who saw them did not learn much; it was rather the act of going to the movies that mattered most" (65). Before 1915, movies may also have been more glanced at than gazed at (Hansen *Babel and Babylon;* Chanan *The Dream;* Mayne *Private Novels,* 68–94).

Largely dependent on those contemporary social and technological conditions I have sketched, this other nostalgic trajectory allows the contemporary or postmodern place as "after history" to find its heritage in a place "before history." Just as the conflicts and excesses of the sixties, all so easily absorbed into an overabundance of media images, seem to mark the end of a modern history, a preclassical parallel seems to offer the contemporary perspective a similar freedom within an unsettled heterogeneity that resists the fixities of historical position. This brand of nostalgia within contemporary film—its institutions and technology—imagines a position that is vacated of subjectivity and is thus truly without bounds; it is a longing of the present (as a future) for another time before historical definition, when a narcissistic wonder seems, in all its emptiness, nonetheless to have the power to re-invent history and historical formations outside the dominant ones (including those of gender, class, and so forth) that have since been put in place.

Following this logic, equally significant social and aesthetic precursors for contemporary movie spectators are the nineteenth-century music halls and the opera. As far more culturally "open" institutions, which gathered a social variety of spectators and participants, music halls represent a kind of fragmented collectivity that muddled official history while it was making it: what Michael Chanan calls a Bakhtinian heteroglossia performed as diverse spectacles. At the other end of the class structure, the operatic describes grand spectacles against which human subjectivity (most often female) must stretch, exceed, and usually destroy itself as a consequence of expressing that subjectivity (Clément, Tambling). An odd cultural and historical pairing, the conjunction and overlapping of these two musical traditions is appropriately forefronted in the visual spectacles and music of *Heaven's Gate* (the title itself referring to an operatic dance hall in the story) to mark the mobility of class differences on this newly opened ground and a kind of grand collapse of the traditional human subject under the weight of history's spectacle.

It is thus fully in keeping with historical returns of contemporary movies that the complement of its music-hall, popular tunes from the sixties, are the operatic arias and scores that have dominated so many films of the last twenty years. From the films of Syberberg, Schroeter, and Losey to *Prizzi's Honor* (1985), *Amadeus* (1984), *Dangerous Liaisons* (1989), the anthology-film *Aria* (1988), and the sudden rush of contemporary versions of *Carmen* (by Carlos Saura in 1983, Francesco Rosi in 1984, and Godard in 1983), the operatic has become the other song of postmodern history. This operatic structure is not, however, the ironic counterpoint to the popular generational songs that might seem to dominate contemporary history, but the full extension of what it means to see history through the generational logic of the popular. In the collapse of history, setting the high-cultural spectacles of operatic crisis (the narcissistic plight of the diva) next to the music halls of contemporary pop (the romance of democratic utopias) aligns and blurs those two strains of pre-classical culture to describe and inscribe a human subjectivity collapsing and dispersing before the narratives of history.[8] When Colonel Kilroy of *Apocalypse Now* (1979) leads his cavalry in a ferocious attack on a Vietnamese village (the horse cavalry from *Heaven's Gate* now in the form of helicopters), a Wagnerian opera replaces the sixties pop tunes that precede and follow it and blares from speakers outside the helicopters, since these soldiers as spectators absolutely need to transcend that historical moment in order to live in it. For them, as for Jean-François Lyotard's postmodern, "it is necessary to admit an irreducible need for history . . . not as the need to remember or to project . . . but on the contrary as a need to forget" (28).

Not coincidentally then, cinematic engagements with that historical watershed event of Vietnam often aspire to the condition of nostalgic songs (from the sixties) and operatic spectacles as the very struc-

Vietnam: Operatic Spectacles and Rock and Roll (*Apocalypse Now,* United Artists, 1979. Tokyo Stills)

turing principle of their representations.[9] Of the many television and filmic examples from *The Deer Hunter* through *Born on the Fourth of July,* two in particular, Oliver Stone's *Platoon* and Stanley Kubrick's *Full Metal Jacket* (1987), serve as good examples of this troubled spectatorial confrontation with the historical moment of the sixties and, in their different relations to that common ground, suggest how those nostalgic trajectories can both narcissistically distort modern history and release, either regressively or progressively, the human subject from its strictures. In varying degrees of self-consciousness, each involves an acute awareness of its attempt to describe historical fissure and loss.

In their forefronting of the problem of telling that story each is more significantly about the melancholic impossibility of coming home to a place in history—or, better put, the impossibility of contemporary subjectivity coming home to a stable history of itself. The narrative voice-over of *Platoon* and the more elaborate structural and imagistic self-consciousness of *Full Metal Jacket* indicate that the overriding subject here is the recuperation of a historical crisis that does not so much resist its packaging but grotesquely reflects and disperses that consciousness across its operatic spectacles and popular tunes. In *Platoon,* the soundtracks of Jefferson Airplane's "White Rabbit," Merle Haggard's "Okie from Muskogee," and Smokey Robinson's "Tracks of My Tears" describe stereotyped social groupings as the sequence cuts from the redneck soldiers who have retreated into cards and alcohol to the more desirable mixture of black and white soldiers who have retreated into a womb-like bunker filled with pot smoke, drugged dancing, and trans-sexual camaraderie. Both visual and audial groupings and the crosscutting between them provide a distracted moment of hazy social and generational identification, for the characters and the audience, with a social and racial heterogeneity. In *Full Metal Jacket,* the stuttering lyrics of the Trashmen's "Surfin-Bird" follow the shuffling dance of a camera crew across the front of the image as the journalists begin their fragmented interviews. As part of a more critical and cynical operation, this last, exemplary song is tellingly nonsensical and identified with vacant images of lost boys; the community regained here is only the community of camera shots whose journalistic truth is reduced to cinematic cliché ("Hey, start the camera; this is Vietnam, the movie").

With equally ambiguous and contradictory ideological positions, both movies concentrate on the events of the war from a soldier's point of view; as mediations for their audience, they are each nostalgic and appropriative (self-consciously and narcissistically so in the persons of their narrators). They differ ultimately, I believe, in their faith or cynicism about that crisis of subjectivity they are describing, their views as to whether that crisis can or should be overcome, and their understandings of that crisis as disturbingly complicitous with a contemporary attempt to retrieve it nostalgically. While *Pla-*

Platoon: The Plenitude of Anonymity in Contemporary History (Orion Pictures, 1986. Museum of Modern Art/Film Stills Archive)

toon depicts the human subject as salvageable in all its traditional, humanistic coherence, *Full Metal Jacket* absolutely empties that subject as he marches into the past.

Platoon clings to a subjectivity that survives historical shattering by transcending history, participating in this sense only in "the anti-referentiality of post-modernism" (Clark 5). Its much-acclaimed realism is the auratic realism of an overabundance of character close-ups: the dominance of expressive faces are able to absorb the wide-shot complications of political and social history by filling the frame with overdetermined moral and humanistic dilemmas, personal emotions and fears that transcend any historical instance. Imagistically, *Platoon* takes place in the smoke and fog of a landscape so claustrophobic with jungle that no narrative context can be seen beyond the thick trees. "It's all a blur," the narrator Chris remarks.

Platoon is an initiation story about an operatic subject wanting to vanish in a religious spectacle, about a boy who "just wanted to be anonymous" while performing in a passion play in which he is "born of those two fathers" (the good, Christ sergeant and the bad, Cain sergeant). Its voice-over address is a series of letters to a grandmother, a generation as much separated in the past as the movie's original audience is separated in the future: this religious melodrama makes historical complexities (from the spring of 1968) into the transcending history of generational differences separating grandmothers and future children ("to fight like dad in World War II and grandpa in World War I"). The last words of the persistently befuddled narrator then offer the audience a vague plentitude of future hopes as beautifully hazy as the jungle fog or the drugged atmosphere of their pot den (where a gun barrel becomes a bong): "I think now, looking back, we didn't fight the enemy; we fought ourselves and the enemy was in us. . . . But be that as it may, those of us who did make it have an obligation to build again, to try with what's left of our lives to find a goodness and meaning to this life." History is reduced to a subjectivity attempting to internalize and subsume the excesses and contradictions of history within its imaginary relation to it. The resulting blur, deferring the past to the future, borders on nonsense. *Platoon* is, I believe, a most powerful and appropriately unaware acknowledgement that "something once happened" in history but that the only relation to it is to map the empty agony of expression but without the truly ethical point of view found in distinguishing images of history. It is entirely in keeping with its address that Lee Iacocca, standing next to a jeep, introduces the videotape version by honoring the spirit of all Americans who have gone to war. The logo of "Eagle-Jeep" then confirms that this is an advertisement, like the movie, for a consumer packaging of history as the vehicle of one's dreams.

Full Metal Jacket, too, describes the Vietnam War as a narcissistic packaging of history through the presiding voice-over of the *Stars and Stripes* reporter Joker. This narrative voice (and the perspective it locates), however, becomes the increasingly detached quips and one-liners of a media man who begins as a stand-up comic mimicking manly John Wayne and ends up in the boy's club of soldiers marching through the night singing "Mickey Mouse." Indeed, screened through the devolution of Joker, the war and its representation become fundamentally about a regressive male sexuality aimed at eliminating all cultural and sexual differences that stand outside that drive, at eliminating, in short, the human subject as anything but narcissistic desire. In part 1, Leonard is transformed into Private Pyle, a television character, just as Jack Nicholson was transformed into Johnny Carson in *The Shining* (1980). Leonard has, through this transformation, become the mechanistic force that destroys anything in his way, even the history of himself. In part 2, the media presence of Joker and *Stars and Stripes* are the distorting gloss that works to make the slaughter of the Tet Offensive into a victory, to make that essential presence of an enemy as an opposition vanish. A colonel remarks that "inside every gook is an American trying to get out," and as Joker's photographer snaps pictures, an American soldier pats his dead Vietcong "bro," already reminiscing about this Titanic beginning of history, about "these great days" when "we're jolly green giants." By the conclusion, the narrative-media eyes of Joker no longer witness the military action but, like the viewer's perspective through the low-angled mobile camera, become the killing technology whose final glory is the death and metaphorical rape of the young girl sniper, the last in a series of stands by the woman-as-

Full Metal Jacket: Eliminating Difference (Warner Bros., 1987. Museum of Modern Art/Film Stills Archive)

enemy Vietcong to maintain a resistance outside a regressive male drive. In the end, Joker achieves the anonymity that the narrator of *Platoon* so longed for, but the distinction between anonymity and heroism, which *Platoon* elides, becomes the essence of Joker's bizarre triumph: a reckless, childless assault on the very notion of difference.

In that final section, the heroics of individualism are fully stripped of any substance or depth by the equation of the mechanisms of war and the technology of image-making. During one startling sequence, the members of the platoon stand around the bodies of two dead comrades. After a crane shot of the group, a series of low-angle head shots from inside the circle records, like snapshots, the comments of each soldier as he stares down at the corpses, again quipping banalities—"Better you than me," "At least they died for a good cause." Surrounding and staring at dead bodies, those vibrant, expressive close-ups of *Platoon* now become parodies of human expression; the faces filling the camera become faceless icons, as emptied of meaning as the corpses at the center of their circle. Like the excessively powdered, neoclassical visages in *Barry Lyndon* (1975) or the wizened, blank look of the dying astronaut at the end of *2001* (1968), social technology has emptied and dispersed the last vestiges of human coherence and subjectivity in the name of imaginary progress.

If *Platoon* depicts an initiation into that blurred historical perspective which is an advertisement for the future, Kubrick's film describes—with the distinctive and peculiarly sharp visual clarity of its war scenes—that kind of perspective as a regression "into the shit" of a boy's club, an absolutely narcissistic return to history as the *imaginary* of sexuality and violent desire, a narcissism ultimately without subjective agency. Following the historical path mapped in *2001*, human history here is the history of technology more efficiently reproducing and extending the human through the conquest of space (Jupiter, Vietnam). For Kubrick, the ultimate and only conclusion to this path can be to expand and extend the human so that it exceeds a fixed subjectivity completely, dispersing human agent into a technological imaginary, a violent infancy that is the death of the humanistic self. Where *Platoon* places its central characters and its audience within that comfortable perspective where history can be melded through a generational imaginary as the transcendence of historical realism, *Full Metal Jacket* highlights the magic of that realism and its regressive trajectory: rather than watching the emergence of an individual through his heroic action (in *Platoon* Chris's titanic last stands in battle), we watch the expunging of the individual within the "full metal jacket" of the solely instinctual group, where the slaughter of a girl-sniper leaves Joker only feeling "alive . . . in the shit . . . but not afraid." In the first, the victorious individual stands for a happily narcissistic vision of history in the name of the future; in the second, the same action becomes the gleeful violence of nostalgic children without the distance or burden of any historical perspective. In a reversal of the self-sacrificing Christian allegory of *Platoon* (where Elias is tragically sacrificed to future wisdom and humanity), these other American soldiers have appropriated the past and "nailed our names in the pages of history."

Full Metal Jacket thus brings into high relief the terroristic anonymity of a contemporary vision, a vision which *Platoon* works so emotionally to displace. For both, the Vietnam War represents a watershed in human history, not just because of the guerrilla violence of a new warfare but because of the new level of media complicity and duplicity in perpetuating that violence. In both the war and its media coverage, the unique horror is the drama of contingencies, of the unpredictable violations of boundaries and spaces: booby-traps explode anywhere at any time; killers remain unseen or faceless or indistinguishable from allies; boundaries constantly give way so that platoons must bomb inside their own perimeters. The only real victories are media victories. According to the drill sergeant in *Full Metal Jacket,* mass-murderer Charles Whitman and assassin Lee Harvey Oswald are "individuals who learned to shoot in the Marines . . . and showed what one motivated Marine and his rifle can do." If terrorism is fundamentally about the mutual anonymity of the criminal and the victim, about a destabilization of public and private spatial securities, and about the promotion of media spectacle as its primary meaning, Vietnam is the quintessential terrorist war and its "regeneration through violence" is critically different from its older manifestations in American history.[10]

The history of this essentially terroristic war, the "first terrible postmodern war" according to Jameson ("Postmodernism" 84), thus parallels the problem of recounting the historical terror that many associate with the crisis in contemporary representation itself.

For both the war and that contemporary perspective on history, a spectacular blockbuster anonymity, propelled by contemporary technology, expulses human subjectivity, as an operatic moment, and undermines any coherent teleology of self and society, as a fundamentally distracted relationship. With both the war and images of contemporary history, viewers either woefully or gleefully struggle against their lack of a stable position or the definition of their position as always and only a passing glance: the crisis of contemporary viewing, in short, has something very much in common, as *Heaven's Gate* dramatized, with the anxiety of a terroristic state and the terrific exhilarations of the music hall. In each case, viewers must now perform themselves rather than decipher the world, and old authorities, interpretive rituals, and ideological positions, fully vacated of traditional coherencies and stabilities, become discourses without walls.

For some (such as Oliver Stone), the only refuge within this state is an extraordinary nostalgia for the timeless history of "lost generations" or "homelands" where the imaginary blur of anxious adults sees through the eyes of children. For others (like Kubrick), there is an apocalyptic clarity about the carnival of self-destruction and the evacuation of humanity of any traditional subjectivity. Yet, for still others, the end is a welcomed beginning, the nostalgia of the contemporary predicament being a sign of a subjectivity in search of more mobile cultural and historical positions, perhaps even those outside the "apocalyptic guarantee" of a generational logic and "the rapacity and melancholia" of appropriative relations with history (Morris 121, 123).

There are, after all, other histories and other viewing positions that now become available within the crisis of contemporary subjectivity, vacated of its old cultural securities. Recently, a 1979 Vietnamese film, *The Abandoned Field,* became one of the first movies made in that country since the war to be shown in the United States. It begins with a tune reminiscent of a Chinese opera and then chronicles the nightmare of a young couple relentlessly and endlessly attacked by helicopters during the Vietnam War. These American helicopters become the technological spectacles oddly displaced and avoided in the film; during one astonishing sequence, the couple seals their baby in a plastic bag in order to push him under water to escape the gunfire from above. In this case, spectacles of technology and the horrific nostalgia captured in the documentary images of history become a song about and spectacle of a people without a generational identity, submerged in other representations of Vietnam, but ultimately surviving them. A small film shown at the Asia Society in New York to a relatively private and passing audience, its greatest significance may be that it produces other origins where audiences can find not some universal human history but other practical glances at localized histories in the making.

REFIGURING AN AUDIENCE

CHAPTER

TWO

ILLEGIBLE FILMS
Texts Without Secrets

□□

"If the old modernising and monumental forms—the Book
of the World, the 'magic mountains' of the architectural
modernisms, the central mythic opera cycle of a Bayreuth,
the museum itself as the centre of all the possibilities of
painting—if such totalising ensembles are no longer the
fundamental organizing frames for analysis and interpretation . . . if we find ourselves confronted henceforth with
'texts,' that is with the ephemeral, with disposable works
that wish to fold back immediately into the accumulating
detritus of historical time—then it becomes difficult and
even contradictory to organise an analysis and an interpeta-
tion around any single one of these fragments in flight."
—FREDRIC JAMESON

"I don't know what a lot of things mean."
—DAVID LYNCH

The historical crisis of contemporary viewing is, most fundamentally, a crisis of legibility. The notion that viewers of films are, in
one sense or another, readers of films is, of course, such a pervasive
and common assumption that it is almost taken for granted. The academic and scholarly scenes have been the usual places where the
legibility and interpretation of the movies have been worked out in
various ways, but a much broader cultural perspective has been
equally informed by this deep-seated, literary sense of how audiences should relate to movies and what it means to decipher a film.

Practically any kind of essay on film, in both scholarly and more popular journals, will today claim to be reading certain textual strategies, and the majority of viewers and reviewers see themselves involved in some sort of hermeneutical operation to make sense of the pleasure or displeasure they experience through the film. Until recently, moreover, most films have willingly accommodated and encouraged this form of reception and have addressed their various audiences along a path whose reading (in one way or another) promises decipherment. How and where this circuit of reading has been disrupted in recent years is the most broadly based distinction of contemporary viewing. If many contemporary viewers have an increasingly distracted relationship with the images that they appropriate in one way or another, today that relationship and those images seem more and more structured to resist legibility and interpretation.

The Commerce of Interpretation

The terms of film reading—and reading in general, for that matter—can of course vary considerably depending on the issues and questions. Here, my emphasis is on reading as a central process in the historical reception of film: according to the traditional formula, to see a movie is to read a movie, and this means *to interpret a film,* in the loosest sense or the strictest sense of interpretation as a mode of decoding a film. The reading or supposed misreading of a film has thus shared the same receptionalist grounds, and these have remained quite consistent through both the modernist and premodernist periods of film history: namely, the need to make meaning. Through the course of (especially recent) film history, according to David Bordwell's formalist account, the dominant mode for responding to the movies has paralleled specific versions of literary reading, somewhere along the axis from comprehending to explaining (*Making Meaning* 1–7).[1]

For my purposes, there are three overlapping modes across which reading as reception has moved, modes that are less cognitive and more cultural and historical than Bordwell's. First, as the most visible form of that socio-historical action, reading is textual practice, and, as such, it necessitates a movement from a system of sounds and images to a conceptual order that purports to reveal meanings within those systems. Most recently systematized through semiotics, reading may work first as a process consisting of a sequence of iconic or audial recognitions of textual combinations founded on similarity and difference, centralities and ambiguities, or contradictions and pluralities. To read a film may mean, in this most basic form, to recognize sounds and images or to identify with a point of view.

Within the temporal dynamics of a film's reception, however, a viewer usually moves simultaneously or retroactively to convert those recognitions into a system of meanings or ideas about what the unities and disunities ultimately refer to. Nick Browne has observed about a movie like *Stagecoach* (1939) that "a guided and prompted performance" of the film text by the spectator becomes a textual interpretation as the viewer reads back through the entire movie: "Reading . . . is, in part, a process of retrospection, situating what could not be 'placed' at the moment of its origin and bringing it forward to an interpretation of the meaning of the present moment" (475, 471). *Young Mr. Lincoln* (1939), *Adieu Philippine* (1962), or any other single film or group of films can yield structural or thematic formations to which a viewer, following the cultural pressures of the past, has then to assign meanings.²

Second, as more explicitly connected to those cultural pressures, film reading is a function of certain socio-historical, often behaviorist, patterns whereby the need to understand a movie and the way a movie is understood are primarily the products of learned cultural codes, both intrinsic and extrinsic to the film. We can interpret a movie like *Meet John Doe* (1941) in a particular manner because we read it through the historical and political referents of the early forties and according to specific cultural expectations about the function of film "to show" to an audience recognizable places and realities. Film reading becomes a kind of historical localizing in which to read means to recognize oneself as a part of a place and time or to discover oneself anew in that place and time, either of which actions can be performed through a sort of coded realism (which of course has little to do with any scientific conception of reality). These kinds of reading formations generally are characterized by a more passive, deterministic stance, but the possibility of cultural and historical collisions—often described as historical or cultural "misreadings" or "readings against the grain" of film—indicate this approach can result in less predictable readings that are interpretive readings nonetheless.[3]

Third, we read and interpret a movie across the movement of subject positions that lean on, for example, psychoanalytic or phenomenological models. In these cases, reading is an *affective* interaction that creates both the subject matter and the reader-subject: this is reading as an interpretation through which the investment of the reader-viewer is repaid by the film through some kind of surplus value, whether the denomination of this value is in terms of imaginative play, an ethical lesson, or the regulating economies of desire (available to both feminist and non-feminist readers). Read with energy, any movie from *Intolerance* (1916) to *The Lady from Shanghai* (1947) or *Lancelot du Lac* (1976) generates, to put it bluntly, measurable value "purchased" by the efforts of reading and interpretation.

Each of these characterizations of film reading is normally founded on a binary relation or opposition, such as the historical one between *now* and *then* or fantasy and reality, as in *Meet Me in St. Louis* (1944), the psychoanalytical or phenomenological move between *presence* and *absence*, as in *Citizen Kane* (1941), or the textual opposition of *signs* and *meaning*, as in *M* (1931). In addition, while any one of these dimensions can seem to privilege either an intra- or an extra-textual position for the reader (the reader is either interpolated into the text or determines from without the meaning of that text), any one of them may be made to work in either direction. Across any of the three formulations, my interpretive reading of a movie can be more or less about myself and my own positions or about the film text and its origins. Together the three dimensions— which certainly can operate at once—might be lumped into a definition of film reading as the "domestication of value through textual interpretation" as a summary of what we do when our readings recuperate films across different histories and cultures, valorize movies or experiences at movies, or assign to images and signs referential and other meanings.

One way to debunk this passion for legibility and interpretation at the movies is to examine exactly how the film medium resists such literary postures. Looked at closely, films throughout the course of their history have never truly had the linguistic or inconographic stability to bear the weight of a legible interpretation. Efforts to codify even the most classical of films invariably run up against textual ruptures, opacities, or "third meanings" that can make reading the film something of a struggle, if not a superimposition.[4] Usually identified with the work of post-structuralist theoretical models, this correction of the interpretive powers of film reading often suggests that the true value of a particular movie lies in some kind of textual residue that contradictorily refuses to be recuperated in a reading. Addressing this contradiction in reading "unattainable texts," Raymond Bellour eloquently stated the problem in 1971: Filmic analysis

> constantly mimics, evokes, describes; in a kind of prin-
> cipled despair it can but try frantically to compete with
> the object it is attempting to understand. By dint of seek-
> ing to capture it and recapture it, it ends up occupying a
> point at which its object is perpetually out of reach. . . .
> The analysis of film never stops filling up a film that
> never stops running out. (28)

Here what befuddles interpretive reading is the promise of a textual secret that most readings claim to retrieve but which can never be semiotically discovered or designated.

Still, however an individual film or group of films may demonstrate moments of excess or resistance to legibility, their definition in terms of their historical reception has, through most of film history, remained circumscribed by the cultural urgency of reading. In fact, often a film resists reading on one level only to be recovered or decoded on another. Where a film may resist a semiological approach, for instance, it may reveal the secrets of a contradictory subject position. Sergei Eisenstein's *Ivan the Terrible* (1944–1946), as Kristin Thompson demonstrates, may indeed be characterized by a textuality that exceeds certain interpretive patterns; yet that excess can ultimately be reinterpreted through the historical framework of Eisenstein's materialist ideology and the film's position outside classical Hollywood narrative (287–302). Similarly, one might claim that a classical Hollywood film like *The Big Sleep* constantly drifts into narrative illegibility, but, historically and culturally, that disturbing drift is reorganized through the powerfully codified presence of the Bacall and Bogart relationship and the genre itself. If films always contain points of excess that frustrate an interpretive reading, those moments have been made legible in both the classical and modernist periods through the cultural and historical formations that surround their reception and demand that movies make sense one way or another. The historical conditions of film reception as a legible formation (including a historical distance from those films) and the address of most movies within that formation have promoted an often varied and subtle but nonetheless necessary interpretive relation between movie and audience.

Relating "reading formations" to larger social and commercial issues, Tony Bennett and Janet Woollacott provide a cultural model for the kind of interpretive reception I am sketching here, a model that, moreover, looks ahead to the root of the interpretive crisis within contemporary film culture. Reading formations are, they argue, "those specific determinations which bear in upon, mould and configure the relations between texts and reader in determinant conditions of reading" (64). Thus, film reading "refers, specifically, to the inter-textual relations which prevail in a particular context, thereby activating a given body of texts by ordering the relations between them in a specific way such that their reading is always already cued in specific directions that are not given by those 'texts themselves' as entities separable from such relations" (4). To some extent, it appears as if "texts themselves" have vanished from Bennett and Woollacott's model, yet, in actuality theirs is a process in which the "text and reader are conceived as being co-produced within a reading formation" (64). Rather than dismissing a text, this reconception of reading simply refuses to prioritize that text any more than it would valorize its reception by a self-legitimizing reader. The exchange between text and reader, instead, becomes defined by fluctuating historical, cultural, and commercial pressures that make the activity of reading (not the text or the reader alone) a various but always legible process of mutual interpretation.

I would argue, however, a revised position to suit the contemporary predicament: emphasizing cultural and commercial formations behind film interpretation not only highlights the predominance of legibility within different reading formations but uncovers those real cultural resistances to legibility that appear throughout film's commercial history. Preclassical spectatorship, again, seems to me to adumbrate the complications in reading and interpretation found within postmodern spectatorship. Situated between an industry and tradition of reading literature that peaks in the nineteenth century and the complementary industry of reading movies in the twentieth century, early movie audiences acted out an unusually active and less codified relation between audience and screen.⁵ Anticipating this relationship, a multitude of significant commentaries by writers like Pierre Macherey, M. M. Bakhtin, and Hans Robert Jauss have, in their variety, mapped how literary production functions in the nineteenth century against a dialogic horizon of reading; each shares the recognition that the action of reading was never more powerfully a function of public modes of production and reception and that reading formations were rapidly being refashioned by cultural and commercial spheres. Thus, for Bakhtin reading becomes "social throughout its entire range and in each and every of its factors" (259).

From the expansion of a middle- and lower-class reading public at the beginning of the nineteenth century to the dispersal of those readers into other forms of public entertainment, like the cinema by the beginning of this century, reading as a reception was becoming much less regulated or more variously regulated within class and gender, while the variety and nature of texts began to describe a plethora of different legibilities and illegibilities within the burgeoning industry of reading: as the place and address of writers from Byron and Whitman to popular serial novelists demonstrate and as Walter Benjamin argues in his essay on Baudelaire, readers were becoming commercial viewers and consumers for whom the interpretation of a text may have been less important than the consumption of its spectacle, similar to the way a viewer is "shocked" by the continuous and discontinuous likenesses of photographs. Similarly, reception at the first movies follows the active multiplicity of its audiences, reflected in the mixed formats of film screenings, which offered films, sing-alongs, and vaudeville acts in no particular order, the widely subjective nature of the nickelodeon machine and text, the performative responses of spectators, and the shifting class lines that researchers are now discovering as the real basis of the fragmented nature of early movie audiences.⁶ For this brief period in film history (that mythical parallel of the postmodern), the reception of the movies appears to have been less a reading than a performance by the audience or a distraction for that audience. In a sense, film reception was too publicly indiscriminate and various to be the receptacle for any secure hermeneutic secrets.

Since those first years, however, film criticism and aesthetics have followed the commercialization of film form in the institutionalization of film reading as the commerce of interpretation. Under the pressure of increasing consumerism and the commercial reification of the relationship between public and private spheres, spectatorship in the cinema openly begins to evoke "parallels between film and reading a novel, and in this sense incorporates readership into classical cinema" (Mayne 120). Indeed, it is crucial to emphasize this connection between cultural commerce and reading, for it provides a common ground for the many reading practices that take place between academic formulations and journalistic reviews, a ground on which the common viewer also engages a film as an interpretive reading. Reading is the commercialization of film reception as a consumerism in that it offers public or semipublic formulas for interpretation determined by ideological, sociological, and economic factors; much like literary readings in the nineteenth century, the success and meaning of these formulas depend on an economics that balances public desire with ideological negotiation. Thus, the history of film criticism could be discussed precisely in these terms of the commercialization of specific reading formations. The work of the *Cahiers du Cinéma* from the late fifties through the late sixties is only one—albeit a most celebrated—example of the successful commercialization of the film viewing as the negotiation of specific reading formations: in this instance, French cold-war ideologies that made auteurism a neat counterpart to American individualism, a reading population gleaned from the cine-clubs and cinematheques, and a publishing machinery inherited from the *Revue du Cinéma* are only some of the historical factors that make those readings less radically romantic and more, in Thomas Elsaesser's words, "a brilliant public relations stunt" ("Two Decades" 199).

Film reading as a commercialization of film reception is often most apparent in journalistic reviews or their television counterparts, where the interpretation or placement of a movie simply replicates the film's own commercial presentation. A typical (uninspired) review reads a movie as all that it should be or a failure to be what it should be. More academic examples may be more interesting for some but are no less a product of a commercial circuit, as their fostering by particular graduate programs or their dependence on certain journals makes clear. Contrary to the charges of exoticism and esotericism, film studies of most sorts attempt to read movies as objects of social exchange. The variations in these readings is in many ways a consequence of the different discourses that function as the more or less popular currencies in a social exchange and the necessity of keeping the movie or movies commercially desirable as new (or perhaps unattainable) text. Put in terms of the commerce of reading, the commercial describes the limits of intelligibility and interpretation across an acceptable economy of popular consensus; the commerce of interpretive reading is based on a binary regulation of semiotic, psychoanalytic, and social excess.

Through this history of film reception as film reading, Walter Benjamin and Siegfried Kracauer seem to me most important as writers who recognize and struggle with the aesthetic and political potential of cinematic illegibility, a semiotics that happens, however, to run counter to other, more political and economically conservative forces that determine commercial horizons of legibility. For Benjamin, the authentic is the transparently legible: "The authenticity of a thing is the essence of all that is *transmissible* from its beginning, ranging from its substantive duration to its testimony to the history which it has experienced" (my emphasis, "The Work of Art" 221). If the aura of a work of art is a function of a distance that creates a ritualistic and abstract relationship between the art object and the spectator, film for Benjamin had, however, the potential to alter this process whereby the spectator and the art object possess and abstract each other in an absorptive reading based in the commodity use-value. In this counterargument, Benjamin uses notions of "closeness," "exhibition," and "testing" to describe a more promising relation: a proximity that militates against the hierarchies of interpretation, a historical and social place that the viewer violates rather than inhabits, a textuality based in the materiality of reproduction rather in hermeneutics.

The sharpest focus for Benjamin's position is his distinction between distracted and concentrated reception. Previous to this he struggles to describe the cinema's break with a classical tradition of reading by drawing a historical parallel with its transformation in the late nineteenth century when "at any moment, the reader is ready to turn into a writer": as the authority and aura of the art object are changed by technology, traditional interpretation gives way "to modern man's legitimate claim to being reproduced" according to the mostly uncodified terms of his or her contemporary needs and desires (232).

Like Roland Barthes's "third meanings" or "obtuse" relation with the film text, these formulations appear to be strained attempts to characterize within a literary perspective a kind of reception that exceeds those interpretive and textual traditions. Benjamin's more accurate tack is his hailing a distracted viewer in contrast to the concentrated reader of movies. Not surprisingly given Benjamin's social and historical penchant, his primary analogy for the distracted viewer is architecture (which postmodernism would also quickly turn to for its models) as a kind of spectatorial habitation: "Architecture has always represented the prototype of a work of art the reception of which is consummated by a collectivity in a state of distraction" (239). Viewing art architecturally and viewing the art of the movies involves a vision—but a vision closer to incidental habits than to rapt attention. Here, the spectator becomes not a mesmerized reader but a distracted critic: "The public examiner, but an absent-minded one" (240).

Benjamin's position clarifies the extent to which even the most radical of film movements, by their involvement in a commerce of reading, remain circumscribed by the conventions of legibility. As Benjamin himself recognized, the surrealists—and for that matter, other experimental and countercultural movements—are a telling case in point. Historically close to the crossroads of preclassical and classical models, the surrealists nonetheless rely on the commerce of an art tradition aligned with the far more conservative tradition of interpretation. In most cases, surrealist films arise out of the desire for illegibility but, through the sociology and politics of an art tradition, they simply displace the terms of their legibility onto a different path (most clearly, a psychoanalytic one or the semiotic one of the silent language of images).[7]

Similarly, despite their subversive stance, the new wave positions of critics like Susan Sontag and filmmakers like Godard dovetail logically: her call to resist interpretation and his early efforts to demand a difficult legibility (through which style supplants content) equally valorize a kind of intelligibility reserved for the hermeneutics of the artist/academic who might enter the privileged place of the text. For her, a film is a sensual subject whose value lies in reading it across a private *erotics* of form rather than content, whose secrets are in the text, not behind it: "What is needed is a vocabulary—a descriptive, rather than prescriptive, vocabulary—for forms. The best criticism . . . is of this sort that dissolves considerations of content into those of form" (12). His films (before the eighties) ask to be read as critical strategies themselves involved in cultural hermeneutics. In 1962, Godard remarked about the analytic posture of his movies: "As a critic, I thought of myself as a filmmaker. Today I still think of myself as a critic, and in a sense I am, more than ever before. Instead of writing criticism, I make a film, but the critical dimension is subsumed" (Milne 171). In both cases, the composition that classically describes film reading has simply become an interpretive decomposition, what Barthes calls reading in slow motion. According to Bordwell's phrasing, "the art-film narration solicits not only denotative comprehension but connotative reading, a higher-level interpretation. . . . Uncertainties persist but are understood as such, as obvious uncertainties. Put crudely, the procedural slogan of art-cinema narration might be: 'Interpret this film, and interpret it so as to maximize ambiguity'" (*Narration* 212).

No Secrets: *Adrift, In a Year of Thirteen Moons, Blue Velvet*

This sketch should indicate the rather consistent stake that film practice and reception have had in the literary terms of legibility as the measure of interpretability (according to which neither readerly nor writerly positions are as countercultural as sometimes claimed). My primary concern with this history, however, is with the distinctive trouble it has faced in maintaining itself through recent years. By this I mean to call attention to how those *conditions* of film reception discussed in the previous chapter—and thus reading formations—have changed so significantly that models of interpretive legibility, from newspapers to scholarly journals, seem to find themselves frequently befuddled. Like all that follows in this study, this argument is not meant to be a sweeping, universal claim: certainly there are viewing conditions and films within the contemporary scene that offer themselves up for readings of one sort or another. Yet, more significantly perhaps, numerous contemporary movies and numerous so-called postmodern films can now be seen addressing viewers across formations that subvert, deflect, or minimalize the very activity of filmic reading. I recognize some of the inherent contradictions in discussing movies that resist reading, and I recognize that my own emphasis on how these movies take advantage of their own problematic reading formations might be misunderstood as a locating of those reading solely in the movie text itself. My textual emphasis here, however, is mainly intended to be an illustration of how films call attention to and address—these movies more consciously than other perhaps—the historical predicament of their own illegibility as a denial or indifference to the secrets of reading. Like more commercial examples, these are films whose transparency or opacity leaves no secrets to discover, whose fragmented mobility mirrors the technological and social conditions that spawned them.

The industrial and cultural conditions that have encouraged movies and audiences to configure themselves in illegible formations are a specific version of those which I detailed earlier. Since the early seventies, the economics of blockbuster production and distribution, along with the inception of many semi-independent companies outside the studio tradition, have joined with the technology of home video to produce either "spectacular" or "distracted" reading formations quite different from the classical and modernist ones of the past. At both the operatic spectacles of the theaters and the home spectacles of the VCRs, audiences now watch movies according to a *glance aesthetic* rather than a *gaze aesthetic:* movies and spectators are indeed "closer" than ever before (in Benjamin's sense) but it is a closeness that encourages viewers to casually test and measure a film as part of a domestic or public environment rather than become part of a concentrated reading. These are small movies directed at a corner of the audience; large movies watched out of the corner of the eye. Whether they create spectacles of technology or are subject to the discriminating technology of home viewing, watching a movie today is "distracted" in nearly every sense, a version of what Baudrillard calls the "exhausted fascination" of watching signs that have lost their authoritative meaning ("Implosion of Meaning" 143).

Within these cultural and industrial formations, many contemporary movies simply refuse to offer or promise interpretive "secrets" to be gained through concentrated vision. In Jameson's version of the predicament, "the postmodern [films] triumphantly succeeded in drawing that 'other thing,' that 'something else,' out onto a unified plane such that they shed their former solidity and depth and become the very images of themselves to be consumed now in their own right, as images rather than as representations of something else." The consequence is the disappearance of a certain "interpretative depth, the idea that the object is fascinating because of the density of its secrets, which are then to be uncovered by interpretation. . . . In short, objects fall into the world and become decoration again; visual depth and systems of interpretation fade away." What remains is "not a meaning that has content but one that seems to be meaningful" ("On Magic Realism" 313; Stephansen, "Regarding Postmodernism" 4, 6).

These contemporary reading formations, which resist legibility, and the secrets that drive interpretation have, of course, no necessary relation with the intentions of a film or filmmaker. A film may aim to be received in the most classically legible way yet find itself a victim of the circumstances of contemporary production and reception. Nor, again, do these cultural formations make it impossible to read a movie in a traditional manner; they merely make that activity unnecessary and difficult for most audiences within contemporary cultural conditions. Certain movies, on the other hand, make this predicament very much part of their discourse in an attempt to address a contemporary audience according to their own communicative formations. This culturally conscious address is what interests me here, specifically as it operates in three examples: Janos Kadár's *Adrift* (1971), R. W. Fassbinder's *In a Year of Thirteen Moons* (1978), and David Lynch's *Blue Velvet*. With each of these, I will concentrate on the textual address, although a variety of extra-textual dramas are also relevant (this is because a semiotics of the "text" has become such a phantom vehicle or lure for a commerce of reading and its promise of secrets). I will also align these particular discussions with the categories of the legible that I have isolated already, although each of these films, as all films, works across multiple formations. Like the films themselves, my analysis here, in short, is a case of scheming to undo the scheme of reading, a reading of how these movies confront a long tradition of reading for interpretive secrets.

The industrial and commercial complications that surround Kadár's *Adrift* reflect appropriately the crisis of how viewing subjects are positioned and displaced through its narrative structure. Produced partly in the United States and partly in Czechoslovakia (during the Soviet invasion), hardly known by a larger public, and now out of distribution in this country, the film was marginalized and excluded by the same commerce of reading that it brought into question. Originally titled "A Longing Called Anada," the story takes place around the isolated riverfront home of a fisherman named János: the narrative recounts the psychological and social chaos that erupts when János, his son, and his father save a mysterious and stunningly beautiful woman, Anada, from drowning. Literally a piece of flotsam, this woman is brought back to life in a shot that prepares for the rest of the film: János's wife Zuska uses a large mirror to detect any breathing, and when she moves the mirror to detect any sign of life, a low-angle shot captures the double and overlapping images of the two women. This split reflection becomes then the metaphor for the *mise-en-abyme* of János's sexual desire, as he is drawn towards Anada and eventually attempts to murder Zuska: a splitting that confuses János's patriarchal stance by metonymically eliding the binary difference between the father and the son, a domestic known and an exotic unknown, dividing and then overlapping his love for the old and his lust for the new. This split look is, moreover, mirrored by a narrative structure that begins with János arriving home with medicine for Zuska and concludes with a version of that same scene. The first perspective suggests János will save his wife and family; the concluding perspective on the same scene indicates that he will poison her with an overdose. All that differentiates the two perspectives are the fluctuations of János's desire as it destabilizes the world he sees.

If *Adrift* is fundamentally about the unlocatable place of patriarchal yearning, the film positions the viewer in the circular perceptions of that chaotic desire as if it drifts free of legal and legible structures like the family and historical time, as it loses sight of a context for a symbolic action that would regulate a *meaningful* relationship between an imaginary world and a real world. In that repeated sequence, for instance, the gestures and words echo and reecho with sliding meanings (about the medicine, the domestic situation, the cry outside the window, or phrases like "I'd burn the house over our heads to save you"). The uncertainty of those meanings forces a viewer to review his or her own capacity to produce and revise shifting and unreliable readings through the changing positions and contexts. Aptly, this doubled sequence features a shot in which János, entering the room, tells his son to stop reading a novel, apt because, framed by this sequence, this remarkably silent movie consistently refuses the stable subject positions required of reading as symbolic exchange. It is only this exchange, of course, that converts one's desires into a meaningful relationship—with another individual, the world itself, or a movie narrative.

A second sequence illustrates, in fact, the extent to which this frustrated attempt to read becomes for the spectator and János the disturbing recognition of the act of misrecognition whereby images are falsely secured as legible, whereby the Oedipal text that normally offers a subject position in this male midlife-crisis movie is foreclosed. In this sequence, János maneuvers a small boat through a thick and dark swampish area near the river; as he approaches a clearing in the river, he sees the nude Anada swimming. A nervous voyeur, János remains hidden behind a tree until Anada disappears for what seems a considerable time, but then she springs from the water and walks unabashedly toward and past the embarassed viewer. The erotics of exchange here begin with Anada as a much too evident imaginary lure and signifier. As on so many other levels of the film, spatial distance from an object tantalizingly on the edge of vanishing, like the flashes on the river's surface, allows the viewer to push and pull that image-object, like the many rack focuses and zooms in the film, through the space of legibility itself. In this particular sequence, however, the circuit of this erotic exchange is strangely interrupted when Anada turns to cross that space and look unflinchingly into the subjective camera (at János and the audience). The structure of the cinematic position is thus revealed (not undermined) by a second position within the exchange. This returned look from the object makes the first, readerly position dumbly aware of the image's refusal to be secured for the pleasure of its voyeuristic value.

Immediately, however, János turns to the dense brush behind him where he hears something rustling. He begins a chase through the bushes, which is shot as a receding frontal track. Finding no one, he remarks that the "spy" will reveal himself by the scratches and cuts from the bushes. Yet, at dinner that evening no one bears those marks except János himself. Just as the thief-voyeur whom János chased becomes literally (but almost unnoticeably) inscribed in the retreating track, the thief-voyeur whom János chased (but whom the self-enclosed blindness of his position prevents him from seeing) is himself. In both cases the reading and recognition of a particular image take place only as a reflection of János's own troubled desires. It becomes a second look that catches the holes, seams, and distances which it tries to cover by reading those gaps from the strength of its position as voyeur. These lacks, excesses, and misrecognitions are frequently signaled in *Adrift* by the carnival music on the soundtrack or the swirling surface of the river across which the darting camera searches. Like the structure of the entire film, they define first and foremost a subject position trying hopelessly to recover itself as a stable reading and self-interpretation.

Within *Adrift* there are several gestures towards securing and reading the excess in which János drifts. Most importantly, the tale itself periodically appears as if it were a flashback told by János to three fishermen, who gradually acquire the status of three wisemen, the critics and reviewers of János's predicament. As they listen to his story, they insist they know only what he knows, that they must share his position to analyze it, that they are interested only in facts. But, since János's story is his inability to secure a position and to make legible the facts of his longings, they, like the folktales that punctuate the film, become mostly ironic structures pointing to what they misrecognize and what escapes them. Towards the end of the film, when János mentions that his wife is deathly ill, this rift between an imagistic excess and its recuperation becomes strikingly clear: as these mythic analysts express surprise and confusion at the news, János erupts, "But I've been speaking of nothing else!" Like the motif of money that runs through the film—spent, exchanged, stolen, promised—symbolic exchange yields nothing here, especially not the use-value of communication.

For János, the discovery of his own position adrift in a flux of images that yield no value is the film's tragedy and the motivation for the celebrated final sequence. Standing at the river's edge, with the house light visible through the twilight, János tries desperately to revise his reading of his illegible situation: to dismiss Anada as a figure who perhaps never really existed except in his own subjective fantasies. As he shouts his wife's name and begins racing towards the framed light in the distant house where he has left the medicine/ poison, the camera tracks with his point of view. Then, suddenly, while the forward track continues accompanied by increasingly strained and high pitched music, there are a series of sharp reverse zooms that bring the film to a dramatic end. This single shot becomes a final, intensely disconcerting exclusion of a spectating subject (János and the viewer) desperately anxious to retrieve the lost security of an interpretive position: while the forward track describes an imagistic depth that is the traditional point of identification for a reading position, the reverse zoom flattens that image as a glistening surface across which subject positions slide with no certainty, caught, as throughout *Adrift,* between the promise of a legible location and its impossibility.

For Fassbinder, the question of illegibility and the crisis of interpretation enter almost every level of his work, most notably as a testing of and confrontation with textual authority. The illegibility of commercial success could very well describe the project of the entire second half of his career, as he alternated with calculated speed and unpredictability between the narrative traditions of commercial cinema and those seeming to align him with the art cinema. Commercial historical efforts such as *The Marriage of Maria Braun* (1978) and *Veronika Voss* (1981) work to make reading within a textual tradition difficult but available according to a syntax and semiotics aligned with a modernist hermeneutics. The more personal and dense films, like *The Third Generation, In a Year of Thirteen Moons,* and *Querelle* (1982), aim ferociously at a textuality that tends to refuse the effort to convert the materials of the film into the explanatory ideas of interpretation.

Of these later films, *In a Year of Thirteen Moons* puts into play densities that do not so much exclude a spectator from the stable place and value of a symbolic exchange (as in *Adrift*) but force the viewer to recognize the materialistic and textual terms of that exchange. The film in effect blocks the search for semiotic coherence and ultimately rewards the spectator with none of the secrets that semiotic coherence usually offers. First and foremost, there is the urgent and strained voice-over of Elvira who desperately tries to tell her own story, its rambling manner emphasizing its own frenzied insufficiency at designating and organizing the multitude of other texts that surround and invade it. As the camera shifts through the dark room of Soul Freida, Elvira's tape-recorded voice sobs on the soundtrack, "What I'm afraid of is that someday I'll be able to put my feelings into words. And when I do. . . ." Stylistically indexed in a mise-en-scène that hides its speakers in its many shadows and complex angles and frames, Elvira's is a story that cannot be told, a body that cannot be represented.

The narrative presents itself from the start as a text about secrets and mysteries specifically associated with the body and emotions. Yet the trajectory of the story's investigation becomes an unraveling of the material of textuality behind which there is no truth. Frustratingly dark long shots and confusing close-ups open the film as a seduction turns into a beating when Elvira is discovered to be a woman rather than a transvestite, the first of many secret discoveries that are themselves lies (Elvira in many ways still being a man).

In a Year of Thirteen Moons: The Crisis of Reading an Identity (New Yorker, 1978. Museum of Modern Art/Film Stills Archive)

In the next sequence, she collapses in the door of her apartment and quietly chants, "Nobody knows that Rumpelstiltzkin is my name. . . ." Elvira/Erwin is the misleading and misread secret, unpronounceable name, the victim of desire and venality and of a social text that cannot possibly understand her/him.

The narrative orchestrates a vast variety of different textual materials meant to assemble and reveal the secret of Elvira's suffering—but those materials never synchronize to make sense. Visually, the mirrored surfaces of a bathroom become a collage of images that shatter the verbal coherence of Elvira's conversation; the trappings of a picnic frame a philosophical discourse on suicide, just before the suicide interrupts the picnic. She watches video replays of her own descriptions of her life, which appear as distanced images of another life. At one point, a group of businessmen-thugs remain mesmerized before a Jerry Lewis film and then act out the choreographed lunacy of a dance sequence. They appropriate and become another discourse whose semantic emptiness and comic inappropriateness to its situation reflects the fragmented, superficial, and arbitrary play of all the discourses in the film. Indeed all of these texts, images, and languages become taken over by their own materiality: much like Elvira's voice-off narration of her own history in a slaughterhouse where the graphic rending of cattle parts becomes a contrapuntal commentary on the pathos of her Romantic discourse and its quotations from Goethe, most of the discourses in the movie become figures torn away from a coherent body to become only grotesque material dressing, textual refuse. *In a Year of Thirteen Moons* is a movie about textual madness, about textualities that lose their ability to naturalize and balance the materials of signification with a sense of meaning. What results is a dense overabundance of materialized markers: too many moons, too many lovers, too much sound, too much spatial clutter, and too many stories.

The foremost textual breakdown in the film is, of course, that of sexual difference. Elvira's crisis and tragedy is the devastating result of misreading sexual difference as text. Like most things in the film, the impetus for her sex change operation is unclear; it appears to be the consequence of a casual rumination by Anton Saitz, his male employer and close friend, that "it's too bad you're not a girl." After Erwin dashes to North Africa to have the operation, Saitz rejects her, and Elvira is left with the realization that she really didn't wish to become a woman: Elvira's mistake is to misread or misunderstand the language of sexual difference as one of simple and reversible opposition and to make her body a text on which those differences can be rewritten as merely a different reading. She takes Saitz's remark literally, as language with a transparent truth (the same mistake that is the basis for the brutal, linguistic games of Chinese roulette that describe the discourses of so many Fassbinder scenarios). Elvira's catastrophe is the not-unusual one of trying to make sexual need and desire a legible and coherent text into which she can inscribe herself, when, in fact, those needs and desires, as they are played out across a social and human material, can only be the victims of a textuality and legibility that have themselves become unmalleable and reified substances. Longing for lofty utopian meanings, Elvira, like other Fassbinder characters, inevitably discovers that all those social discourses that surround her do not discover meaning but rather strip human longing down to its most grotesque physicality. In that famous slaughterhouse sequence from this film, there is no disjunction: Elvira's pleading narrative becomes the longing for textuality that is slicing her to pieces.

Ultimately then, it is the ubiquity, weight, precision, and disassociation of the multiple textual registers that make this and other Fassbinder films resist interpretive readings so rigorously. Especially in this film, the material force of so many discourses fully obliterates the meaning of its human subject and the demand for meaning that describes its human tragedy. The finale features a sudden gathering of the entire cast of characters and stories that Elvira has been investigating in order to make some sense of her life. This variety of human figures includes the Catholic nun of her childhood, his daughter and former wife, Saitz, and her prostitute companion, and the newspaper reporter and his wife. Visually and aurally, the sequence is typical of the entire film: the soundtrack is layered with so many different songs, sounds, noises, and voices that none can be distinguished clearly; the spatial continuity is disrupted and confused by the angles of intruding walls and windows. In the midst of this overwhelmingly precise textual clutter, Elvira, barely noticeable, is dead. It is a moment in which the material of textuality batters the need to make sense of it, just as those last images refuse any acknowledgment or explanation of Elvira's death. At best, the viewer is left with his or her own frustrated longing to respond to the alluring display of so much evidence, yet with an accompanying sense of how nonsensical and destructive it is to try to interpret contemporary social formulas through the perspective of human sense and meaning. For the Fassbinder of these later years especially, to interpolate oneself into the machinery of that textuality in search of semantic secrets becomes the physical slaughter of the subject within the incoherence of so much excessive textual material.

Thus, viewers confront the two-edged sword of Fassbinder's aesthetic: the overdetermined textuality continually frustrates efforts to make it legible in any traditional sense. Or, in the terms of the more public reception of and responses to his movies, the presentation of a socially critical text becomes unreadable by the multiple audiences who attempt to interpret the films through a conventional oppositional grammar of, for instance, left versus right, Hollywood versus alternate cinema, patriarchal versus gay/lesbian sexuality, or aesthetic expression versus aesthetic victimization. For him and his begrudging fans, the social and political imperative to read movies is the ultimate sadomasochistic project.

In David Lynch's *Blue Velvet,* there are no politics because there are only illegible social configurations: unlike the difficult and exotic places found in a Fassbinder film, here a viewer casually inhabits a familiar neighborhood where violent distraction is a way of life. Situated in Lumberton, the film is a perpetual construction site built of representational waste that is immediately taken apart: "It's a beautiful day, get out your buzz saws," the radio announces at the beginning of the film. Here, that localizing structure of reading—whereby to read and interpret a movie is to locate oneself, fantastically or realistically, in or against the environment of a movie—confronts a locale that appears so extraordinarily strange because it is so extraordinarily familiar, a pastiche of too many distinctive generational images (from the fifties through the eighties) made oddly familiar by the rapidity with which those distinctions decay and meld together in this temporary place. Like Jeffrey's invasion of Dorothy's apartment (after he has previously disguised himself as an exterminator in order to become familiar with its geography), viewers find themselves in a different, almost exotic world. But, as the subsequent discovery of Jeffery reveals (voyeuristically hiding in the closet, watching the rape of Dorothy), those viewers become strangely at home there, made "neighbors," like Dorothy and Jeffrey, through the pleasure of the narcissistic distractions and vacant violence that makes each of them familiar to the other.

Lynch's neighborhoods have always been built on a familiarity that stubbornly and violently refuses the comfort of psychological or historical meaning. What disturbs about *Eraserhead* (1976), *Elephant Man* (1980), *Dune* (1984), and *Twin Peaks* (1990) is a shared preoccupation with a historical evaporation of social or psychological meaning beneath the surface of seemingly normal places, things, and people, an evacuation that leaves only grotesque shells. The nostalgia of *Elephant Man* is for some meaningful human presence under the skin of a boy encrusted with inhuman deformities; in *Dune* these physical and social distortions of humanity's search for their redemptive substance in the excrement of worms, the only presence underneath a desert world. In each case, the past and the future contend for the same place, a historical reality that, missing any kind of depth of historical spirit, becomes only a violent collection of images and clichés in search of stability and meaning. In Jameson's words about the historical "aimlessness" of *Blue Velvet* and *Something Wild* (1986), they "show a collective unconscious in the process of trying to identify its own present at the same time that they illuminate the failure of this attempt, which seems to reduce itself to the recombination of various stereotypes of the past" ("Nostalgia for the Present" 536). "I don't know what a lot of things mean," Lynch blithely claims (Bouzereau 39).

As in a Hitchcock film that likewise problematizes familiar terrains, in *Blue Velvet* Jeffrey investigates a crime and possible murder in hopes, it seems, of discovering more about the nature of his town. Finding an ear, he begins his search for the crime behind it and along the way becomes sexually entangled with Dorothy Vallens, the sultry wife of the kidnapped victim. Unlike a Hitchcock film, however, in these neighborhoods there is only one nature for Jeffrey to discover, a horizontal rather than vertical "second nature" that flattens and evacuates all human and natural depths. In this contemporary version of a "second nature" (as opposed to Benjamin's), there is no nostalgic yearning for a lost place or a hidden meaning (even the darker ones of Hitchcock). What the bland, semi-conscious Jeffrey discovers is that he himself is a violently mechanical reproduction, a shimmering surface (like blue velvet) of a decaying environment. "I don't know if you're a detective or a pervert," Sandy observes without concern.

The Violent Decay of the Too Familiar (*Blue Velvet*, De Laurentiis Entertainment, 1986. Museum of Modern Art/Film Stills Archive)

Highlighted in the sometimes extreme metallic colors of the film, those reproductions of a violent second nature—its vociferous birds, its severed ears, its knife-point sexuality—are the violences of gestures and communications separated from a primary motivating context that could "naturalize" their grotesque logic. Characters communicate through advertising slogans, which seem alternately stupid and threatening because they are so excessive to their situations. Frank's horrific ecstasy over Ben's lip-synched version of Roy Orbison's "In Dreams" has much to do with the song's double removal from natural expression (as a performance of a recording of a performance). The pleasure and violence of living in Lumberton (as in going to a shopping mall) is that one continually acts outside of a motivating context, pursuing distractions that lead away from any sense of place (which is how of course Jeffrey first notices the ear—

while tossing stones across a field). Walking through this cozy neighborhood, Jeffrey suddenly sees a home where "a kid with the biggest
tongue in the world lived"; pausing suddenly, he reflects, " . . . but
he moved away." He then quickly asks Sandy if she knows "the
chicken walk" and immediately demonstrates it. She replies with as
powerful an interpretation as his neighborly position makes available:
"Interesting."

An exaggerated drama of supposed initiation into experience,
the film becomes then a postmodern variety of Benjamin's allegorical world: the allegorical describes here a place that has become
so familiar that it is no longer historically meaningful. "Allegories are, in the realm of thoughts, what ruins are in the realm of
things," Benjamin says (*German Tragic Drama* 178), suggesting,
as Gregory Ulmer points out, that "something becomes an object of
knowledge only as it 'decays,' or is made to disintegrate" (97). If
allegorical meanings are usually a product of discursively mobile
formations set against their historical cultural emplacements,[8] in
Lumberton those formations, like the severed ear that initiates the
detective search or the mocking pastiche of images from different
times and places, are always artificially severed from a localizing and naturalizing context. What Jeffrey learns by the end of the
movie and what this allegory teaches is therefore the most contradictory of knowledge: that this neighborhood is made up of nothing
more than fragmentary images that were once meaningfully distinct
and motivated but which continually lose those meanings because
they are always in the process of decaying into sameness. To understand this is to know that historical and geographical differentiations
are fruitless since they are always subject to an insidious decay onto
the same flat plane. The vision of this understanding is accordingly
what motivates the concluding utopian image of so many violent
forces (especially Jeffrey himself) and contending women (Dorothy
and the innocent girlfriend Sandy) blissfully reconciled across the
undifferentiated haze and glow of Jeffrey's home, a home where
robins still, in a final close-up, mechanically devour worms.

Trying to read the allegory of Lumberton thus becomes an odd
exercise of reading an allegory that refers to everywhere (small-
town America) and nowhere (imagistically disseminated and antiquated) at the same time. Even trying to understand these markers
ironically or satirically becomes the most uncomfortable of stances,
most recently noted in Peter Brunette and David Wills's Derridean

reading that toyfully argues "the limits of reading" the film and the "abyss at its centre" (145, 147). If there is the promise of distinguishing revelations and secrets here, discovery of those revealed secrets releases no real information, only the displaced promise of other secrets that are never revealed. By the time the narrative reveals the climactic tableaux of the dead husband and corrupt cop, it appears almost incidental to the drama of Jeffrey and Dorothy. These and other revelations (such as an admission of love for Sandy) become merely private (but passionate) stagings of environments and trivial formulas—like Frank's desperate claims for Pabst Blue Ribbon beer over Jeffrey's favorite, Heineken—whose revelatory meaning has long since decayed into a familiarity. The refrain of the film, "It's a strange world, isn't it?", has nothing hermeneutically strange about it. Like even the kinkier scenes in the film, it is as unprovoking and familiar as "There's no place like home." In *Blue Velvet,* according to Jameson, "despite the grotesque and horrendous tableaux of maimed bodies, this kind of evil is more distasteful than it is fearful, more disgusting than threatening: here evil has finally become an image" ("Nostalgia for the Present" 535).

Since all meaningful differences have grotesquely merged across the shifting but similar locations of *Blue Velvet,* the awkward crisis becomes if and how one can signal one's presence in that place. Faced with this temporal and geographical sameness, every thing and person in Lumberton needs, like Frank, to shout its presence as the only way to distinguish it, and it is especially appropriate that Frank loudly and regularly greets Jeffrey as "neighbor" since to be a familiar neighbor here means to bond across the violence of becoming a vacant figure. The measure of reading this place thus becomes the manager of the hardware store who sees everything and knows his environment intimately—despite or because he is blind: here there is nothing to be recognized or distinguished. Everything is known but nothing is understood, and therefore the only available interpretive gesture is to violently disturb the surface of the place.

No wonder most viewers of *Blue Velvet* feel blandly exiled from its locale, destabilized within all its familiarity, and yet able to participate in it as the moderately popular commercial success that it was. For, to search for an interpretive position in *Blue Velvet* means finally accepting a reading formation in which all secret depths and meaningful differences share an enervated, familiar sameness, devoid of provocation or mystery and so allowing and perhaps absolutely necessitating some kind of demonstration of a viewer's own distinguishing position. In more concrete terms, this helps explain, I think, the peculiar social and commercial place into which this Lynch film has been received since it appeared, where its (and later *Twin Peaks*'s) strange and diverse popularity is certainly not specific to it alone in contemporary culture. In this place, the commercial showcase can accept the leftover inhabitants and structures of an art-film tradition as a location where that tradition does not need to make sense; here a modicum of commercial success is based on the attraction of going out to experience the location of otherness as the familiar place of personal distraction; here viewers seem taunted to interpolate themselves, with no textual guidance, as the only way of locating the terrain ("What *is* the proper response here? Nervous laughter? Bemused horror?"). The frequent feminist readings of the sexual violence in *Blue Velvet*—even those as imaginative as Laura Mulvey's in *Visual and Other Pleasures* (196–200)—are thus a provoked and often uneasy intervention. They become, at their best, aware that, similar to the psychoanalytic or semiotic readings of *Adrift* and *In a Year of Thirteen Moons*, differences in *Blue Velvet* (gender and other kinds) trade places so violently that reading them is ultimately reading one's own position and place, quite profitably excluded from the film.[9]

Indeed, the interpretive illegibility of each of these three films can be measured to some extent in the critical reception they have provoked. Both institutionally and rhetorically, they have proved peculiarly difficult to designate and recuperate, peculiarly difficult to comfortably interpret. This is not, I would underline, the traditional problem of a mistaken or wrong reading but a case of a group of movies, and the conditions through which they are viewed, troubling and refusing the standard paths of interpretation and hence eliciting multiple interventions. *Adrift,* for instance, was, oddly, released in showcase cinemas in this country after attracting huge audiences in Czechslovakia, where it was, apparently, seen as a folktale. In the United States, however, it mostly bewildered spectators who, like Roger Ebert, bemoaned it as psychological surface with no depth, but grinningly admired the posed beauty of Paula Prichett, the parodic center of the film. The case of Fassbinder extends well beyond *In a Year of Thirteen Moons* but in many ways is highlighted by it: squeezed between *The Marriage of Maria Braun* and *Berlin Alexanderplatz* (1979), it was largely ignored by critics and the public, and, when discussed, it was uncomfortably relegated to the art cinema where even there its textuality had to be displaced, inappropriately, onto the theatrical autobiography of the auteur. *Blue Velvet,* on the other hand, has achieved a bizarre public success in showcase cinemas as well as art houses and, later, video stores, reviewed ten times by *The New York Times* and a range of magazines and journals from *The Village Voice* to the *National Review* and culturally embraced by Europeans and Asians alike. These reviews, moreover, have been as contradictory, stuttering, and contentious as their institutional presentation has been uncertain: they range from the desperate ("turns the viewer's passivity into furious cognitive activity") to the stunned ("demands respect"); and the most accurate praise of its illegibility becomes the most severe condemnation of its illegibility ("a piece of mindless junk").[10]

Again, these are not simply instances common throughout film history where spectators and critics simply read a movie differently, some more correctly than others. Nor are these films that create just another version of what has been called an "open text" that allows for a variety of writerly readings. These are films, as I have tried to show, whose texts explicitly acknowledge the conditions of their reception by confronting and befuddling reading as it has been traditionally structured around certain historical principles and formations. These films, that is, are more self-conscious engagements with a larger pattern of illegibility in the international movie industry today as it responds to widespread changes in production and distribution of film texts whereby viewing becomes an odd combination of distraction and appropriation.

The more troublesome question is what do we then call and how do we then generate commentary on these movies, movies that seem more to discard interpretation than to invite it, to reside more in their excessive surplus than in their legible value.[11] Although the illegible address within the contemporary film industry certainly does not disallow interpretive readings of the traditional kind, these interpretive readings will, consciously or not, be antagonistically engaged with the history and conditions of watching movies in the eighties and nineties. Reading a film today therefore is usually done in spite of what our historical and cultural conditions seem to allow and, in the case of many postmodern films, in spite of the textual positions these movies offer.

This predicament is not, however, reason to devalue interpretive readings, although it clearly makes it easier to justify the bad faith implicit in constructing meanings for films. Rather, if reading texts without secrets today means to recognize formations that seem to exclude the authority and hierarchies of interpretive reading, it forces audiences to turn to the contours and choices of their own responses within those formations as the chief subject of their read-ing—responses today that range from inarticulate silence to more elaborate theoretical propositions to the social and cultish games that surround the reception of many films—as is especially evident in the responses to shows like *Twin Peaks* or *Dick Tracy* (1990). This is a call to discuss movies not as texts, positions, or places but as multiple cultural and commercial processes through which spectators, like performers in a cult, construct largely a version of themselves as a way of acting out a narcissism across different sub-jectivities. I would align this revised stance before movies with what Gregory Ulmer calls "post-criticism" whereby one kind of reader-viewer's position is as a parasite/saprophyte who performs a re-sponse as an "interruption" that "grafts itself onto" the decay of tradition and textual authority. In Barthes's words, viewers might now "produce simultaneous theory, critical combat, and pleasure; we subject the object of knowledge and discussion—as in any art— no longer to an instance of truth, but to a consideration of effects" (*Roland Barthes* 90). My readings of three films here are, conse-quently, hardly meant to be authoritative interpretations of textual secrets but admittedly limited and antagonistic readings of how those texts reflect the illegible conditions of their reception, inter-pretation (including mine) an uneasy search for its own positions and strategies. I am not discovering any textual secrets in any of those films but only mapping both the relevance and irrelevance of our frustrated search for such secrets.

Within this contemporary scene where a traditional legibility gives way to different performative interventions, misreading or misinterpreting a film is perhaps no longer even a question or at least not the primary question anymore. At their best, readings of and writings about movies today are dislodgments and interruptions (the actions Benjamin associates with essay writing) that regroup and make sense around particular audiences. Subjecting the illegible to the legible may no longer be interpretation (at least in a classical or modernist sense) but, as Benjamin might say, a testing or digression on the narcissistic limits of both. The space of those limits, of course, is where contemporary social and cultural life take place— and that is what the humbler action of trying to read the illegible makes available to us. After all, as Gayatri Spivak has reminded us in speaking of *Sammy and Rosie Get Laid*, "There are positive misreadings" and real lessons to be learned about ourselves in "the stalling of a programme of reading" (86, 83).

FILM AND THE CULTURE OF CULT

□□□

"A person in the 20th century can exist honestly only as a foreigner."

—JULIA KRISTEVA

What people have called cult films have usually been designated such and valorized, I think in far too vague a manner, precisely because they have been seen as marginalized or eccentric. They are what they are because they are peculiar, excessive, self-indulgent: movies watched at midnight, movies that appeal to outsiders of one sort or another, movies that exist beyond the canon of classical or showcase cinemas. As Umberto Eco points out in *Travels in Hyperreality,* in one of the few rigorous essays on cult movies, these films create, by definition, a private world whose furnishings can be acted upon "as if they were aspects of the fan's private sectarian world"; they are postmodern movies, he argues, in the sense that "the quotation of the topos is recognized as the only way to cope with the burden of our filmic encyclopedic expertise" (198, 209).

Aligning these movies even more radically with that postmodern impulse, I would argue, however, that the so-called eccentric status of cult movies is precisely what has made their particular reading formation so central during recent years. Resisting traditional inscriptions and legalities, most movies are now watched by audiences as private, domesticated performances or spectacular backgrounds to public lives. Unlike Eco, moreover, I believe that these cultish formations and viewing activities are *primarily* a product of the excessive historical burden of a contemporary audience's viewing conditions (spread across blockbusters and VCRs) and have less to do with any strictly textual features of those movies than with *how these movies are historically acted on from outside their textual peripheries.* Unlike B-films, the public precursor of cult movies, any movie today can become a cult film. Cult movies are those films that become the property of any audience's private space, and in this assumption of public images into private space, they become furnishings or acquisitions within which any modern viewer temporarily inhabits and acts out different subjectivities.

On this central point, my position differs quite significantly from Eco's argument that these films are *"born in order to become cult objects"* (209). No film, I would say, is naturally a cult film.[1] All cult films are adopted children: they are chosen from an excess of images that all say "choose me" and placed in a relationship with the viewer that, as a denaturalized and private performance, is beyond a naturalized and mutually possessive collectivity, "after ours." In this capacity of any audience to become the temporary parents of these temporarily domesticated children, those traditionally marginalized cult audiences have thus themselves expanded across culture and been reborn as the primary audience position of contemporary movies. Instead of reading movies, contemporary audiences now adopt movies, create cults around them, tour through them.

The Spectator as Tourist

With cult movies, as opposed to most other films, audiences seek out and discover not only the unfamiliar character and story but the unfamiliar style, frame, and imagistic texture. Once discovered and identified, though, the cult film and its strange images are then brought home, made familiar through the appropriative action of the viewers who make those images privately and personally meaningful while finding their own meaning in those images (Belmondo and Allen each take home parts of Bogart for their own fantasies, and Bogart inhabits both of them). In both classic and modern film theory, these viewers have usually been characterized as urban natives, individuals who, for better or worse, are able to find themselves at home in the vast architecture of images before them: the factory worker of Eisenstein, who lives the environment of *Strike* (1925); the city flaneur of Stanley Cavell, who wanders wide-eyed but comfortable like Chaplin in *City Lights* (1931); the courtyard voyeur of Christian Metz, who watches the city from his own *Rear Window* (1954); and even Teresa de Lauretis's female spectator remains unhappily trapped at home in one of Calvino's invisible cities. My cult spectator here, however, is more like a tourist whose relationship with the city of images on the screen begins from outside and who inhabits that city only by taking parts of it over. He or she stands in this city like a visitor in a photograph before the Eiffel Tower. For cult audiences, films are all stranger than paradise (often illegible just because they are so familiar), and it is the ability of these audiences to make a personal paradise out of that strangeness that marks them as cinematic tourists, so different from the urban natives who learned to read films by locating themselves in them.

On this tour, there are, for all of us, some easily identifiable examples. In low-budget films, from *Night of the Living Dead* (1968) to John Sayles's more elevated efforts, the economics of their production and distribution become a means of distinguishing these movies from a typical Hollywood production yet also a way of claiming a kind of common/secret ground for audiences who might feel closer to Pittsburgh and grainy stock than to the glamour of Hollywood. These are cult films as home movies. Similarly, there are the technological peculiarities that, for modern audiences, define 3-D films, silent movies, or the wizardry of *2001*, and so take the opposite route to a similar position. Here audiences establish their relationship with technology itself, and even when that rapport is only metaphoric (as with early sci-fi films) cult spectators are allowed the fantasy of their own position as technological participants. These are cult films as video arcades. Whether the audience focus for these films is economics, technology, or some other material dimension of the text, cult movies are always foreign films: the images are especially exotic; the viewer uniquely touristic; and in that relationship, viewers are permitted to go places, see things, and manipulate customs in a manner that no indigenous member of that culture or mainstream filmgoer normally could. Why Jerry Lewis is so loved in France follows from the same reason that Lina Wertmüller, despite her mediocre reception at home, became so

popular in the United States: cultural distance allows for the transformations of and by cult audiences. To adapt Susan Stewart's remarks, such films "allow one to be a tourist in one's own life, or
allow the tourist to appropriate, consume, and thereby 'tame' the
cultural other." Often displaying the mobility of their text through
the quotations, tee-shirts, or posters worn or claimed by their audience, these films "speak to the possessor's capacity for otherness: it
is the possessor, not the film, who is ultimately the curiosity" (146,
148). Indeed, what is centrally curious about the cult spectator and
the tourist is their ability to simultaneously appropriate images and
relinquish themselves to those possessed images.

Cults of any kind, especially those made up of film audiences,
are cultural revisionists. Their primary signifying practices are to
wrench representations from their naturalized and centralized positions and create what Eco terms "glorious ricketiness" (198): cru-
cifixes with motorcycles; lace over leather; Maoists in America;
Woody Allen as Bogart. Here any sense of a legitimate or true place
for the original representation becomes exactly what is under attack:
for film audiences and other cult groups, cult action is radical *bricolage,* the play with and reassembly of signifiers from strikingly
different cultures and contexts. With these films, the thematics—no
more than any notion of spiritual essence in a religious cult—are
only slightly relevant. Of course, these are often films about outsiders, yet they are vastly different from the large number of mainstream films where the rebels always have a cause. Of course, these
movies commonly dramatize a clash between different cultures or
subcultures, yet they share nothing essential with movies like *Mos-
cow on the Hudson* (1984) where the clash is in fact a thinly disguised assimilation into American society and, more importantly,
conventional audience positions where one interprets the movie
across legible places, characters, and actions.[2] If one wishes to
privilege a thematics, the most important motif in these movies is
the debris and excess that define characters and environments that
never quite relate to each other as natural or textually motivated. Yet
this excess is important mainly as a textual signpost to the real action in the film, the audience's use of the film text as debris in and of
itself.

Far more than thematics, what defines cult films is the materialization of the text in two related senses. Through the actual trans-

formation of the film into a kind of physical fabric (most clearly dramatized, in one instance, through the imagistic manipulations that repeated viewings or VCRs allow), the textual materiality of the images largely replaces the sense of visual presence and textual transcendence through which the viewer simply accedes to the movie. In a more theoretical sense, this material dislocation of a cult film can be described as a perverse swerve from the Oedipal trajectory that underlies a psychoanalytic model of the cinema. With that model, a spectator becomes positioned by the play of images whose *real* absence make their illusory presence more mesmerizing. With cult films, however, any sort of presiding, determining, or patriarchal relationship is displaced between audience and screen; the acquisition of those images as a material and moveable substance in their own right becomes their chief significance for the cult spectator. Like a mythical pre-classical viewer, the diverse, physical presence of the audience becomes a presence that overrides any other epistemological absence. Whether through the redefinition of the cinematic apparatus as an adult toy (a domestic game rather than a public ritual) or through the perverse materialization of the logic of an Oedipal imaginary, cult movies are the product of a viewer who acts out simultaneously the vision of child and adult. Rather than making the perspective of the audience the figurative child of the imaginary world that he or she reads a self through, that audience's perspective now becomes itself a shifting and temporary dominant that at once claims movie images and releases its perspective to them as its actively adopted children.

What this unique audience-screen relation testifies to and why I believe it is so significant as a description of how viewers watch movies today (significant enough to pass over the dubious quality of the films themselves) is its unusual disregard for textual authority and systemic coherence. It pinpoints, in short, an instance of dominant viewing and a semiotic practice that willfully refuses to play by the traditional rules of the game. These interpretative disruptions cannot, moreover, be simply dismissed as the "subjectivist madness" of post-structuralist angst, since this action is not only collective and based in a peculiar release from subjectivity, but, additionally, it is often the very terms of the texts it engages. Certainly one of the most obvious and crudely exemplary cult films of the last decade, *The Rocky Horror Picture Show* (1976) is a low-budget, "hysterical" mish-mash of genres from the musical to the sci-fi film. Centered on a sexually random family of media outsiders, it presents a chaotically intertextual range of subcultural clichés literally as social debris. Yet its true, if unsubtle, mark as a cult film, for my purposes, is how, in the first years of its fad, it generated a variety of representational distortions (squirt guns, toilet paper, etc.) from different urban audiences who in their excessive take-overs of that film nonetheless established a shared set of responses, responses that quite materially dispersed that movie and the performances that appropriated it in the clutter that then surrounded it. (In contrast, one might argue, the standardization of these responses as a type of mythology today has pretty much redefined this film as mainstream, not cult.) Here the audience narcissistically acquires images of self as a socially foreign image (transvestites from outer space) but only as these collective subjectivities can be quickly discarded as material debris.

Cult Movies and the Performance of History

If this kind of viewer response to cult films operates in general not just as textual disjunction but as disjunction that materializes the text as a tourist's souvenir, I will now map and specify a few varieties on the historical tour: to suggest that to explore both the different ways cult films have evolved and how the dynamics of cult viewing have recently been adapted to create sometimes more complicated and more serious strategies is to aim at the center of contemporary viewing.

One of the most prominent of these types is the historical cult film that locates itself precisely along that edge where the temporal and historical distance of a representation initiates audience reaction. *Casablanca* (1942) is one too-familiar choice, and we could all list similar choices that might appear on a "ten-best" list and which, depending on the catholicity of taste, might serve as a cult catalogue of revival films. These too are always and ironically marginalized products, if only through the label "best"; and as these lists change, sometimes dramatically according to the groups making them, the entire notion of a canon begins to waver through the instability of its status as a less-familiar sort of movie cult. To be most polemical, one might say that the historical valuation of films is frequently no less fetishistic about deep focus or auteurs than a teenage audience might be about rock music or kinky sex. Indeed, even when our relation to historicized films is purportedly based on more intellectually rigorous thinking, this relation is, of course, made across historical disjunctions that force these films to be recuperated and reconstructed through the mobility of our perspective. In these films particularly, the debris and waste always at the heart of cult activity is, most apparently, the materialization of history itself, whether in the form of film stock, lack of color, ancient props, or the presence of a dead actor. Indeed, Paolo Cherchi-Usai describes the distortions and transformations that early archivists and recent television have visited on original films by, reluctantly, admitting the cultish significance of any recuperation: "Every copy, so long as it is on film, remains a unique object, distinct from others; and the only truly possible aesthetic history of cinema is the enumeration and explanation of the circumstances that have made film so different from what it was (or may be supposed to have been) at the outset" (174). The rebirth of Fritz Lang's *Metropolis* recently (1985) thus becomes the archetypal adopted child that is cult: a historical souvenir dramatically materialized in tinted film stock and reconstructed through the fabric of contemporary rock video.

Welles's *The Magnificent Ambersons* (1942) might be a more subtle example, whose regular appearance as part of the canon might not be "despite" its clearly truncated and butchered look but "because of" that look. Appropriately, this is a film about the ravages and losses of history, marked with nostalgic references to an even older cinema—like the long iris-in that signals the end of George's innocence. It is a film in which the soft-focused edges of the first shots look intentionally like old photographs or, as Manny Farber complained, like a succession of postcards (McBride 102). While images such as these may point the way for a contemporary viewer, the harsh cuts and breaks that resulted from the studio's taking the film and its editing away from Welles provide the crucial openings for its success as a kind of cult movie: these are the material scars that, in only partly a metaphoric sense, allow the viewer to remake the film as what might have been under the guidance of its original auteur-father. From the perspective of the present, historical films of this kind always lack the continuity and verisimilitude needed to represent history authentically for that viewer, and through the ma-

Postcards from the Past (*The Magnificent Ambersons*, RKO, 1942)

teriality of their representational discontinuities the audience constructs his or her own history within the gaps and omissions of the movie. History is wasted by history itself—or, more exactly, its representation is torn from an original context and reconstructed, sometimes recklessly, through the historical presence of the viewer. Thus, the historical cultist in Scorsese's recent *After Hours* (1987) who does both: pretentiously referring to "the film" *The Wizard of Oz* (1939), she tells of the lover who was able to have an orgasm only by shouting "Surrender Dorothy." Where the lover performs a piece of the film as his own private movie, the teller of this tale casually exhibits herself through the film as a valorized fragment of film history: the twin action of historical cult.

This quiet violence implicit in a contemporary audience's rapport with historical cult films becomes much more explicitly a part of the image in my second category, those films called "midnight movies." These are also a somewhat arbitrary group. Anything from the quirky surface play of *Harold and Maude* (1971) to the bizarre nightmare of *Eraserhead* might figure here (while admittedly glossing over important distinctions). But, as a recent popular newspaper list indicates, the most cultish of this group generally tends towards what that writer calls "outrageous trash": *Attack of the Killer Tomatoes* (1980) and *Blood Sucking Freaks* appear alongside such classics as *The Texas Chainsaw Massacre* (1974), *Pink Flamingos* (1972), and *Liquid Sky* (1982).

What these have in common is, unmistakably, that they are after-hours films in every sense and usually rough cut even in the final cut. It is, I expect, unnecessary to detail the violence and very real trash that pervades these movies, often in films like *Blade Runner* (1982) and *Mad Max* (1979), as indications of how history "has already" or "will have" laid history to waste. More telling, perhaps, is the proleptic rock-video form of some of these movies and, even more than historical cult, the potentially infinite repetition of their social reception. Anticipated by older musicals and anticipating television shows like *Miami Vice* or *Cop Rock*, these narratives nearly dissipate their own narrative structure, undermining it with loosely connected non-narrative events whose excessive display either of the visuals or the music becomes a perceptual or audial format and invitation for the audience's own performance. Whether these non-narrative, usually musical, scenes announce the preparation for or the acting out of love or violence, they offer the viewer a private exhibitionist's space, not a voyeur's. The star performers in these films, such as David Bowie in *The Man Who Fell to Earth* (1976), are, after all, realizable, like the music, off the screen and beyond the fiction, and that, in large part, supports their attraction as cult concretely and erotically in excess of the narrative fiction and frame.

If these performances become vacuously repeated both in the

films and at their Friday night reception, this repetitious structure and its referential flux—corollaries perhaps for the random violence in these films—are the formula that allow an audience to perform the film as an exhibitionist's stage, where an individual can be both fully narcissistic and selfless. Here an encounter with a "foreign image" of other worlds and other selves is contained like a postcard sent again and again with the viewer's personal signature: as his own varied stage personas clearly reveal, David Bowie is a cult figure only because he repeatedly falls to earth, an avatar made through the different desires and imitations of his audience. If the recreation and mixing of archetypes or stereotypes becomes a central signifying practice in cult films, it is certainly not in the traditional sense of these types but only as they are reified, made material, and offered up to their audience for mechanical reproduction. *Road Warrior* (1981) might employ a conventional flashback technique to tell the story of a classical hero from another time, but what distinguishes that film and describes this hero is his special identification with and performance of the scattered waste and debris of some other, lost culture—ours to take hold of and release ourselves into because that culture is and is not ours, again and again in this film or in its serial repetition from *Mad Max* to *Mad Max Beyond Thunderdome* (1985).

To speak of interpretively reading either of these two types of cult films (as Eco seems to suggest) is to misunderstand them, just as to talk about "camp," cult's first cousin, is, according to Susan Sontag, to betray it. As a measure of much contemporary viewing, cult films, whether by nature or choice, invariably subvert and run contrary to the immobility and stability that regulate standard viewing and reading practices. If they initiate a kind of identification, it is quite unlike the usual internalized identification based in fantasy. It is rather identification with the materiality or material history of the image, an externalizing of those so-called imaginary signifiers as the material markers that give that image significance: specific lines of dialogue, a gesture, a piece of clothing. These images and markers thus do not have any essential stability or balance (or stability provided by some essential difference), and without this essential stability they lack, as the previous chapter argues, that binary structure which has supported most notions of reading (now and then, presence and absence, signs and meaning). Instead, these are al-

Cult Audiences and the Midnight Performances of *Rocky Horror Picture Show* (*Fame*, United Artists, 1980. Manayunk Pictures)

ways, at best, "re-readings" of the viewer's own position, for in these cases the audience always comes armed and overprepared with a text of its own that makes the film text pretty much secondary. There are, for cult films, no first-time viewings, since these movies by definition offer themselves for endless reappropriation: their worn-out tropes become the vehicles not for original connotations but for the viewer's potentially constant re-generation of connotations, through which the audience reads and re-reads itself rather than the film. In a more complicated sense than most critics have recognized, these films are indeed trash but trash as it refuses the domesticated place of cultural reading. This is historical junk like repossessed cars that the spectator experiences as an exotic monument to his or her own present; consumer art like generic food that accommodates not just an artist's name but the names of multiple spectators who have (metaphorically or actually) purchased the film; touristic texts, like a videotape memoir of Paris or New Orleans, which even when it is first shot is already a "misreading" of a city or an individual as memory and souvenir.

What these films are about, though, is more than the distortion of memory. Today, the historical appropriations and cultural exhibitions that these first two categories map have become socially central. In a day when movies of any type are more and more in the remote-control hands of domestic viewing, the textual play of cult viewing has moved steadily across media cultures as a third category of cult, a contemporary commercial cult. With this commercial cult, films aim to manipulate that audience through the very terms that audience itself created in its assaults on the movie screen and on movie history. The provocation for this play with the material of the image has now, however, shifted its source (at least partially) back into the text in a decided attempt to elicit the kind of reckless and self-conscious audience response that I have associated with more recognizable cult films. When these contemporary films work as cult, their seams, gaps, and instabilities often look slicker and more aesthetic than their prototypes, yet, imagistically and narratively, they remain materially overdetermined and ultimately about the performance of the spectator.

Viewing as Choosing: *Choose Me*

Specific examples of this contemporary cult movie are Alan Rudolph's *Choose Me* and Scorsese's *After Hours*. To indulge in a bit of cultish bricolage, *Choose Me*, for instance, might be seen on a line from *Casablanca*, with its Hollywood counterpart in *Play It Again, Sam* (1972). Thus, while *Casablanca* achieves its cult status through the fragmenting pressures of history that make its text a mosaic of different filmic representations and through the action of audiences that, in many ways, liberate it from that history, the Woody Allen film simply absorbs that cult status and audience to refocus them on the intellectual and dramatic irony that Allen's character can orchestrate. *Choose Me*, on the other hand, eschews even that ironic stability. The always-mobile center of this film (which is in fact no center) is the media cult that develops around Genvieve Bujold as Dr. Nancy Love, a radio talk show host who seems to affect everyone's romantic and sexual life. As long as her encounters are confined to phone conversations, she is the emblem of conservative stability; when she enters the visually excessive world of "Eve's Place," however, that stability begins to shake loose; and she, like the characters around her, begins to live out the random obsessiveness that characterizes a truly contemporary cult. Indeed, Micki, the protagonist who first initiates her, crystalizes this odd obsessiveness when he asks every one he kisses to marry him and then points out that he only chooses to kiss women he would marry. For Micki, a kiss is not just a kiss in any sense.

In *Choose Me,* this tough-guy Micki aligns unmistakably with a Bogart archetype—a spy, a Yale professor, a jet pilot. But, if Eve is his Ilse and her place his cabaret, all those types on Micki become a function merely of material evidence (magazine covers, blurred signatures, etc.) that may or may not be fraudulent. This world is as far from Casablanca as it is from any realistic Los Angeles: here the touristic intrigue and exoticism evolve around not mystery but the material instability of the place itself and the exhibitionism that is the only way these characters can relate to one another. Eve owns the cabaret/bar only because "Eve's Place" was for sale and her name happened to be Eve; she meets Micki only because he returns

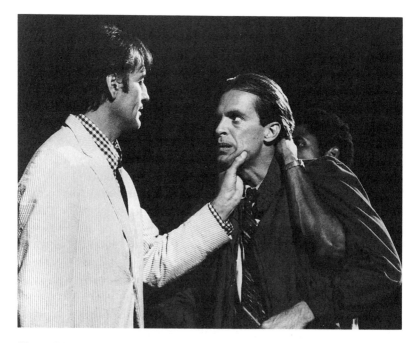

Choose Me: The Drama of Too Many Choices (Island Alive, 1984. Tokyo Stills)

looking for the original Eve, but is just as happy with the new version he found "under the blinking sign"; finally, the two are married only because of their willingness both to relinquish themselves to what material coincidence offers them and to accept marriage as both sacred and sordid. If the Nancy Love–Eve relationship focuses this film as a remake of *All about Eve* (1950), this Eve and her companions exist and communicate only in the terms and substance of that 1950 movie as it appears as a poster in a character's apartment, as, that is, cult material.

The last scene in this film is consequently far more than forty years from Rick and Ilse's farewell. This is not, though, because the final choice of *Choose Me* is so much less noble or idealistic or that this Rick stays with this Ilse. Rather, it is because these characters have realized that truth, love, and idealism can only be cult gestures today, and, if one is to commit oneself to these it is only for as long as that passion remains aware of its material instability. In the medium close-up of the final shot, there's no "looking at you" for these characters, sitting side by side with shifting eyes. Yet, there is still, if ever so tentative, commitment to and passion for someone beyond one's self. In *Choose Me,* the Oedipal trajectory of the narrative is not, in the end, rejected or even interrupted, but rather split in a way central to cult logic: *Choose Me* describes the state of having it both ways, of participating without confinement, of active commitment without a central presence, of narcissism without subjectivity, of appropriation as relinquishment.

In the same way, the spectator of this film remains oddly inscribed as the adopting parent (possessing and not possessing) a perspective that refuses to anchor itself in any secure sense of an authentic or naturalized reality—whether that reality be fiction or fact. This unusual position reflects the film's unconventional production and distribution strategies on the outer fringes of Hollywood, and in turn predicts the consistently different and uncertain reactions that the film has generated. Made for $800,000, *Choose Me* was produced and distributed through the semi-independent channels of Island/Alive and consciously aimed at the more "private" audiences of commercial cult who, in Rudolph's words, want "to work a little bit" (Siegel 38). Specifically, this work must take place across the spectacularly artificial sets and carnivalesque narrative of *Choose Me,* which dislocate an audience especially from

Hollywood's public fantasy and relocate it in the free play of a sort of hyperrealism. Dramatized through its false depths and dense surfaces, which at once attract and arrest vision, *Choose Me* engages its audience through a billboard perspective that aims to collapse the distinction between private and public space, the illusory and the real, the imaginary and the symbolic. Towards the end of the film, Micki and Eve appropriately act out their reconciliation before a rooftop billboard with an audience of prostitutes watching from below, while, in a parallel fashion, the entire film works to inscribe us, their second audience, between the no-point-of-view of the advertising image and the exhibitionistic stance of its wandering audience— sexual and cultural tourists performing public images as a private space. Just as this romantic union is materialized in all its "obscenity," the perspective of *Choose Me* forces its audience to assume its public images only as the property of private consumption: like a music video where the imaginary materializes in the viewer's endlessly repeated and theatrical performance of it. In *Choose Me,* an audience does indeed choose a temporary narrative and cultural home, but only as it defines itself as a constantly mobile, private scene.

After Ours: *After Hours*

Whether we describe this home in terms of the remains of film history, the repressed activism of the me-generation, or the redundancies of VCRs, it is a home-away-from-home where we glancingly perform the images around us as a way of releasing ourselves from our contemporary narcissism and its drive to appropriate. Here we watch the world across the circus of multiple screens and shows, as in *After Hours,* where individuals are all tourists in their own cities, trying to adopt a temporary home. Here, culture looks more and more like the collection of the cults that wander through the Soho of *After Hours:* a film whose title should have a very silent "H" in that second word, indicating the disappearance of a cultural screen that once could have coordinated the broken family of all those separate exhibitionists, tourists, and adopted children.

Paul, the protagonist in *After Hours,* is the quintessential uptown native who finds he has become the absolute downtown tourist when a chance encounter deposits him in the streets of Soho, a part of his town that is a pastiche of many other worlds. A word processor, he begins as a character who has successfully and comfortably situated himself within a neatly programmed life. But, while romantically pursuing a chance encounter with the stranger Marcy to a downtown rendezvous, the world and its objects suddenly come alive with images that do not so much respond to his perspective and desires as truly assault that perspective with a material and independent aggression. During the taxi ride downtown, high-speed images turn the city into a carnival, and, as the comical start of his misfortunes, his last twenty-dollar bill leaps out the cab window. When he does find the loft where Marcy is staying, her friend Kiki tosses the keys from the fire-escape balcony. The point-of-view shot from below exaggerates the fall of the keys into a frighteningly disproportionate image that seems as if it will crush Paul. From then on, the environment is actively foreign to Paul: a tourist in a town that is his own town and where he must perform its images in order to survive them.

The comedy and horror of the movie results from an unsettling play between what could be a series of disturbing coincidences and what could be a terrifying master plan to persecute Paul, the paranoid suspicion of a grand narrative to which he has no interpretive access. His original romantic motivation for entering this world is explicitly related to the fetishism of romance. He aims to seduce the unknown Marcy, but soon flees from the suggestion of some kind of grotesque burn or scar on her thigh, the first of several castration fears that haunt Paul. He simply cannot look—especially at that which could unsettle or break down the romantic centrality of his place in the world, his coherent and patriarchal subjectivity. As long as he maintains the traditional centrality and reality of a single point of view in a contemporary city, as long as he inhabits the city as a reflection of himself, the relay of events and images necessarily supports both persecution and paranoia: Marcy's death later *does* seem his fault and he is, for good reasons, mistaken for the burglar who is everywhere because Paul projects himself everywhere. As the narrative unfolds, however, Paul becomes increasingly the victim of that which is beyond his limited, fetishistic perspective: specifically a wild array of self-subsisting, foreign, and disconnected worlds ranging from the sixties sanctuary of Julie to the obsessive vision of a Mr. Frosty vendor. Eventually, Paul's notion of a coherent subjec-

Paul at Club Berlin: An Initiation into Cult Survival (*After Hours*, Geffen Film Co., 1987)

tivity with a personal integrity is, in every sense, chased, harassed, and haunted by an eclectic force of different cults, who are intent, as he reads in a newspaper fragment, to tear that self apart.

His escape occurs only when he learns to perform himself as a changing identity and figure in the images, scenes, and art objects that appear randomly to invade his life with a life of their own. He learns to give up old hierarchies and authorities and become himself an active cultist who can adapt to material circumstances. His demand to enter the punk Club Berlin is finally granted but the unexpected price to go there is his partial transformation into its punkish, cultish images (he is marked with a botched mohawk haircut); temporarily rescued when he pretends to pick up a nervous gay man, he buys time by performing his adventures as a stand-up routine, staged and shot through a series of demonstrative dissolves. If at the beginning of the film Paul can smile wryly at the computer trainee who secretly harbors an artistic life, his adventures in Soho teach him that, although artistic control (in a traditional sense) is impossible, survival in contemporary life means having a performative relationship with the contingencies that overtake any sense of control. In Paul's first encounter with Kiki, she asks him to work on her papier-mâché construction of an agonizing Munch-like human figure. Paul's shock at how nonchalantly Kikki gives away her artistic authority becomes the first episode in his transformation into a cult artist self-subjected to the life of material circumstances. By the end of the narrative, Paul finds his way out of Soho by recreating himself as a material figure in the terms of whichever scene presents itself. In the final climactic sequence, he gives himself up to another woman artist (reversing the sexual dynamics that began the film) who saves him by making him into a version of the sculpture that he had helped construct at Kiki's. He becomes a piece of energized flotsam, a postmodern work of art to be stolen and circulated indiscriminately (like all the money in the film), merely a material object who has come to recognize that (in the apocalyptic words of the jukebox song of this sequence) "that's all there is." Greeted by his computer after his touristic nightmare, Paul knows better than ever the irrelevancy of traditional humanistic authorities and unified social myths.[3]

Structurally, the narrative refuses logic in the same way that the different images—of the characters and the filmmaker—refuse coherence and realistic motivation. For the viewer, the story appears almost as a series of separate, performative dissolves, like the summary of his tale, which Paul performs for his bored and disappointed host. It appropriately follows the logic of a computer-game narrative, which works to undermine the teleology of humanistic narrative itself and replace it with an aleatory set of circumstances that require an always-different set of judgments in order "to figure oneself out of" the situation.[4] Unlike with classical or modernist narratives, viewers of *After Hours* anticipate and find a series of disconnected and discrete situations that seem to parody (through Paul's own vision) an audience's antiquated need to connect times and places as a familiar place. The result is, in Scorsese's words, a "swirling effect . . . in the audience's mind" (Lopez 19). In this narrative, the suspense is always the shock and surprise of the tourist's present moment, the crisis of how to appropriate and adapt oneself to the foreign situation.

Whether through revivals, midnight movies, or commercial cult, all that the cult films like *After Hours* and cult relations with any movie may put into play is, like Paul's dangerous liaisons, the rare and suspect coincidence of meeting glances. Midnight people, we become audiences desperately and comically mobilized across a shared singularity, seemingly freed from the burden of truth or authenticity or any other "ours"; a large part of film audiences today may now only perform and relinquish itself again and again in order to give not images but itself a certain but temporary cultural significance. At the beginning of *After Hours,* the camera drifts perversely from a conversation (in which a new word processor assures Paul that he eventually intends to start a literary magazine) and creates a wandering focus on marginal objects: a photo, a doll on a desk, *souvenirs of a personal and family life displayed in a public space.* For Andrew Sarris, this camera action is bizarrely inexplicable in its material take-over of the point of view, and concomitant tittering of the audience was equally annoying ("Stranded" 54). Yet this kind of distracting irrelevancy, cut loose from a central perspective, is exactly what this film is about and why it might be described as an allegory of the contemporary cult audience. As Paul eventually learns, spectators today embrace and revel in material connections and chance meanings, which may be there or which may be generated only by their choice to perform a relationship with those images.

Appropriately, there seem to be two lines of response to this Scorsese film: if you're not from New York it's a paranoid fantasy; if you live in New York it's a documentary. Either way, of course, it's a tourist's view of the city, any city, where we adopt its images as part of us and not part of us and where our marginal and temporary places are always its only center. Finally understanding what we have in common as tourists here and how we now figure ourselves in this city of images—through, for instance, directors, genres, and narratives—may be more central today than any attempt to make an accurate map of it—let alone feel at home there.

DISSOLVING VIEWS

THE COMMERCE OF AUTEURISM
Coppola, Kluge, Ruiz

□□□

"As soon as you become that big, you get absorbed."
—FRANCIS COPPOLA

"Subjectivity is greater than someone's intentions."
—ALEXANDER KLUGE

"I thus partly failed because they had given me a television
assignment and I had made, anyway, a film by an auteur."
—RAOUL RUIZ

Despite the continuing prominence of the *auteur* as a heuristic category, theories and practices of auteurism have never really been
untroubled. Their spread from France in the fifties through America
and elsewhere in the sixties and seventies was tightly bound to
changes in production and distribution strategies, such as the rise of
an international art cinema and the introduction of an Arriflex camera, all of which encouraged reconceptualizing films as more personal and creative documents. While these changes in production
technique frequently presented auteurism as a more accurate way to
cut through the complications of mass entertainment and to locate
the expressive core of the film art, they also offered, less visibly, a
more historically appropriate method for negotiating the reception
of films. The historical adaptability of auteurism, back through the
works of early filmmakers like Von Stroheim and Eisenstein and
forward through the present generation of Spielberg and Cimino,

identifies mainly the desire and demand of an industry to generate an artistic (and specifically Romantic) aura during a period when the industry as such needed to distinguish itself from other, less-elevated, forms of mass media (most notably, television). Auteurism offered not just new audiences, retrieved from the modernist art communities, but new cultural sanctions to old audiences, alienated and awash in an indistinguishable spate of media images. Despite its often overstated countercultural pretentions, auteurism became a deft move in establishing a model that would dominate and stabilize critical reception for at least thirty years. The subsequent auteurist marketing of movies whose titles often proclaim the filmmaker's name, such as Bernardo Bertolucci's *1900* (1976), David Lean's *Ryan's Daughter* (1970), or Michael Cimino's *Heaven's Gate* guaranteed a relationship between audience and movie in which an intentional and authorial agency governs, as a kind of brand-name vision that precedes and succeeds the film, the way that movie is seen and received.[1]

The Multiple Children of Truffaut

Indeed, one of the chief mystifications or omissions within early theories and practices of auteurism has been a valorization of one or another idea of expression, mostly disconnected from its marketing and commercial implications. Despite their large differences, theories and practices of auteurism from Astruc and Peter Wollen to Foucault and Stephen Heath, from John Ford to Jean-Luc Godard share basic assumptions about the auteur as the structuring principle of enunciation, an organizing expression of one sort or another.[2] Whether one locates that auteurial presence as a source for stylistic or other textual consistencies and variations or as a figurative authority supplanting a lost or "dead" source (as Barthes would say) in the form of a textual enunciation, the place of the auteur within a textual causality describes a way of organizing spectatorial positions in a transcendent or trans-subjective fashion ("The Death of the Author" in *Image–Music–Text* 142–148). To view a film as the product of an auteur means to read or to respond to it as an expressive organization that precedes and forecloses the historical fragmentations and subjective distortions that can take over the reception of even the most classically coded movie. The often strained attempts to make consistent or evolutionary the British and American movies of Hitchcock or the German and Hollywood films of Fritz Lang are governed by some sense of a historically trans-subjective and transcendent category that authorizes certain readings or understandings of those movies. In David Bordwell's analysis of auteurism as an interpretative cue,

> the overt self-consciousness of the narration is often paralleled by an extratextual emphasis on the filmmaker as source. Within the art cinema's mode of production and reception, the concept of the *author* has a formal function it did not possess in the Hollywood studio system. Film journalism and criticism promote authors, as do film festivals, retrospectives, and academic film study. Directors' statements of intent guide comprehension of the film, while a body of work linked by an authorial signature encourages viewers to read each film as a chapter of an oeuvre. . . . More broadly, the author becomes the real-world parallel to the narrational presence 'who' communicates (what is the filmmaker saying?) and 'who' expresses (what is the author's personal vision?). (*Narration* 211)

Formalist and cognitive critiques of auteurism, such as Bordwell's, can vanquish most of the myths of expressivity in the cinema in favor of more formal and heuristic uses for the auteur. Yet, these too do not fully attend to the survival—and, in fact, increasing importance—of the auteur as a *commercial* strategy for organizing audience reception, as a critical concept bound to distribution and marketing aims that identify and address the potential cult status of an auteur. Today, even these modernist corrections, discussions, or deconstructions of the romantic roots of auteurism need to be taken another step toward recontextualizing them within industrial and commercial trajectories. Illustrating this need to investigate how "the author is constructed by and for commerce," John Caughie has noted that this question has been overlooked since Brecht's 1931 account of *The Threepenny Opera* trial in which Brecht "brilliantly exposes the contradiction in cinema between the commercial need to maintain the ideology of the creative artist and the simultaneous need to redefine ownership in terms of capital, rather than creative investment"(2).[3]

This attention to a commerce of auteurism is especially critical in keeping pace with the auteur as a practical and interpretative category during the last fifteen years, the period when the play of commerce has increasingly assimilated the action of enunciation and expression. Certainly such a reevaluation of auteurism as more than enunciatory expression or heuristic category could and should take place across any of its historical variations and to a certain extent has already been implicit in the social and historical emphasis of a "politique des auteurs." Yet the international imperatives of postmodern culture have made it clear that commerce is now much more than just a contending discourse: if, in conjunction with the so-called international art cinema of the sixties and seventies, the auteur had been absorbed as a phantom presence within a text, he or she has rematerialized in the eighties and nineties as a commercial performance of *the business of being an auteur.* To follow this move in contemporary culture, the practices of auteurism now must be retheorized in terms of the wider material strategies of social agency. Here the auteur can be described according to the conditions of a cultural and commercial *intersubjectivity,* a social interaction distinct from an intentional causality or textual transcendence.

Models of agency are useful here precisely because they are models of intersubjectivity that aim to undermine the metaphysics and the authority of expression and intention, the cornerstones of a stable subjectivity. They delineate a model of action in which both expression and reception are conditioned and monitored by reflective postures towards their material conditions. Charles Taylor, for instance, has argued a model of human agency that foregrounds "second-order desires" where the "reflective self-evaluation" of "the self-interpreting subject" has as its object "the having of certain first-order desires" (43, 28, 15). Similarly Anthony Giddens suggests a materialist model of expression as self-reflexive action. The motivation of expressive action, the rationalization of that action, and the reflective monitoring of action concomitantly interact to map the structure of expression as a reflective social discourse that necessarily calls attention to the material terms of its communication. In both cases, *agency* becomes a mode of enunciation that describes an active and monitored engagement with its own conditions as the subjective expresses itself through the socially symbolic. In the cinema, auteurism as agency thus becomes a place for encountering not so much a transcending meaning (of first-order desires) but the different conditions through which expressive meaning is made by an auteur and reconstructed by an audience, conditions that involve historical and cultural motivations and rationalizations. Here, even hopeless auteurs like Coppola, reluctant auteurs like Kluge, or chameleon auteurs like Ruiz may strategically embrace the more promising possibilities of the auteur as a commercial presence, since the commercial status of that presence now necessarily becomes part of an agency that culturally and socially monitors identification and critical reception. Auteurs such as these can be appropriated only across the gap between their agency and their subjectivity.

The Auteur as Star

Where the practice of the auteur as a particular brand of social agency initiates its revision of its relation with film audiences is in the contemporary status of the auteur as star. This idea of the auteur-star may appear merely to hark back to the earlier avatars of auteurism who were placed in certain aesthetic and intellectual pantheons: from Orson Welles to Robert Bresson, the celebrity of the auteur was the product of a certain textual distinction. As generally consistent as that tradition of the textual auteur is, more recent versions of the auteurist positions have swerved away from its textual center. In line with the marketing transformation of the international art cinema into the cult of personality that defined the film artist of the seventies, auteurs have become increasingly situated along an extratextual path in which their commercial status as auteurs is their chief function as auteurs: the auteur-star is meaningful primarily as a promotion or recovery of a movie or group of movies, frequently regardless of the filmic text itself.[4] Like Michael Cimino's *Heaven's Gate,* auteurist movies are often made before they get made; and, like Coppola's *Tucker* (1989), a director's promoted biography can preempt most textual receptions of a movie.[5] In a twist on the tradition of certain movies being vehicles for certain stars, the auteur-star can potentially carry and redeem any sort of textual material, often to the extent of making us forget that material through the marvel of its agency. In this sense, promotional technology and production feats become the new "camera-style," serving a new auteurism in which the making of a movie, like *Fitzcarraldo* (1982), or its unmaking, like *Twilight Zone* (1983), foreground an agency that forecloses the text itself. As Godard has parodied it so incisively in *King Lear* (1989), in today's commerce we want to know what our authors and auteurs look like or how they act; it is the text that may now be dead.[6]

Placed before, after, and outside a film text and in effect usurping the work of that text and its reception, today's auteurs are agents who, whether they wish it or not, are always on the verge of being self-consumed by their status as stars. By this I am not suggesting merely some brand of egotism or self-marketing posture but that the binary distinctions that once formulated most models of auteurist expression against textual organization have collapsed into what Dana Polan has called, in a larger context, the postmodern "evacuation of sense" ("Brief Encounters" 167–187). The oppositional calculus of expression to text, psychology to meaning, or authority to interpretation no longer sustains the contemporary auteur film. Instead, institutional and commercial agencies define auteurism almost exclusively as publicity and advertisement, that is, as both a provocative and empty display of material surface that intercepts those more traditional oppositions. Meaghan Morris has noted (in language similar to Richard Dyer's description of stars), that today "the primary modes of film and *auteur* packaging are advertising, review snippeting, trailers, magazine profiles—always already in appropriation as the precondition, and not the postproduction of meaning"(122–123). To respond to a movie as primarily or merely a Spielberg film is, after all, the pleasure of refusing an evaluative relation to it—a pleasure that might be equally true of the standard reception of Herzog movies—and much of that pleasure lies in being able to already know, not read, the meaning of the film in a totalizing image that precedes the movie in the public images of its creator.[7] An auteur film today seems to aspire more and more to a critical tautology, capable of being understood and consumed without being seen. Like an Andy Warhol movie, it can communicate a great deal for a large number of audiences who know the maker's reputation but have never seen the films themselves. This, not surprisingly, is what so exasperates neoromantic Marxist critics of postmodernism who cling longingly to the high-modernist conception of filmmaker as expressive artist, to a time before "art becomes one more branch of commodity production" and "the artist loses all social status and faces the options of becoming a *poete maudit* or a journalist" (Jameson "Reification" 136).

Of the several tacks within the commerce of the auteur-star, the two that are most pertinent here are: the commercial auteur and the auteur of commerce. Although the first category could theoretically include a vast range of stars as directors and directors as stars (Stallone, Kevin Costner, Clint Eastwood, and others), more purportedly respectable names in this group would include Spielberg, George Lucas, Brian De Palma, David Lean, and, with different agendas, John Sayles, Woody Allen, Truffaut of the later years, Lina Wertmüller, the Bertolucci of the latest Academy Awards, and the Spike Lee of Air Jordans. My argument so far would assimilate most of these names since what defines this group is a recognition, either foisted upon them or chosen by them, that the celebrity of their agency produces and promotes texts that invariably exceed the movie itself, both before and after its release.

The second category is, I believe, the more intriguing variation on the first, for there a filmmaker attempts to monitor or rework the institutional manipulations of the auteurist position within the commerce of the contemporary movie industry. If normally the auteurist text promotes and recuperates a movie, these filmmakers now run the commerce of the auteurist and autonomous self up against its textual expression in a way that shatters the coherence of both authorial expression and stardom. Motivations, desires, and historical developments—which are frequently dramatized in critical readings of films as at least semi-autobiographical—now become destabilized and usually with a purpose: did, one asks, the same Fassbinder who made *Maria Braun* give us *Querelle?* While a more traditional auteurist position could describe these changes in perspective and expression according to some coherent notion of evolution, an evaluation of many contemporary filmmakers must admit fissures and discrepancies that consciously employ the public image of the auteur in order to then confront and fragment its expressive coherence.[8]

As a specific example of the contemporary auteur's construction and promotion of a self, I will concentrate on one "semi-textual" strategy that is often taken for granted in the relation between a filmmaker, the films, and an audience: the interview, which is one of the few, documentable extratextual spaces where the auteur, in addressing cults of fans and critical viewers, can engage and disperse his or her own organizing agency as auteur. Here, the standard directorial interview might be described according to the action of promotion and explanation: it is the writing and explaining of a film through the promotion of a certain intentional self; it is frequently the commercial dramatization of self as the motivating agent of textuality. But the transparencies of this logic are exactly what many contemporary auteurs necessarily trouble, confuse, or subvert through the agency of their commerce.

The Economics of Self-Sacrifice: Coppola

Certainly Francis Coppola is one of the more celebrated and bewildering examples of auteurism as it has evolved through the seventies and eighties. In an essay on the evolution of Coppola's career, Richard Macksey astutely makes the connection between Orson Welles and the more recent child prodigy of Hollywood, the first anticipating and the second following the heyday of auteurism as Romantic expression and independent (if not transgressive) vision. Yet, as Macksey observes, distinctions between the two filmmakers are even more compelling. On the one hand, "Welles has been a presiding model of Romantic genius, the myth of the explosive, comprehensive talent challenging corporate power and ultimately becoming the victim of its own genius." On the other hand, there is Coppola's marketing of that myth:

> If he has inherited something of the Romantic artist's impatience with the system, his powers of persuasion and need to take risks have led him toward the boardroom rather than the garret, back toward the old putative center of power in Hollywood (and the financial centers off-camera) rather than toward exile and "independent filmmaking." His perilous if uncanny power to enlist bankers probably depends upon his temperamental inability to fold in a poker game; movie-making and risk-taking are synonymous for him. (2, 3)

As a romantic entrepreneur, Coppola becomes a self-exiled and stridently independent auteur who claims in one sentence "I need to be a solo guy" and then for *Tucker* humbly surrenders the film to George Lucas's "marketing sense of what people want" (Lindsey 23–27). Straddling the margins of European art cinema and the center of commercial Hollywood, he is one of the original directors of the contemporary blockbuster (*The Godfather*) and the one whose experimental goals seem most threatened by the financial and commercial exigencies of his blockbuster successes. This ambivalent double image as the auteur-star of goliathan productions and the auteur-creator victimized by the forces of those productions defines Coppola's central place within the commerce of auteurism, characterizing him, in Andrew Sarris's offhand portrait, as a "modern dissonant auteur" ("O Hollywood" 51).

Coppola's career has followed an almost allegorical path. It begins confidently as a commercial talent with *Finian's Rainbow* (1968) and *The Rain People* (1969), transforms itself through the commerce of auteurism with *The Godfather* and *The Conversation* (1974), suffers the contradictions of that position with *Apocalypse Now* and *One from the Heart* (1982), and most recently settles uncomfortably into the aims of the commercial auteur with *Tucker.* Jeffrey Chown has described these commercial pressures and contradictions, beginning with Coppola's first appearance as the auteur-creator of *The Godfather:* "It is curious that the film that put Coppola on the celebrity map, that gave him the magic adjective 'bankable,' is also extremely problematic in terms of authorship. . . . Coppola coordinated diverse creative agents in this production, he was clearly the catalyst for the film's success, but, in a career view, his creative control and originality are far less than in other films that bear his directorial signature" (59). Even Coppola's most artsy and individual film, *The Conversation,* demonstrates major industrial complications within auteurism, at least as it is applied to the control of the filmmaker. Walter Murch, who engineered the brilliant soundtrack and much of the editing of that movie, can claim, for many critics, the most important part in that film. With *Apocalypse Now,* moreover, this most celebrated of contemporary American auteurs surrenders the choice of three different endings to a battery of advisors and miles of computer printouts that surveyed the expectations and desires of different audiences (including President Carter). In the most industrial and textual sense then, Coppola has become the willing victim of his successful name: as Chown observes of the critical slaughter that greeted *One from the Heart, The Outsiders* (1983), and *Rumble Fish* (1983): "The name Francis Ford Coppola connotes spectacles, Hollywood entertainment combined with artistic sensibility, Italian weddings, and napalm in the morning. Coppola the individual seems stifled by those expectations" (175). As with his capitulations to Army censors for *Gardens of Stone* (1987), self-destruction seems part of his "creative compromises" with the contemporary terms of auteurism.

His commercial compromises with the agency of auteurism mean, more exactly, a kind of sacrificing of that self as a spending and expending. In 1975, Coppola summed up his perspective on auteurism this way:

> The *auteur* theory is fine, but to exercise it you have to qualify, and the only way you can qualify is by having *earned* the right to have control, by having turned out a series of really incredibly good films. Some men have it and some men don't. I don't feel that one or two beautiful films entitle anyone to that much control. A lot of very promising directors have been destroyed by it. It's a big dilemma, of course, because, unfortunately, the authority these days is almost always shared with people who have no business being producers and studio executives. With one or two exceptions, there's no one running the studios who's qualified, either, so you have a vacuum, and the director has to fill it. (Murray 68)

Coppola's emphasis here on the word "earned" is especially significant, since for him the expressionistic privileges of auteurism are directly related to financial actualities of investment and risk: an auteur earns his status by spending himself, and both gestures involve the aggrandizement, demeaning, and "expending" of oneself through a primary identification with the agency and exchange of money. Thus the complement of a self that is constructed as a financial agency is degradation of that self as *merely* a financial product. For Coppola, "the artist's worst fear is that he'll be exposed as a sham" (Murray 65), namely, that an audience's financial investment in his agency will be revealed as only commercial advertisement.

This image of self curiously mirrors the obsessive geniuses found in Coppola's liturgical and operatic narratives. From the two *God-fathers* through *Apocalypse Now* and *Tucker,* his visionary charac-ters invariably pursue grandiose spectacles that reflect their desires but which either literally or metaphorically then serve to destroy them. While these spectacles frequently echo their nineteenth-century origins (lavish visuals and operatic soundtracks), the more exact terms of their agency as cinematic characters are the contem-porary spectacles of industrial technology as a financial investment (for war, for corporate industry, for the business of the family). *The Conversation* is the most appropriate example: driven by the pas-sions of the protagonist Harry, it is a conversation through technol-ogy that leads to the absolute collapse of a sacrosanct individuality. Coppola's description of Harry, the devout and tortured Catholic, could indeed describe Coppola himself as auteur: "He's a man who has dedicated his existence to a certain kind of activity, to technol-ogy, and who in a part of his life experiences regrets and realizes that the weapon he uses for others in a certain fashion is destroying the man himself. . . . The single reason for which he is destroyed is perhaps that he has started to question all that" (Belloni and Codelli 51). If Hollywood's commercial industry is the financial agency that makes and unmakes Coppola the auteur, Coppola remains driven to invest and lose that self in ever-grander forms of its technologi-cal spectacle. Perhaps the most extraordinary and thus indicative examples of this tendency are Coppola's technological dream proj-ects: a giant domed theater in the Rocky Mountains or an imagined film *Megalopolis* where four elaborate video films would draw on Goethe's *Elective Affinities* to tell the story of Japanese-U.S. relations.[9]

Not coincidently, I think, an interview with Coppola becomes a media performance focused on the technology and the business that define and threaten him. Worried about the casual nonchalance of his meeting with this auteur, for instance, one interviewer notes Coppola's immediate identification with the technology of the per-formance, "I needn't have worried. The minute I switched on my tape recorder, Coppola came to life. This was *work.* First, he cor-rected the position of the machine, then he fiddled with the volume and tone controls till he had them set to his satisfaction. Finally, he allowed me to question him" (Murray 54). More generally, Coppola frequently constructs himself in an interview as an entrepreneur orchestrating the forces of technology or as a character lost in the improvisations of Hollywood business. In the same interview, he describes his expectations and frustrations about the Academy Awards, his struggles with Paramount executives to have Marlon Brando cast for *The Godfather,* and then acknowledges that this most famous vehicle for his agency as an auteur had less to do with his control of the film than with submission of self and the loss of energy: "A lot of the energy that went into the film went into simply trying to convince the people who held the power to let me do the film my way" (59).

Francis Coppola: Success as Self-Destruction

Ultimately, of course, it is this expenditure of energy as the loss of self that is the contradictory measure of Coppola as auteur. Evaluating the ratio of his position as artist against his possible decision to actually assume the full agency of a studio (which he would do with phoenix-like Zoetrope Studios), he casts himself according to the finances of running a large piece of technology:

> If I were running a studio, it might take me 100 B.T.U.s worth of energy to bend something a quarter inch; if I stay independent and use my own resources, those 100 B.T.U.s could bend something a foot. . . . But look: The average executive of a movie studio may make $150,000 a year, and have a corresponding power, over his company. As a film artist I make much, much more than that and, consequently, have that much more power over my company. . . . Perhaps the wisest thing to do is to use all my energies to make a film that grosses some stupendous amount, then go out and buy a major company and change it from the top. (Murray 68)

Appropriately, for this elaborate characterization of himself at the turning point in his commercial career, Coppola begins this 1975 interview by claiming "this is my last interview" (54). Within this glossy, high-tech conversation with *Playboy*, he must naturally be given up from the start.

Attempting to synthesize his relation to his movies in the manner of the Big Picture, Coppola's interviews often make him into the film itself. He becomes the presiding genius of the film of himself; however, this genius is represented not in expression or productive control but in expenditure and loss: loss of control, loss of money, loss of vision, and loss of self. His renowned posture as a risk taker thus becomes a bombastic effacement of any differences between his intentions and the films. In 1982, Jonathan Cott asked Coppola about the publicity gained from adopting this posture of loss during the production of *One from the Heart*. His response resembles the hysteric in trouble with his language and in trouble with the distinction between self and the agency for that self:

> The real answer, from my point of view, is that I just say what the facts are; in this case, that I'm working on a

film, I'm told that the money's gone, and that if I want to go ahead, I'll have to risk something of my own. And by that point, I'm so far into it that I say okay. . . . And then that tends to be the story that the people who write about me want to go for. If they ask me, "If the picture's a flop, will the company go out of business? and if I say yes, it's because that seems to be the case. But it's not the idea that I want to push out into the public. In fact, I regret that I'm treated more as a charlatan or a con man than as a professional person, and to be honest, my feelings are hurt. I feel that I'm not reckless or crazy. It's just that I'm primarily interested in making films more than amassing money, which is just a tool. If someone suddenly gave me a billion dollars, for instance, I'd only invest it in my work. I will say yes to anything that seems reasonable to me, and sometimes I get in a little deep because I want to participate so much. (24)

A key moment in this interview, as with others with him, is the appeal for sympathy, not the distance of authority. It elicits a kind of social and psychological identification between Coppola and an imagined interlocutor, like that between a spectator and an actor-victim in an epic movie. For Coppola, the auteur communicates from one heart to another, and, for him specifically, the self-portrayal of the auteur as one who has been persecuted and dismissed by the operatic conglomerates who have made him a powerless vehicle becomes the basis for a sympathetic identification: "I've done so much for them, and yet they resent even putting me in a position where I don't have to go to one of them with my hat in my hand and have them tell me what movies I can or cannot make" (76). At other times, with astonishing dexterity, he rhetorically moves between an image of himself as the powerful agent of a financial and technological machine and an image of the completely insignificant individuality that inhabits that agency—oddly sounding like Rupert Pupkin in Scorsese's *The King of Comedy* (1982):

You know what I think? I think people are afraid of me, basically. They're afraid if I ever got like too much power, I'd change their lives, and they're right! . . . I'm only a minor representative of the times. I may be a schmuck, but you can be sure that some other people somewhere are going to start doing the same kind of stuff, and the world is going to change. . . . As for myself, I'm not worried. What the hell! If I don't do it with this film, I'll go and invent some little gadget that will make billions! (Cott 76)

The sympathetic enlistment of an audience now becomes the path for locating multiple subjectivities ("other people somewhere") within an agency that disallows the authority or stability of any single organizing perspective. In this action, Coppola puts into play the central problem of contemporary auteurism as an interpretive category: while it remains a more powerful figure and agency than ever, it is invariably forced to disperse its authority in terms of its "sympathetic" reception across a commercial agency.

In the end, Coppola remains the most utopian figure within commercial auteurism, for whom the spectacle of self-destruction becomes a way back to self-expression. For him, the destruction of the authority of the auteur will mean the resurrection of an audience of private auteurs, an intimate yet goliathan network of electronic communication. Speculating on the future of new technologies, which regenerate themselves through money made and money spent on them, he imagines artists and audiences as a home-video exchange that retains the aura of auteurist agency, the expressive "I" becoming a multiplying and sympathizing third person plural:

Everybody will use it, everybody will make films, everybody will make dreams. That's what I think is gonna happen. You'll ship 'em over to your friend, and he'll ship one back. . . . I think that, very shortly, there's going to be a whole new approach to things, and the designers and the architects and philosophers and artists are going to be the ones to help lead the society. (Cott 76)

The Politics of Self-Fragmentation: Kluge

Far from the combination of bombast and self-abnegation that characterizes Coppola's auteurist image, Alexander Kluge is a grudging auteur, a reluctant personality who seems to engage any and all historical issues more than the history of himself: since the famous

Oberhausen manifesto that has become a mythic starting point for the New German Cinema, he has been one of film's most famous international signatures yet has accepted that label only with great hesitation and careful qualification.

To locate Kluge within the troubled category of auteurism has always required revision, but as Kluge has moved across the contemporary international film industry, placing Kluge the auteur has meant increasingly complicating that position to fit the shifting grounds of postmodern culture. His trouble with and redefinitions of auteurism have, to be sure, already been remarked within modern German cinema as a whole. As Miriam Hansen and Eric Rentschler have argued, one of the most important collective gestures of contemporary German cinema may have been to re-situate the very notion of the auteur: Rentschler has shown that Kluge has been part of an effort to enact a variety of cultural subjectivities in which different enunciatory relations with history have decentered the conventions of auteurism ("Cooperative Auteur Cinema" 89–101); Hansen has noted that for the New German Cinema "the emphasis was necessarily more on a 'politique des auteurs,' the political struggle for independent film making in a country which did not have a film culture comparable to that of France," this new direction calling for a "revision of *Autorenkino* through a collective politics of production" ("Cooperative Auteur Cinema" 41).[10] Accurate as these assessments are, I would like here to add to them by suggesting another way in which Kluge has mobilized auteurism as a critical category, to suggest less a critical subversion of auteurism as a production strategy than a critical exploitation of auteurism as a category for reception. Indeed, the marked shift in emphasis on auteurism as a way of viewing and receiving movies, rather than as a mode of production, has been the central change in the meaning of auteurism from the sixties to the eighties. It is along these lines that Kluge has begun to make specific use of the commerce of his own singularity and subjectivity.

Many of the relevant terms in this revised stance—fragmentation, diversification, multiplication—are not new to studies of Kluge. But I will enlist them here as part of an exploration of a specific commercial strategy in which a politics of agency takes its place as much in an extratextual as in a textual business, more exactly as a "semitextual" practice where Kluge admits to performing himself as an image of the writer/producer/filmmaker but primarily as a strategy for eliciting certain relations with his audience. In a crucial sense, Kluge's writing of a self in today's national/international film industry situates itself between the more social and political work surrounding the films (his involvements with government policies or television networks) and the reception of his film practice (whose material textuality refuses to be the authority for its reading). As an extension of his early attempts to dismantle the aura of auteurism as expression, Kluge's more recent engagements with the practice of auteurism have been to use it as a textual material in its own right, a textual material through which he can act out and disperse the specific problematic of an authoritative agency.

Within this commerce of auteurism is where I believe Kluge has been positioning himself more and more, admitting and reworking the institutional impostures and excesses of an auteurist position today in a way that aligns him somewhat peculiarly on this front with filmmakers like Coppola and Raoul Ruiz (as well as Nagisa Oshima, R. W. Fassbinder, and the Godard of the eighties). Walking a tightrope between the image of a romantic auteur and his recognition of its commercial conditions, Kluge has recently described himself as a "demolition artist" whose position under the Big Top today alternates between a highwire artist and a performing clown: "I'm Robinson Crusoe. If I'm an artist, I am alone, and individually I can work only this way. I'm esoteric like Adorno is, like every artist is. But I would like to have camouflage, mimicry. I think it's important not to show one is an artist nowadays, because it's a very dangerous status" (Rainer and Larsen 21). Again, this claim both to be an artist and to mimic its image does not contradict Kluge's aesthetic programs in revising the needs of "Autorenfilm" as a cooperative cinema nor his other efforts to generate the multiple perspectives of a public sphere. Yet, if in the sixties those efforts emphasized political and formal strategies that leaned towards a countercultural utopia, this particular engagement with the commerce of auteurism indicates a more conscious confrontation with his own evolution into the mainstream of film culture. If, comparing Kluge to Wenders, Schlöndorff, Fassbinder, and Herzog, one could previously make, more reliably, the claim that Kluge stood outside the international auteurist circle, that is less true today as Kluge carefully promotes his politics through the promotion of his name: his 1988 premier appearance in New York, for example, has featured radio interviews, university symposiums, negotiations with *Paper Tiger,* a special issue of *October,* and the overseeing of an American collection of his films and television programs at the Anthology Film Archives. A growing television presence in West Germany, Kluge has become a reluctant star within the international auteurist circle, and the question has now become for him, I believe, the inverse of the American political scene today: not how can a star absorb the political but how does a star reactivate a materialist politics within his or her commercial agency.

The answer for Kluge and others is that there is a business and politics of agency that permits auteurism to remain a useful tactic in engaging commercial or semi-commercial patterns of identification. Although auteurism today has effectively vacated the agency of a metaphysics of expressive causality and textual authority, the shell of auteurism—which remains in the form of a material publicity— opens a space for the dramatization of subjectivity refusing its own expressive authority, for a dramatization of subjectivity as, in fact, a material intersubjectivity responsive to the action of self-interpretation and self-critique. To put this in linguistic terms, the mechanisms for identifying with a speaking subject, usually a director, have become as important to communication in film culture today as the so-called textual statement of a movie itself or the different ways it is received by different audiences: the commercial drama of a movie's source can say as much today as the drama of the movie and the dispositions of its viewers. As important as the text of a Kluge film becomes the work of critical reception that Kluge initiates across his name, that is, his auteurist status and his public's knowledge of it.

Kluge thus finds in the contemporary agency of auteurism one of several postmodern grounds from which to initiate a modernist critique of contemporary cynicism and vacancy, a way of reorganizing a devalued and emptied auteurism as a critical subjectivity.[11] As early as 1979, he claimed, "I have always believed in auteur cinema." But "auteur cinema," he continued, "is not a minority phenomenon: all people relate to their experiences like authors—rather than managers of department stores" ("On Film" 206–207). Implicit even in these remarks is an understanding of auteurism as a process of identification that can reflect itself as an agency for critical "self-interpretation" in its audience; such a reception of auteurism is possible largely because a putative creative presence has been commercially dislocated from textual authority and refocused as the mechanisms of agency. Indeed, an especially concrete and anticipatory version of this critical use of the agency of auteurism can be seen in Kluge's release and re-release of perhaps his most commercial undertaking, *Strongman Ferdinand* (1975): he followed the film from theater to theater, the authorial source repositioned as a critical interlocutor defined by the diversity of his audience. The auteur becomes literally realized as an agency constructed across the diverse response of a genuinely public sphere—not unlike one of Charles Moore's postmodern buildings, constructed through the interaction of community planning.

Kluge's aesthetic and ideological play with the agency within the commerce of auteurism may be seen acted out across a spectrum of other artistic and social texts: from public appearances and social and political commitments to literary and nonliterary writings, from rumored histories of one's past to one's penchant for a certain camera person or a particular star.[12] A recent television program he produced, for instance, features a collage of different "auteurs" from the New German Cinema (Helke Sanders, Margarethe von Trotta, Herzog, Volker Schlöndorff), yet the show refuses to identify the specific product of any particular director. Indeed, for Kluge, the very multiplicity of his own personae, as a university professor, novelist, aesthetician, politician, lawyer, disciple of Adorno, and businessman becomes a fortuitous instability within the auteurist perspective on his filmmaking career. Other, more textual dimensions, would include his early use of his sister as a familial counterpart in films like *Yesterday Girl* (1965–1966), his place as adaptor of his own stories, such as *The Patriot* (1977–1979), and the books that reassemble movies like *The Patriot* and *The Power of Emotion* (1983) around Kluge's own voice and promulgations.[13] Like the wry voice-over whose "useless remarks" introduce *The Patriot,* his expressive agency through most of these tactics achieves a "prismatic effect" that tends to assert and then disperse its own authority (Rainer 23–24).

With Kluge, the interview becomes a dialogue about complications and deferral in which, in his words, he, "like a catalyst, . . . disappears from the process" (Kluge "On Film" 208). Indeed, much of the attraction of the interview format for Kluge may be precisely that dialogic or polylogic structure that is ignored in most auteurist encounters but which for him is enacted as something between a conflictual debate and the relational experience of "chatting" (which Kluge oddly associates with women). This kind of encounter obviously parallels Kluge's work with textual montage and his other efforts to replace creative authority with a more cooperative and conflictual exchange. Yet, here it has the specific advantage of reformulating the coherency of intention and the opacity of celebrity that attaches independently to the agency of auteurism, the path which in the contemporary film industry has become increasingly important in forming modes of identification as expressive action.

For Kluge, the interview regularly accentuates that presentation of agency according to a series of rhetorical and structural strategies. As early as 1974 Jan Dawson recorded this tendency when she introduced a long interview as "a fragmented, three-day conversation." After reading the transcript of that interview, Kluge distanced himself further from it by complaining about its abstractions and asking Dawson "to cut down the generalisations and explicate his meaning with more concrete illustrations from the films." Confronted with all these dislocations of her speaking subject, Dawson took proper refuge in Kluge's film aesthetics, asking the reader to "create their own interview from the text that follows" (*Kluge* 206).

More specifically, one finds in Kluge's interviews a tendency not only to alternate the abstract with the concrete but to embed that concrete in a disconnected montage of seemingly digressive stories, placing oneself as an empty agent at the center of "not one story but many stories" (206). Serving to fragment the speaking subject rather than synthesize (like Coppola) diverse matter through that speaker, these anecdotes can range from accounts of the filming of an eviction in Frankfurt to stories about the "history of the plow, which in 8 A.D. already looked like it does today," to pseudo-confessional fantasies of lovemaking in the deserts of Africa (216–217). Sometimes, these episodic digressions can serve as illustrations of certain points, but just as often they stand out as Brechtian gests that seem to trouble intentionally the historical and cultural place of Kluge himself as speaking subject: the apparent failure to maintain a consistency in subject matter or historical episode monitors a speaker whose agency is regularly being fractured by that matter. This is the presentation of Kluge as historical raconteur who, unlike the Reagan paradigm, does not use the historical anecdote to fabricate himself as a transcendent or opaque agent of discourse ("Anything I say is important and true simply because *I* say it") but to disperse or dislocate his agency through the material variety of history's "histoires" ("Because anything could be said, it surpasses any coherency I can give it").

A second characteristic of the Kluge voice is its ability to absorb or deflect a centered, critical position. As has been common from the beginning, an interview with Kluge is an interview with a complex plurality manifested in his third- or first-person plural voice and the deflection of most questions about his specific work towards larger financial, artistic, and political issues. In an interview with Stuart Liebman, for instance, Kluge consistently redefines his own alliances, relocating himself as a filmmaker within a variety of odd bedfellows. He accepts Herzog as an ally, as "an amateur like me." "Even films like *The Boat, The Never-Ending Story, The Name of the Rose,*" he allows, "are made the Oberhausen way." Yet he finds Straub and Huillet's *Moses and Aaron* (1974), a film that would seem close to Kluge's own materialist aesthetics, too visual in its recreation of the opera (Liebman 31, 49, 25). At one point, cinemas are declared dead; television hailed as the future; but, he then acknowledges, "We will come through television to cinema again." With typical mobility and contrariety, he refuses full identification with either the modernist or postmodernist school, and instead declares his work "classical" in its faith in a counter public sphere (Liebman 43). His objections and agreements always appear as only qualifiers, making waffling seem strict political program: "We have no objections," he says of his and Negt's disagreements with the historical focus of Habermas's work, "but we have a different field of employment" (Liebman 42). In a 1989 interview with Yvonne Rainer and Ernest Larsen, Rainer pursues the elusive "we" that Kluge becomes, and the response only diffuses the agency further before it paradoxically joins ranks with *Der Spiegel:*

> We have organized ourselves. We have organized all opera houses and theaters in Germany, book publishers and independent filmmakers. In other words, the traditional media—not newspapers or broadcast artists—the

books, cinemas, theaters, and the circus. They belong together. And on television they look very different. This is
understandable because originally they had nothing to do
with television. We also have a partner, the news magazine *Der Spiegel*. (Rainer and Larsen 19)

To paraphrase his own words, this auteurial voice—mobile, critical,
and generous in the sense he applies it to Adorno—is a voice of continual differentiation in which it becomes more a predicate and a
"porous" agent than an authorizing expression.

   Interview tactics such as these are not, obviously, radical political
gestures. As a part of the diversified confrontation that is Kluge's
project, however, they can mark a significant move within the critical reception of agency. Indeed, the questionable possibility of a
"radical gesture" itself may be exactly what is implicit in a perspective on auteurism as critical agency. As Charles Taylor notes about
the subject/agent of Sartre's "radical choice" (who might equally be
the classical auteur or the textual auteur of the sixties):

He would be utterly without identity. . . . The subject of
radical choice is another avatar of that recurrent figure,
which our civilization aspires to realize, the disembodied
ego, the subject who can objectify all being, including
his own, and choose in radical freedom. But the promised total self-possession would in fact be the most total
self-loss. (35)

Instead, as I believe Kluge recognizes on all fronts, the preliminary
question to all other questions of symbolic form within today's international culture must concern the material conditions and agencies
of intersubjectivity. This is a politics of agency that moves beyond
radical choice towards that of the radical evaluation and openness of
a public sphere, towards, in Taylor's words, the "deepest unstruc-
tured sense of what is important."

   Kluge has said of the style of his films, "One doesn't see the
cut, but my signature resides in it." Likewise, one might say of
his agency as an auteur, one hardly sees the expression because
the speaker resides so rigorously in the material politics of its
predication.

Scattering a Phantom Self: Ruiz

Raoul Ruiz appears to have little ambivalence about the commercial and postmodern status of his signature. If he too dramatizes an auteurist self as a version of self-sacrifice or self-dispersal, these strategies are much more than Coppola's call for "self-creativity" within the technology of agency or Kluge's eliciting of "self-interpretation" across his own mobile persona. They are, rather, a cultural exercise and intellectual game meant to make all notions of self disappear within a hall of mirrors.

Despite his characterization as one of Europe's most celebrated auteurs, identifying with Ruiz's image as an interpretive category is never more than a temporary sighting of the ghost in the machine of the culture business. Most prominently, Ruiz uses his shifting international citizenship to position himself as a dislocation of the geographical parameters that usually anchor identity as part of a single culture (Coppola as essentially American, Kluge as essentially German). A Chilean exile with an ambiguous heritage, Ruiz has made his auteurist reputation largely in France and other European countries, but only as it has rubbed against the grain of those adopted cultural identities. Gilbert Adair explains the origins of this always adoptable figure:

> Raul Ruiz was born in Chile, i.e. nowhere. Indeed his earliest memory . . . is of being actually 'discovered', while mooning around the doorstep of his parents' home, by a party of English explorers, whom he conjured up for me as scanning the horizon in Jungle Jim safari outfits, earnest hands cupped over noble brows. (When on telling of another, no less outrageous anecdote, I asked him point blank if he was lying, he vigorously protested his innocence—as, of course, would both a liar and an honest man.) Since the military coup of 1973, Ruiz has lived in exile, i.e. everywhere—for, from that point on his filmography has imposed a different geographical entry after virtually each entry. (40)

Between nowhere and everywhere, Ruiz the auteur becomes a kind of relativity machine who represents mostly the changing conditions that surround him, projecting himself into those cultural conditions as only one of their always shifting variables.

"Raoul Ruiz" is a continually scattered and suspended place, a Chilean auteur-filmmaker whose exile in France made television work for different countries his primary activity. Following the coup of 1973, a number of Chilean filmmakers set themselves up, mostly in Europe, as a cinema of resistance. For Ruiz and his films, the oppositional position, especially after *Dialogue of Exiles* (1974), became increasingly inappropriate, his place as an "international exile" describing too much movement and variety to be geographically defined as oppositional in any sense. For Zusanna Pick, this identity as a geographical wanderer and collector who views the world as museum has something particularly Latin American about it but in the person of Ruiz it becomes a central site for upsetting stable notions of subjectivity and its association with territorial authority as a discursive formation: "In the case of Chilean cinema in exile, the reformulation of the boundaries of culture and place opens the way for the notion of exile. Its intervention in the critical space traditionally assigned to nationality has the potential of expanding the strict link to 'geographical' and 'territorial' boundaries. . . . The notion of culture would contain the interrelation of other elements—those located both inside and outside its original boundaries—even if they seem incompatible at first" (45, 47–48). Hence, his cultural identity as an exile acquires for a filmmaker like Ruiz the portability of a document (such as a passport) whose discursive possibilities mean especially that it can be forged and altered to assimilate heterogeneous elements and situations.[14] This is the auteur as tourist.

Within this formation, Ruiz the auteur becomes the essential nowhere man who willingly gives up the expressive authorities of a filmmaker and becomes (with tongue in cheek) the television *metteur en scène* who assembles what the conditions around him provide. Whereas usually "auteur" connotes creative activity, Ruiz makes films as an "inventor" who is continually aware that his inventions assemble very tentative constructions that have only a fleeting relation with reality. Like a tourist, he energetically simulates locations and environments before moving onto another—a troublesome tourist who destabilizes whatever location or conditions he inhabits. If the more oppositional filmmakers from Chile are moti-

vated by an inherent sense of what they *should* do as Chileans loyal
to their origins, Ruiz has described himself as motivated by what he
can do within the location and conditions he finds himself ("D'Une
Institution L'Autre" 19).

A Chilean situated in France but involved with other European
and some American projects, Ruiz has succeeded by adapting and
relinquishing his own personal vision to a wide variety of opportuni-
ties and conditions. Through various projects from film features
to short television documentaries, he becomes, in his words, the
"holes to be filled" (Ehrenstein 2). Far from claiming to have the
unique control of an auteur, Ruiz characterizes himself as a laborer
who loses himself in the "interior of the assignment":

> I realized that we were considered auteurs, thus like
> people somewhat on the outside of the mainstream. But
> what interested me [about working in television] was to
> work like an employee of television and to shoot the
> whole time, since I love only that. I consequently wanted
> to make a reputation for myself as job laborer. For that,
> after having made *The Suspended Vocation* (1977) and
> *Hypothesis of the Stolen Painting* (1978), I asked that I
> be given a job assignment. Even a stupid assignment. I
> liked very much that I do everything that was assigned to
> me, so that I could look for a place at the interior of the
> assignment. . . . As soon as they offered me the oppor-
> tunity to make a film like *Of Great Events and Ordinary
> People* (1979), I took it as an assignment and experi-
> enced some problems in my relationships with people:
> I realized that work of a television director was very
> different from the work of what one calls an auteur.
> ("Entretien" 41).

Ruiz is the auteurist as the free-lance laborer who simulates the
position he is offered. Again distinguishing himself from any oppositional avant-garde, he notes that "there is a see-sawing in my
work as my themes and problematique have changed, whereas Littin
makes the same films in exile that he made in Chile. . . . For me, I
recognize that it's impossible to make a film without taking account
of the conditions in which I am making it, thus my situation itself,

the conditions of an exile who must make films in France with the French and on French subjects" ("D'Une Institution" 21).

An auteur absorbed by the eclectic assignments of a media industry, Ruiz recognizes that the authority of his address becomes dispersed not only in the different demands of a multitude of production enterprises but concomitantly by the unpredictability of its reception. Scattered throughout different cultures and countries, his projects are sometimes never shown and when they do appear the vehicle was "not simply TV" but "ten different TVs." Television networks and their audiences vary throughout Europe, and one "can never be sure where your film will be shown when you make it." Unlike Fassbinder, that other astonishingly prolific auteur of the seventies, Ruiz claims he is an auteur without a defined market or audience: "Sometimes my films work for one or two people but not a whole audience" (Ehrenstein 6). If an auteur's audience becomes part of his or her definition within the commerce of auteurism, Ruiz's success is fabricated, according to him, by a lack of material definition. "We don't have an audience at all," he claims at one point. "*La Ville des pirates* (1983) for example was rejected by all the European TV networks. At the same time it was accepted as the official representative of France at the Venice Film Festival. After that it got distribution. Another film we made in four days, *Pointe de fuite* (1984), was just a joke. But it was sold to German television and the Netherlands and ended up paying for *La Ville des pirates*. In each case it's something like that" (Ehrenstein 5).

Educated in law and theology, Ruiz has acted out the role of a filmmaker as a vocation suspended between the certainties of its material and cultural practice and his own personal yet fragile speculative propositions (about reality, about communication, about the human figure itself). His vocation as auteur is not unlike that of the characters in his 1977 film, *The Suspended Vocation*. In that film, a young seminarian finds himself embroiled in an ideological feud between the Jesuits and a cult to the Virgin Mary (which is itself subdivided into two groups). The vocational direction of the young seminarian becomes, however, far more a structural and formal problem as the film gains speed. The movie becomes two movies, one whose cast and setting are located in the black-and-white conditions of a forties film, the other materializing in the color stock of the sixties. Actors wander from one film text to another, the seminarian

The Suspended Vocation: Authority Caught between the Certainties of Law and the Speculations of Religion (New Yorker, 1977. ICAB)

himself is played by three different actors, anachronistic cars and television programs intrude here and there, and spatial demarcations between the two mutually reflecting films are frequently blurred or overlapped. The religious blasphemies that appear throughout this film are, more than anything else, the blasphemies of figures who refuse to remain stabilized within a textual, religious, or ideological scheme (neither St. Bernard's nor Trotsky's). Here the coherence and personal commitment of a vocation becomes shamelessly and hilariously suspended and dispersed by the material of a heterogenous agency it can never control: "The whole may be seen," Ruiz acknowledges in a description that could apply to *After Hours,* "as the image of a missed vocation as much as the chronicle of a paranoia" (Christie 123).

Ruiz, in turn, acts out blasphemies—or to use his other word, "irresponsibilities"—against traditional auteurist positions. He gleefully suspends himself between the visionary agency of the auteur as artist and the invasions of that position by aleatory events, discourses, and situational predicaments that unbalance and often debunk its claims as a coherent expression. In suspending himself this way, he literally plays himself out—scatters himself—as a set of formal propositions whose rigorous logic is undercut by the material and cultural predicaments that surround and invade that perspective. Suspended between the myths of "religious" totalities and the exigencies of "legal" contingencies, this auteur becomes a Borgesian gamesman whose passions for a unity that responds to the multiple options of a material world end up canceling out the coherence of his own position as they cancel out each other.

An identity spread across cultures, a vision dispersed through a multitude of industrial conditions and forms, and a voice that addresses an unknown and changing audience, Ruiz is an unanchored and nomadic auteur defined by the fatherless ghost that informs both his persona and the narrative images of his films. This fatherless status might first reflect Ruiz's consistent disassociation from the usual auteurist conflict with a "cinéma du papa." His narratives then parallel that historical dissociation by evolving from a lost or parodied father figure, such as his filmic adaptation of the marooned boy of *Treasure Island* (1986): "I've put in the idea of all the other pirates having affairs with Jim's mother. So every ten minutes one of them comes to the boy and tells him 'Listen, I've got something to tell you—I'm your father!" (Ehrenstein 7). Directly or indirectly, this forsaking of fatherhood with its subsequent narrative confusions and pleasures figures in the plots and perspectives of many other Ruiz works, such as *Hypothesis of a Stolen Painting* with its missing master image and *Three Crowns for a Sailor* (1982) where Ruiz conflates a group of exiled patriarchs and lost seafaring sons drawn from tales such as Coleridge's "The Rime of the Ancient Mariner" and Conrad's *Secret Sharer*. The textual result is a visual context made confused by phrases of irrelevant dialogue and characters who wander through images and environments without a sense of direction or place. In many of his films the dialogue detaches itself entirely from the characters and the situation, just as the plot itself becomes less important to the film. Here, and throughout most of his films, Ruiz's fantastically baroque stories and mise-en-scène, in Pick's words, articulate "the disjointed subjectivity of exile" (56), a subjectivity—much like his own—deprived of the symbolic and representational agency of a patriarchal order and so free to make its temporary home in multiple narrative and imagistic forms.

The phantom figures that proceed from this fatherless auteur and his unanchored narratives occupy what Ruiz describes as a "zone" where any affirmation of identity is also a denial. With his usual flare for geometric abstractions, he characterizes this logic:

> Sometimes, when there is the unexpected association of one image which is shown to us with another which we have in our heads, we must make a jump across a zone where images are bound in a provisional manner. Images then organize to constitute themselves as phantasms. Fantasy is not the bridge between the hidden images and the ones we are shown. Nor is it what permits the rescue of other images which form a temporary bridge. There is a mutual stimulation: images come to fill a zone formerly occupied by the phantasm as a void. And when it appears, the phantasm terrorizes because it is a kind of *affirmative denial*. ("Les Relations" 32)

The appearance and disappearance of these phantom images proceed therefore not so much as part of motivated hierarchy but as an aleatory and provisional drift in and out of background "sets," progressing, according to Ruiz, through their centripetal and centrifugal movement in and out of those sets, which function as temporary agencies: "The strength of the images which constitute the fantasy derives from the fact that one chooses an object from a set extremely quickly, not necessarily the most conspicuous object, and one uses this object as a pivot with which to propel oneself to the next scene. The feeling of *affirmative denial* arises because in moving so quickly from one set to another by means of a rapidly chosen object, we remember only that object" ("Les Relations" 32). These fatherless phantoms, exiled in a zone of perpetual tourism, thus affirm themselves only against a shifting and continually vanishing agency, the monetary background of the set.

The suspended image of Ruiz as wandering auteur, I am arguing, projects itself within the institution and agency of the auteur across a similar phantom zone. Like his characters and his phantom images, his auteurist character "starts a project, stops, goes back, and starts out again animated by another project" (Buci-Glucksmann and D'Allones 91). Especially as he constructs himself in an interview, Ruiz as an authoritative agent and vision follows the rhetorical logic of the fatherless phantom: "It is first haphazard or aleatory, but it is especially polysemantic and polyphonic. . . . One presents a phrase, retreats from it, then remakes it. . . . I am continually playing with that, and with the gesture, with the ambiguity of the gesture in a situation" (Buci-Glucksmann and D'Allones 90).

This analogy between the phantom images of his characters and that of the interviewed auteur seems entirely appropriate since, more than most filmmakers, Ruiz has made the structure of the dialogue and interview a repeated part of the narrative structure of his films. In *Of Great Events and Ordinary People,* for instance, Ruiz accepts a television assignment to inquire among the citizens of his *quartier* in Paris about their personal opinions of an upcoming election. With the finished product, however, the whole interview process starts to be questioned and suspected. As Ruiz himself points out, the film finally describes only the impossibility of locating any sort of authentic subject or private life within an interview process that functions within an official background or set:

> When someone is interviewed, me for example, I give
> only official answers. I act as much like the President as

Raoul Ruiz: The Everywhere and Nowhere Man (ICAB)

myself. . . . What we see of these private lives does not
in fact reveal anything. Ordinary situations are "official": shooting in a factory, for instance, one always
shows workers working, officially engaged in work, officially discussing, officially stating their personal problems; but one never sees the accidents which call into
question what those people are doing. To do this it is necessary to fake things. (Christie 126)

Accordingly, these documentary interviews become a series of theatrical encounters with phantom presences (80 percent of those ap-
proached declined to be interviewed); as a local dialogue with
private lives, it, in the spirit of Ruiz, disperses itself: "the actual
tendency is towards dispersion. I have taken advantage of this dispersion to begin my film in a district in Paris and end it in New
Guinea" (Christie 126). Finally, even the auteur-interviewer himself
in this film is defined as the material fiction of a wandering witness:
written originally in Spanish, Ruiz's commentary is haltingly sight-
translated on the soundtrack by another Chilean exile.

In his own, more conventional interviews, the filmmaker appears
and disappears primarily through calculations and abstractions that
explain the movies yet contrast with a variety of material predicaments surrounding those speculations. Quite unlike Kluge, Ruiz
seems to relish his flights of abstraction (about history, representation, and so forth) as a way of presenting himself through what Ian
Christie has called a rhetoric as "impersonal speech" (84). Set
within those more material anecdotes, however, these register as
simulated explanations, phantom propositions that seem to deny
and to affirm the concrete realities and multiple sources of his films.
Just as he contends that his movies are without an audience, he thus
cavalierly obscures auteurial speculation within the play of circumstances (in a passage that could easily be referring to Coppola):

An American director I like very much came to Europe
and said 'I just need a little bit of money—a million dollars.' Now a million dollars is really a lot, even for someone like Bergman. But this director was concerned with
specific elements—like say for example a scene with a
hundred horses. You shouldn't think like that. For ex-

ample I wrote a scene for a helicopter and we got a car instead. So we changed it to a car. If you are making films my way, like a novel, you can use everything. (Ehrenstein 5)

In this same 1986 interview, when the interviewer comments on Ruiz's interest in children's films and how that seems to coincide with Hollywood's interests, Ruiz obscures the logic as a chain of accidents: "It's completely accidental. But most of my films come from accidents. My coming to Hollywood is an accident. . . . As for the connection with children's films, I'd say that I haven't so much made films for children as with children and about children. Ordinary childhood doesn't interest me. And as for any relationship between my films and Hollywood the only connection would be Truman Capote whose work I liked" (Ehrenstein 4–5). Shortly after this remark, he describes his "dream to create a kind of centrifugal force in the midst of these different levels" and illustrates it by rapidly shifting from this abstraction to "a wonderful moment" in *Cleopatra* "when you can see in the background of one of the shots an airplane. True surrealism! For me to combine that sense of awareness with the visual elements of the *qualité française* would be wonderful" (Ehrenstein 6).

In this simulated play between speculation and aleatory conditions, the quintessential Ruiz interview may be his dialogue with Jean Louis Schefer, that philosopher of representational bodies on the margins of discourse. In this dialogue, the two figures both constantly move in and out of definitions and propositions in the play of affirmative denial:[15]

> R.R.: . . . although the three points which you've made are sometimes marginal to the subject, every, absolutely every cinematic image, and all the elements of that cinematographic image in its alignment with any other cinematographic images, all of these are only ellipses.
>
> J.L.S.: Yes, agreed, but even then there are several things assumed about continuity in the image. . . .
>
> R.R.: Yes, that it is the effect of a *continuum*.
>
> J.L.S.: Which belongs to which?

R.R.: The one which is not a vacancy, since a vacancy is impossible to show: you cannot make a film about the non-death of Napoleon in Paris.

J.L.S.: Yes, that's it! But that wouldn't be a vacancy! The non-death of Napoleon in Paris.

R. R.: No, no, that is not a vacancy. I mean the events that have not happened. The darkness, the obscurity, the whiteness, the light, the idea of a fragment which is so difficult to make felt in the cinema. (68)[16]

Featured in a special 1980 issue of *Ça, Cinéma* titled "The Image, Death, Memory: An Imaginary Dialogue," this structured dialogue between Ruiz and Schefer features short philosophical meditations and fictional exercises constructed alternately by the two, occasionally these sections being entirely a collage of quotations from Vico, William James, Artaud, Jean Paul, and others. Here the author and the auteur overlap and counterpoint each other's speculations and literally disperse themselves through the ellipses and conflicts within the formal agency of the collection. Punctuating the whole volume are film stills of medieval knights in battle or in a jousting tournament. As a kind of extreme paradigm of the presentation of Ruiz persona, this dialogue-interview is more exactly a combat about trying to remember a human figure lost across cultural history; it is a disjointed reflection on a human figure whose presence is lost beneath the overdetermined cultural shields and armor that he moves in, the temporary agencies through which he affirms himself in death.

Even in interviews less extreme than this one, Ruiz the auteur frequently resembles the host of *Hypothesis of a Stolen Painting*. Standing before a number of "tableaux vivants," his whimsical, alternately concrete and abstract, and often complicated explanations ultimately draw attention away from the living images and towards an absent, speculative scheme, centripetally pointing at a central product but then centrifugally spreading his own agency into the surrounding space, which keeps moving, changing and losing definition.

That difficult and playfully elusive space is, I believe, the shifting cultural space through which the wandering tourist is always mov-

ing and always being refigured by a new background. For spectators
in search of an auteur, Ruiz engages and escapes his agency, leading
us through sometimes frustrating linguistic and imagistic forests.
Never actually locating this fatherless child/auteur for adoption, audiences of the auteur watch, perplexed:

> A child lost in the forest and everyone searches for him.
> They call, they cry. . . . There are several paths. Now
> we spectators, who are not the people who search, we
> watch the process. One can imagine diverse ways to-
> wards that lost child. One is imagining all this at the
> same time and there are several things which happen.
> You can surely interest yourself in one thing or another,
> but the fiction is more than ever there. While one pre-
> tends that the fiction is tied to a succession that follows
> a thread, one "loses the thread." ("Interviews" 79)

Escaping that path of auteurist agency, Ruiz pipes his readers and
viewers down the path of his own touristic exile, back into the
changing backgrounds of the world. In his endless tossing and turning of the image of the auteur, the auteur cracks open its agency,
making the world he inhabits dart through in a variety of forms and
from a variety of directions. To identify and enlist with the authority
of this phantom agency is then to become subject to the touristic
vicissitudes of an always-changing world: "The smallest crack
allows spaces created by the direction of other people's looks to escape, and these spaces go around the world several times. From this
point of view it is important that the earth is round" ("Les Relations" 29).

Auteurs are far from dead. With ghostly auteurs like Ruiz, they
may in fact be more alive now than at any other point in film history.
Although this particular interpretive category has never addressed
audiences in simple or singular ways, within the commerce of contemporary culture it has become, as both a production and interpretive position, more critically central yet massively different from
what it once may have been. Since the early 1970s, the commercial
conditioning of this figure has successfully evacuated it of most of
its expressive power and textual coherence; simultaneously, this
commercial conditioning has called renewed attention to the layered

pressures of auteurism as an agency that establishes different modes of identification with its audiences.

Not all filmmakers, of course, work through this particular agency, and the ones that do have potentially a large variety of relations they can fashion with it. The three examples I have used here have taken different paths: from Coppola's Romantic self-sacrifice within its industrial and technological conditions, through Kluge's fragmenting of its central and dominating agency, to Ruiz's phantom reincarnations in many different cultural locations. However vast some of their differences as filmmakers may be, they each, it seems to me, willingly or not have had to give up their authority as authors and begin to communicate as simply figures *within* the commerce of that image. For viewers, this should mean the pleasure of engaging and adopting one more text that surrounds a movie without the pretenses of its traditional authorities and mystifications.

CHAPTER
FIVE

GENRE, GENDER, AND HYSTERIA
The Road Movie in Outer Space

□□□

> "With regard to many of these photographs, it was History which separated me from them. Is History not simply that time when we were not born? . . . History is hysterical: it is constituted only if we consider it, only if we look at it—and in order to look at it we, we must be excluded from it."
> —ROLAND BARTHES

> "Hysterics suffer mainly from reminiscences."
> —BREUER AND FREUD

If hysteria is a body in trouble with language, historical place, and a failure to adequately repress, genre may always have been on the edge of a hysterical history, a shifting marker of history's troubled relation with the way it represents itself. While genre has always struggled valiantly to accommodate within its formulas the social and cultural contradictions of history as if they were a single story— a western, a musical, a sci-fi film, in that action genre has often appeared strained or uncomfortably aware that any "true," "real," or "natural" cultural history persistently remains outside its excessively codified borders, ready to break apart its monolithic stances: the extraordinary ending of *Mildred Pierce* (1945) describes, in its excessiveness, its formulaic impossibility; the fragile, often confused narrative structures of so many films noirs—such as *The Big Sleep* (1946)—refer ultimately to their generic desperation in confronting all the implications of postwar history.

Indeed, the very idea of genre seems to reflect the excess history that it cannot accommodate, since there never could be a film that represents the pure or classical genre that genre criticism and theory seems to need in order to sustain itself. But, especially with the generic pastiches of contemporary movies (the blending of sci-fi, romance, and the western as one film, for instance) and the current critical positions that relentlessly try to use it (thematically more popular than ever in journals and at conferences), genre seems invariably to overdetermine, mimic, repeat, and shuffle its structures so excessively that what is mostly designated is a contemporary history that insists that it cannot be ritualized according to a single transhistorical pattern. The image of genre seems to taunt contemporary reception with its utopian possibilities only to turn those audiences back before its historical impossibilities.

In this sense, road movies have become a primary and incisive marker not only of how contemporary genre reflects the contemporary moment, but, more specifically, of how that crisis of genre is also the cultural and psychoanalytic crisis of gender. As an explicitly desperate genre, the contemporary road movie (and its first cousin, the buddy movie) responds specifically to the recent historical fracturing of the male subject, who has traditionally been the main support of those institutional walls of a dominant cinema. This cultural fracturing has made this subject insist all the more on its representation at the movies while at the same time making that representation impossible. When in a recent comic film, *The Big Picture* (1989), a small-time producer informs an aspiring director that buddy movies are "happening" and urges him to look at a script about Lincoln and Babe Ruth (*Abe and the Babe*), the joke, in all its silliness, is also a serious comment about contemporary generic representations of history and the hysterical but impossible need to stabilize male identities within history.[1]

Generic Hysteria

Rarely is there a discussion of genre that does not take into account the historical pressures which lurk behind a particular form or, in Stephen Neale's words, the historical "pressure of genre" on that cultural history. On the one hand, social history informs and troubles most genres: an economic depression and the musicals of

the thirties, the discontent of a female work force and the melo-
dramas of the forties, the Red Menace of McCarthyism and the
sci-fi films of the fifties. On the other hand, genre enacts a counter-
pressure that Neale describes

> in terms of the relations of subjectivity involved; in terms
> of the structures and practices both of the cinematic in-
> stitutions as a whole and of that sector known variously
> as "Hollywood" or as "commercial cinema"; and in
> terms of the determinants and effects of each of these
> within and across the social formation and its component
> areas. (17)

In the majority of cases and in the majority of critical models, it is
this second tendency, the power of genre to recuperate, ritualize,
and mythologize cultural history (its forms and representations),
that has been the key to its stability and security. What has interested
most critics about genre is its uncanny ability to reflect and create
rituals of social history and thus to intensify a culture's relation to its
social histories.[2]

For me, however, this ability to ritualize has, especially recently,
become less the heart of genre and more a side effect produced by
assimilating genre's drive to repeat itself into the naturalizing action
of narrative. What has increasingly come to complicate film genre
as an interpretive category, as well as a production model, is its drive
to repeat specific signifying materials, an obsessive drive to repeat
in reaction to the *resistance* of cultural history. Normally and classically, of course, narrative regulates this generic drive. The implicit
demand to produce or see the same story, the same characters, and
same historical referent within a genre movie is offset by the variations inherent in narrative structure (Altman "A Semantic/Syntactic
Approach"). Narrative, in this sense, structurally contradicts as it
naturalizes the generic impulse, a contradiction that is probably
most evident in musicals and sci-fi films, where the key markers of
the genre are instances of technology and spectacle that run counter
to narrative continuity. If genre has always been a way of organizing
stories and expectations for film audiences (Schatz 3–14 and *passim*), it is the overdramatized redundancy in that formulation that,
with a large number of contemporary films, now represents the true

nature of genre and distinguishes it from other models of production and interpretation: organizing stories and expectations that are necessarily already organized has developed into a kind of theatrical redundancy, and in the material theatrics of that redundancy are the signs of a compulsive potential perhaps always present in genre but recently its presiding term, pointing towards what Jim Collins formulates (in regard to the Western) as "the diverse consciousness of a heterogeneous culture" (97). While many contemporary narratives—I will argue in the next chapter—engage that historical heterogeneity by refusing narrative motivation and naturalization, contemporary genres often obsessively repeat themselves in order to reflect a history now figured as refusing to become public ritual. In both cases, the standard mechanisms for interpretation and reading are turned back on and point towards the uncontainable historical variety of the audiences employing those mechanisms.

Consider *Singin' in the Rain* (1952), an archetypal genre film about the historical trouble with genre, but one whose narrative naturalizes that trouble (in way that *The Singing Detective* will refuse to do). The central plot—a romance generated by the generic nightmare that Kathy articulates when she claims all Don's movies look the same—is how to naturalize at least two different film genres that threaten to collapse into gibberish before the demands of historical representation and its technologies: the silent swashbuckler films on which Lena and Don build their reputations and the musical itself whose historical adjustments from vaudeville through Busby Berkeley to Stanley Donan and Gene Kelly form the largest part of the film's background.

Yet, there is another way, I think, to regard these self-reflexive maneuvers than as Jane Feuer convincingly does when she describes them through myths of integration and spontaneity (166–168). The other side of what that battle of generic forms points to is the potential hysterical figure that haunts them as they attempt to balance themselves against other historical pressures. With the first genre, the silent swashbuckler, the most revealing image in this regard is the preview of *The Duelling Cavalier,* which goes out of sync, literally out of sync with the historical technologies it struggles to recuperate; the result is the comically "hysterical" shot of Lena speaking with a man's voice and saying "yes" while shaking her head "no." With the other—the musical—genre, which operates at the center of *Singin' in the Rain,* the primary theme and work of the film is a successful attempt to naturalize or make "real" (in a strict historical sense) its generic conventions. In the narrative success of that project, however, there appear numerous moments in which the generic conventions of the musical become visibly desperate before the so-called natural or "real" world they work to recover: Kelly's brilliantly choreographed number for the title song, for instance, dances a thin line between an acceptable generic engagement with the reality of the dark and rainy streets (of postwar society?) and pure, compulsive lunacy; the suspicious glance of the policeman who enters at the end of the scene suggests how close the convention comes to a clinical violation of the law and how close Kelly may truly be to Alex in *A Clockwork Orange* (1971).

In *Singin' in the Rain* the success of the genre in textually inscribing cultural and historical change is explicitly a function of the film's relation to its audience (Feuer 168–171). From the beginning of the film, the fans that make up the movie audience within the narrative sustain the regenerations of the stars and the re-production of their movies. The renewal and naturalization of the genre depends on the audience's fantasizing as natural (that is, historically appropriate) the genre's conventions: those conventions traditionally must be possessed by an audience as adequately representing their own cultural history. When the distinction between narcissistic fantasies and historical reality becomes unmanageable, hysteria threatens: early in *Singin' in the Rain* a crowd of fans nearly tears Don apart in hoping to retrieve a material relic from the generic star. Yet at the conclusion, this generic aberration is corrected: as Kathy—the "natural" girl who is clearly the emblem of a changing historical audience—flees stage and screen, Don calls on his audience to stop her; she is then returned to that stage through a musical number that reintegrates her into the now renewed and naturalized musical genre. Quite literally, through the drama of Kathy, the audience is able to read itself back into the theatrics of the genre; the film then appropriately cuts to Don and Kathy, surrounded by a sunny natural world, regarding themselves in a billboard advertising *Singin' in the Rain.*

With contemporary genre, however, a naturalized public ritual has been replaced by the performance of denaturalized and appropriated generic conventions. In this case, audiences act out a kind of a cultural crisis as the theatrical repetition of the conventions themselves, watching generic formulas again and again and again as the symptoms of their contemporary history. In this contemporary audience's relation to its genres, participating in a generic ritual has less and less to do with socially sharing a public entertainment ritual that integrates a cultural and historical community and more and more to do with participating in fragmented, narcissistic obsessions with pieces of generic conventions that cannot be naturalized across a large narrative community. For this audience, the sacramental ritualizations of genre (Braudy 17–25) become the material props of separate cults trying to return themselves to a place in history.

What interests me here is, to summarize, the central, lurking potential within genre to manifest itself within contemporary society as a symptomatic look at its cultural history, the potential within its repetition compulsion to dramatize its failure to repress and contain. Although a constant threat since the mid-thirties, this failure occurs consistently only in films made in the last twenty years. Recently, that regulating action of narrative has begun to lose its force within a variety of films within the generic tradition (chapter 6); and genre has accordingly begun more and more to dramatize its historical love affair with its own symptoms. Road movies, I will argue, are a genre that crystallize this action more clearly than any other.

I do not, of course, pretend to be clinically precise here; I am not trying to present film history and texts as patients on the couch of film theory. I am using the notion of hysteria as a way of getting at certain, often-overlooked implications within contemporary film genres, implications that directly involve the actions of representation and its trouble with a referent. For these purposes the presiding symptoms of hysteria in this context are: a failure to repress, which leads to obsessive repetition; and a crisis in representation whose excessive theatricality attempts to simultaneously accept and reject the signs of a given world, to claim at once its narcissism and a release into a symbolic reality.[3] In short, I am using this notion of hysteria partly as a metaphor that can locate extreme psychoanalytic and formal demands next to their inevitable social and historical inadequacies, a conjunction that, according to the metaphor, produces excessive theatricality and symptomatic repetition. My notion of generic hysteria here is similar to Jacques Derrida's sense of the madness of genre: " 'Do,' 'Do not' says genre, the word 'genre,' the figure the voice, or the law of genre" (56). For Derrida, the law of genre is a law based in "excess, the law of participating without membership, of contamination" (81, 63).

Generic hysteria is a historical body in trouble with its representation of itself and its historical place. Indeed, if one wants an instant emblem of it, remark toward the end of *Paris, Texas* (1984) the large mural on the wall of a building in which the face of Nastassia Kinski inhabits the icon of the Statue of Liberty; or recall the Travis of *Taxi Driver* (1976), the mohawked Indian from Vietnam, trying to network romantically in a yuppie culture. Separately, each describes one history and culture madly trying not to fit into but to hide behind the representations of another history and culture. What I like about both these twisted road movies is that they make generic and gender hysteria such a transparent vision of the present and the breakdown of male subjectivity.

The Road to Contemporary Culture

The road movie is the genre most demonstrative of this contemporary trouble with genre for two reasons. First, as a relatively recent generic form, it is especially close to the historical conditions that have destabilized interpretive viewing in general. As a film genre, road movies are frequently bypassed by some of the best studies of genre, and one explanation for these omissions could be that it has only recently appeared as a major direction in film history, the modern descendant of westerns such as *The Searchers* (1956), and so is recognizably less stable than most so-called classical genres. There have been important prototypes such as Raoul Walsh's *They Drive by Night* (1940) and Fritz Lang's *You Only Live Once* (1937). But it seems clear that the road movie is very much a postwar phenomenon and is rooted in the institutional turbulence that describes the cinema after that war, with its foundation in the fifties and its maturity in the sixties and seventies. Second, as a genre traditionally focused, almost exclusively, on men and the absence of women, the road movie self-consciously displays the crisis of gender, so central in stabilizations of any genre, around the seemingly peculiar and historically recent proliferations of the threat of male hysteria (Theweleit vol. 2, *passim*). In keeping with the back-to-the-future position of the contemporary spectator, it is accordingly appropriate that Lynne Kirby aligns "cinematic hysteria" with males and trains in the late nineteenth century, a preclassical version of the postmodern crisis played out by the contemporary man on the road: "The male hysteric . . . might then be seen as the boomerang of male, technological culture against itself, a vision of the railroad neurotic as a man reduced to female, or non-male state. . . . The paradox: investment, or, overinvestment in the male 'culture of time and space" was emasculating" (125, 124).[4]

What most of the films of this genre share is, quite obviously, a quest motif, which propels the usually male characters along the road of discovery. With this limited definition, road movies might have their precursors as far back as Homer's *Odyssey* where Odysseus appears as the first Western road warrior; and the heritage could easily be traced through Chaucer, Voltaire, Fielding, Goethe, and Hogarth to Joyce's reincarnation of that original street wanderer. As with the later road movies, the heroes of these travelogues embark on a learning experience that becomes most historically determined in bildungsroman tradition: the familiar is left behind or transformed through the protagonist's movement through space and time, and the confrontations and obstacles that he encounters generally lead, in most cases, to a wiser individual and often a more stable spiritual or social state. In these early treatments, the road invariably represents the inscription of a superior (usually patriarchal) perspective that keeps the protagonist from wandering into dangerous unmarked space. Whether it is God's way or the author's, the road limits and circumscribes desire as a way of mapping meaning, and the vehicle or sign for this mapping, even when it is displaced onto a ship or a horse, remains the human (invariably male) body, whose transformations become a metaphor for growth or progress.

With real road movies, however, the terms change in ways that seem superficial only at first. Besides the specifically postwar anxiety that gives these films a distinctly existential air, road movies are, by definition, movies about cars, trucks, motorcycles, or some other motoring soul-descendant of the nineteenth-century train. They are peopled with male buddies, usually a pair whose questing will only be distracted or, at best, complemented by the women who intrude from time to time. Edgar Ulmer's *Detour* (1945), for example, combines film-noir and road-movie narrative, as it tells the unhappy tale of Al Roberts's attempt to get to Los Angeles from New York; he is picked up hitchhiking but unfortunately the driver of the car dies of a drug overdose; after dumping the body, Al returns the favor by giving a ride to a woman who then tries to blackmail him; she too lives in a world of hostile inanimate objects and unluckily strangles herself with the telephone cord when she tries to call the police. Poor Roberts waits dejectedly to be arrested for two murders he simply found along the road. That the director Ulmer, a displaced German, had apprenticed with Lang on both *Metropolis* (1927) and *Spies* (1928) explains much of the dark economy in the film, but *Detour*, I believe, is a thoroughly postwar, sexually haunted vision in which an automobile becomes the sign of a psychic and social dispossession spread across Europe and America, where identity becomes lost in violence. By 1953, Henri-Georges Clouzot's *Wages of Fear* makes this vision much more historically transparent. The vehicles of adventure this time are trucks loaded with nitroglycerin, driven by an international group of Italians, Germans, and French through Central America. Permeated with hints of American exploitation and a sexual instability left over from the war barracks, the road film focuses on the trucks that must deliver a remedial explosive to stop an oil fire. With their lives defined by oil, money, energy, and explosives, the men of *Wages of Fear* think they are driving to freedom but instead die in a variety of ghastly ways, victims of their own vehicles and monstrous environment.

   With these two films as backdrops, some of the distinctive characteristics of the genre begin to emerge as it developed through the fifties. (1) More and more, the family unit, that oedipal centerpiece of classical narrative, begins to break apart, preserved only as a memory or desire with less and less substance. (2) Unlike other genres, such as the detective film where characters initiate events, in the road movie events act upon the characters: the historical world is always too much of a context, and objects along the road are usually menacing and materially assertive. (3) As this genre develops through the fifties, the quest motif becomes increasingly mechanized through those central vehicles in a manner far different from even the industrial quests of the nineteenth and early twentieth century. By the mid-sixties, the protagonist's identity is almost fully displaced onto the mechanized vehicle as that vehicle becomes transformed into a human or spiritual reality. Peter Fonda would become his motocycle, and both become something transcendent. More importantly, the perspective of the film as relayed through the central characters becomes a function of those vehicles. If the thriller makes the camera a weapon and the melodrama makes it a family member, in the road movie the camera adopts the framed perspective of the vehicle itself. In this genre, the perspective of the camera comes closest of any genre to the mechanical unrolling of images that defines the movie camera. As with the movie experience, time on the road becomes figurative space, and the buddy system, which informs most road movies, could be seen similarly as a reflection of the voyeuristic mechanisms of a historically patriarchal medium through which all the world might be seen as "male" while being founded on heterosexual desire. In the mechanics of its narrative structures and concerns, road movies are doubly self-reflexive and excessively self-conscious, both inside and outside of oedipal structures and inside and outside of the tropes of a cinematic realism.

With just these anchoring points, the link between road movies and a war-torn midcentury becomes a bit more graphic and more historically complex. If the search for an obscure object of desire— even one that is never named or known—is not particularly new to art, literature, or film, it seems to me that the mechanical agency that now moves that search is very much a modern image. After a war in which most signs of traditional culture were actually or figuratively blasted away by the relentlessly mechanistic forces of modern warfare, Europe and America moved towards a new industrial and technological future, and what becomes a ubiquitous symbol for that so-called progressive energy is the automobile. Surely there are other signs of the burgeoning materialism that, in the late forties and fifties, becomes a way of covering the spiritual destitution that World War II represented. But motorized transportation carried an unusually large number of historical resources that the shared structures of cinema might engage—ones dramatically troubling to the humanistic body. Cars and motorcycles represent a mechanized extension of the body, through which that body could move farther and faster than ever before and quite literally evade the trajectory of classical narrative and twentieth-century history.

As a perspective and frame, the road movie embodies the endless potential of future space, outer space, and a past that is continually fleeing. The car becomes the only promise of self in a culture of mechanical reproduction. As in the economic politics of most postwar societies, boundaries and borders disappear (at least temporarily) in a car and with them the sanctions, securities, and structures of a family tradition. Most importantly, unlike Westerns or sci-fi films, the space that is explored in these films is usually familiar land that has somehow become unfamiliar: the road and the country may be known, but something has made it foreign.

Energy becomes the key metaphor but that energy, as in *Wages of Fear,* has nothing spiritual or intellectual about it: energy is gasoline; energy is material, and to have it concretized in the form of a car is the surest sign that the past is disappearing in your rearview mirror. That mirror, along with the window frames of a car, also assures a kind of perceptual self-consciousness that identifies a generation whose present, past, and future is more and more mediated by the images of visual technology and whose ultimate aim is to possess those images within the frame of a moving body. For the children of the fifties and sixties, the world viewed is always and anxiously viewed as image, distanced, disenfranchised, and eventually possessable. The distinction between public and private space becomes less and less meaningful.

To summarize this reductive plot, the material progress of the postwar decade can be seen as a function of the fears of historical regression. As the ideal represented by the family begins to crumble and dissipate in the explosion of World War II, the most secure and likely replacement for that heterosexual unit is the male buddy-group left over from that war. If a friendly horse became the way a person would gallop through the Wild West, a train the way to cross nineteenth-century industrial landscapes, and a silly jalopy the way to get through the newly risen urban jungles of the first quarter of this century, the car of the fifties and sixties becomes a consumer tank. If in the fifties, the road spawned social outcasts that the film's narrative tried to socialize, this narrative action is then the naturalizing of a visible anxiety that would become an (hysterical) excess of indeterminable possibilities contained only by its self-consciousness in the road films of the sixties. By 1953, the United States had six percent of the world's population and sixty percent of its cars. By 1959, 1.25 million Americans had died in car accidents, more than in all U.S. wars combined. The strangers on the trains of the early fifties begin hopping into cars by the turn of the next decade and acting out a psychodrama in which cars were the vehicle of escape, as well as the grim reminders of repression and death. Indeed, perhaps the finest overture of the threat that drives men to repeat and keep moving through the road movies of the fifties, sixties, and seventies is the key sequence in *Rebel without a Cause* (1955). Shortly after watching an astronomer's demonstration of man's insignificant presence within the galaxies of outer space, James Dean prepares to do battle with his local rival Buzz, who in a twisted way is also his buddy. As a test of their manhood, their cars are lined up to race toward a cliff that plunges into the ocean below. Dean, a traditionalist even then, naively asks, "Why are we doing this?" His rival, who would have been a man of the future if he had survived, replies, "You gotta do something."

In the sixties and seventies, road movies, like all genres, adjust their anxious relation to the sociocultural fears and complexities that threaten to make their codes and formulas at best fragmented languages and at worst the meaningless debris of history. One obvious index to this historical movement is the emphasis in these films on social rebellion and the mostly token appearance of women—who usually appear as ways of emphasizing the unrecuperable spectacle of the road. In this context, there are, I believe, two notable changes in the road movie genre: first, the humanistic transformation of that material vehicle begins to break down entirely; and, second, the traveler or traveling pair loses that James Dean–like innocence and embraces, with increasing abandon, its own definition as material image. This commodification of the image as vehicle underlines, in brief, the central crisis that is developing: it increasingly marks the separation of human perspective and the genre from any sort of logical or natural relation with the history of culture, forcing each to take as its subject only its own symptoms, the material excess of a culture's failure to naturalize its rituals. As Guy Debord suggested about this relationship between driving and culture:

> When culture becomes nothing more than a commodity, it must also become the star commodity of the spectacular society. Clark Kerr, one of the foremost ideologues of this tendency, has calculated that the complex process of production, distribution and consumption of *knowledge* already gets 29% of the yearly national product in the United States; and he predicts that in the second half of this century culture will be the driving force in the development of the economy, a role played by the automobile in the first half of the century, and by railroads in the second half of the previous century. (par. 193)

Bonnie and Clyde: The Crisis of Male Subjectivity (Warner Bros., 1967. Tokyo Stills)

A telling evolution in this regard is the development of the genre from Penn's *Bonnie and Clyde* in 1967 to Malick's *Badlands* in 1973. *Bonnie and Clyde* remains, of course, one of the premier examples of the genre, an infinitely more intelligent and eloquent film than the more popular *Easy Rider* (1969) and one that demonstrates a more historical sense of its own historical neurosis. In true sixties fashion, Bonnie and Clyde are road rebels as odd heroes whose travels are a media tour of meaningless violence. As travelers, they are as displaced from any sense of place as they are from any sense of their own subjectivity: as that fifties nostalgia for character and morality fades, all experience becomes the mechanical reproduction of the road through a real or metaphoric windshield, and these perspectives then become redundantly relocated in the images of themselves that they see distorted and reproduced in the local newspapers. The putative documentary look of *Bonnie and Clyde* is thus aptly a ruse and a red herring: the focus is instead on how the conjunction of road, vehicle, character, and perception becomes a collection of sensational, mass-produced consumer images, the material of a documentary on a desperate consumer culture. Bonnie and Clyde's feverish repetition of crimes is largely an attempt to see themselves in the newspapers, sensationally and therapeutically separated from the historical Depression outside their ken, and Clyde's response to Bonnie, when she asks him to imagine another way of life, is that of a man theatrically passionate about his own symptoms—he imagines different strategies for committing crimes, not a life outside crime. The celebrated conclusion to this film—the grotesque, multi-angled, slow-motion execution of Bonnie and Clyde—describes the end of the road only in that the road has become fully merged with the mechanical vehicle of the car and the ironically popular images of the film—both torn apart in the final sequence: a ritualistic slaughter of the material of these characters as characters defined by their material and an ironic ritualistic destruction of the "natural and transparent image." If *Bonnie and Clyde* is based on a historical account, it is more accurately a historical account of modern perception, perception that in the sixties is already beginning to reduce history to the material of images, material in which a culture must obsessively act itself out in order to displace the return of more threatening histories. (Like so many other genre films of this era, such as *The Wild Bunch* [1969], the confused and uncertain reception of *Bonnie and Clyde* suggests the significant problems in trying to address political and social issues through forms whose tendency towards hysteria always theatricalizes the relation of genre and history.)[5]

Malick's *Badlands,* in fact, takes this logic and perspective to an even more disturbingly witty conclusion. Whereas *Bonnie and Clyde* borrows enough from the French New Wave to make it look as if it could or should be "read" through its irony, *Badlands* suggests, more accurately, that hysteria is always one of the most difficult texts to read and analyze. The movie contains a plethora of road-movie markers, which display themselves too obtrusively and densely. Martin Sheen playing Kit postures himself not as an ironic James Dean but as someone who totally inhabits the image of that character: he makes that image physical by becoming it, with little regard for an ironic distinction between image and world or with any sense that there is some human individual who precedes that character. What drives Kit and Holly, his strangely passive accomplice, seems to be nothing more than the accumulation of dramatic but completely unmotivated images as they arise arbitrarily and violently out of coincidental situations: killings or courtesies, there is little difference when motive or reference is unimportant. Where the sensational materialism that motivated Bonnie and Clyde remained linked to the narrative history that they were making through their own exploits and which Penn is ironically exploiting in his narrative film, in *Badlands* that narrative voice, which is the road that structures images in road movies, dislodges itself through the flat, uncomprehending voice-over of Holly. On this road, action and character stand out like roadside billboards that believe themselves true or like debris that has been discarded. This new James Dean does not ask why but simply accepts and revels in the materiality of predicament: he suggests that they smash their hands with a large rock as a ritualistic monument to their love; when he is about to be captured, he builds a mound of stones by the side of the barren highway. Only debris has ritual meaning along this road with no other signals or signification.

In *Badlands,* the formulas, characters, and images often look like generic waste, multiplying as representations overdetermined by their materiality and no longer even interested in accommodating historical and cultural change. It is no accident that this James Dean

Desperately Marking Space in *Badlands* (Warner Bros., 1973. Museum of Modern Art/Film Stills Archive)

starts the film as a garbage man who, instead of wagering before a cliff about life and death, bets his partner that he can't eat a dead dog. Nor is it insignificant that the road in this film, in one of its most striking sequences, ultimately becomes the borderless waste-land of the Dakotas. Both suggest how far the road movie has traveled in a culture where images of history now only recycle themselves. Now the representations that once secured a place are neurotically cut loose of any referent but themselves.

The historical journey of the road movie might consequently be described through an obsessive itinerary that moves through the prophetic tales of Ulmer and Lang, prototypical road movies that were not yet generic, through the postwar formulation of the genre, characterized by amnesia, hallucinations, and theatrical crisis. In the mid-seventies and eighties, the genre has made its very action and subject its own historical hysteria: if genre is the prototype of classification and interpretation, it now becomes the *mise-en-abyme* reflection of an audience that can no longer imagine a naturalized history. The environment, conditions, and actions of the road movie have become a borderless refuse bin, limning the state of contemporary perception, both in- and outside the movie theaters. If the road movie traditionally subsisted on gasoline as a metaphor for restless energy, when that gasoline begins to dry up in the seventies the vehicles it propelled become scrap by the road. One reason the road movie has remained a culturally central genre today may be because the oil and energy crisis in the world reflects the much larger historical and cultural crisis in which traditional images of male identity and significance have also become generic debris.[6]

Off the Road, Into Space: *Paris, Texas*

Paris, Texas is a remarkable example of a road movie that has embraced its hysterical relation with history, made by a displaced master of the genre, a filmmaker who seems to grow successfully more and more in love with the generic symptoms of that displacement. The ten years that intervene between *Badlands* and *Paris, Texas* are cataclysmic years for Hollywood and narrative movies in general, the prophecies of *Badlands* spreading rapidly through a culture now permeated with VCRs, blockbusters, and the consumption of non-narrative images. Whereas before, the crisis of genre was how to naturalize (which also means to defer) its materially overdetermined relation to history and culture, now the excesses of history and culture have essentially become reflected in the material forms of the very images they previously could pressurize into a humanistic and ritualistic form. The crisis is now not between the language of images and the body of cultural history but between multiple conflicting languages that pretend repetitively and desperately to some meaning, yet without anything to refer to. This is the state of things from which *Paris, Texas* is born, where the disappearance of roads and boundaries and narratives has left the characters with little but undefined space. In this state of things, space is all outer space, a sci-fi road movie in which the increasingly undifferentiated global culture of earth is the garbage of the galaxies.

The story of *Paris, Texas* focuses itself as a desperate need to reclaim a family and a language through a paranoid narcissism. Produced in a cultural no-man's land as a German-French-American project, a melange, not a dialectic as in *The American Friend* (1977), it was written by at least two script writers and spurred appropriately multiple responses from viewers who either loved it (as at

Cannes) or detested it (as with some feminist responses), but always seemed to read it differently. The film itself looks like the quintessential road movie in some ways: the story concerns Travis, a wanderer who has not only lost a family and an identity but, more importantly in some ways, a road and a car. As the film opens he marches resolutely across a desert landscape going nowhere, but going there with hypnotic purpose. What Travis might have been searching for once is what most road questers invariably want: an authentic home, a lost origin where what you see is what you are. In 1984, however, that kind of authenticity is simply impossible: Travis's lost home is a photograph of a barren plot in Paris, Texas, where he thinks he may have been conceived. The name of the town itself represents a blurring and final confusion of cultural identity, a sacred origin which is, in effect, nothing more than a mechanical reproduction, possessed and carried in his pocket. The joke of the title, repeated a couple of times in the movie, is based on the exotic expectations associated with Paris, France, but, with the punch line, that space is then reduced to substance: the aura of an image becomes the waste of historical reality, whose ultimate significance for Travis is that he possesses it as a material image. Like Barthes's photograph, history here is "that time when we were not born. . . . History is hysterical" (*Camera Lucida* 64–65). But, for the contemporary Travis, that hysterical history can be gathered up as a concrete possession and put in his pocket.[7]

In *Paris, Texas* the road goes nowhere except, in a very literal way, to "outer space." The driver is a backseat driver (where he sits when his brother first retrieves him). He does not desire even to see the road and does not particularly wish even to talk to his buddy except maybe through walkie-talkies (as he does with his son Hunter as they travel in search of his mother). In one odd sequence the vehicle itself becomes identified with rusting pieces of junk, off the road in the desert, not even capable of being recycled. Outside the borders of family and "beyond rage," Travis returns to childhood where, if there is a bond formed with his wife and son, it is totally regressive to the end—before speech at the start of the narrative and situated in imaginary images through to its conclusion. With Travis's surrendering the object of his quest, the reuniting of mother and son, the ending is, possibly, ambiguous but, more likely, the confirmation of a state of things in which all that has been affirmed

Postmodern Buddies: Off the Road and Broken Down (*Paris, Texas*, 20th Century-Fox, 1984. Manayunk Pictures)

is Travis's ability to recycle his family as an empty image, his need to be in love primarily with his own symptoms.

As opposed to the usual readings of the movie, I would describe the pathos of this film as the pathos of post-humanism, the inability to distinguish human subjectivity from its mechanized vehicle: not that of Henry Fonda on the run in *You Only Live Once* but the comic and hysterical pathos of a man who would insist on exactly the same rental car he once had as he makes his way through a sea of rental cars. This is not, as Richard Kearney would have it, an "unresolved quest" (328–329), anymore than Jane and Travis's encounter in the peep-show club is about "the art of mutual dis-possession," reaching "toward a form of genuine communication, however brief, by abandoning the image in favor of the world" (327). This narrative, like that climactic confrontation between husband and wife, only parodies a road quest and its search for communication, while in fact Travis remains absolutely adrift in his own narcissistic play with the images of family and home. From beginning to end, Travis stands beyond any cultural road that could socially ritualize history: he is in the desert of "outer space," and can no more communicate with his history than he does with Jane, his back turned, separated by a mirrored glass, and telling only *his* story of their tragedy. Like the central shot in this climactic sequence, which superimposes the reflection of his face on her body, he sees her only in the image of his failure to have any history but his own, again blindly in love with his own symptoms.

Images in *Paris, Texas* thus constantly call attention to themselves as images, not in the usual Wenders manner as self-conscious perspectives through which a character sees and encounters the world but as the exclusively material terms of the world and identity. The tension and difference on which the road movie once built its drama is collapsed into an equivalence: outside the frames of the cars in this road movie there are only more frames; the wild west is a neon landscape where the lack of spatial depth makes everything look a bit like a postcard or a movie quote; a father becomes a father through his imitation of magazine images; the family discovers a shaky and temporary presence only through the material images of home movies and scrap books. Indeed, this collapse of the subjective into the ubiquitous and undifferentiated images of a consumer culture is best summarized in a passing remark between the two buddy-brothers: as they drive into L.A., Walt explains that he runs a billboard company (like the patriarch in *Badlands*); Travis then responds like a Chancey Gardner raised exclusively on television and finding subjective intention dispersed everywhere in a world of simulacra: "Oh, you're the one who makes those. I love those. Some of them are just beautiful."

In the last part of the film, one witnesses the climactic instances of this imagistic bind, of this hysterical paralysis. Travis has it both ways: at the end of the road he has reconstructed his symbolic family under his gaze, but concomitantly he has remained narcissistically free of that structure, possibly on the road to the desert again.

Reunited in Male Narcissism: The Peepshow in *Paris, Texas* (20th Century-Fox, 1984)

As the graphics of the embrace between mother and son make clear, Travis is allowed the reality of being at once father and son, lover and child—a much more muted and masculine version of the horrific child-mother-sister in *Chinatown* (1984). In these final revelations there is therefore also the final reduction. As Wenders's script describes this ending, only the mirror remains: the doubling of Travis's position becomes more than just an imaginary projection of himself, as the glare and frames of so many reflecting windows make that imaginary scene into a new kind of symbolic order whose excessively and exclusively material construction becomes the only means of mediating and designating a contemporary history.

If the road in *Kings of the Road* (1976) led to modern Germany

and the road in *The American Friend* led always to the same city
which is Hollywood, the road in *Paris, Texas* goes from a photographic home to the space city of Houston where banks need no
people, where the future is the electronic perception of no one's
point of view, and where the dialectic between a male subjectivity
and a symbolic historical order collapses into the identity of material
images. The logic of looking is no longer the road-movie track, out-
wards towards something. In *Paris, Texas* it is now a combination
of the slow horizontal pan of (usually) empty landscapes and the
strange vertical tilt up (often) empty skyscrapers, neon, and American flag poles, twin actions that describe the direction of this road.
Together it maps a visual trajectory that points off the road and into
an outer space where this way of looking expects to see only its own
frames emptied of objects and to encounter other equally empty
frames. Clearly driving this road is a different sort of road movie in
a different culture, characterized astutely by Baudrillard as the emp-
tying of an appropriative drive into the ecstasy of open space:

> If one thinks about it, people no longer project them-
> selves into objects, with their affects and representations,
> their fantasies of possession, loss, mourning, jealousy:
> the psychological dimension has in a sense vanished, and
> even if it can be marked out in detail, one feels that it is
> not really there that things are being played out . . . little
> by little a logic of "driving" has replaced a very subjec-
> tive logic of possession and projection. No more fan-
> tasies of power, speed, appropriation linked to the object
> itself, but instead a tactic of potentialities linked to usage:
> mastery, control and command, an optimalization of the
> play of possibilities offered by the car as vector and ve-
> hicle, and no longer as an object of psychological sanctu-
> ary. . . . The vehicle now becomes a kind of capsule, its
> dashboard the brain, the surrounding landscape unfold-
> ing like a television screen. ("Ecstasy" 127)

Changing Drivers

But let us not forget what this end of the road often obscures as it
drifts into space: that the vehicle here is still a historically pressurized vehicle, pressurized quite specifically in terms of a male

subjectivity in crisis. Earlier, Marlon Brando, James Dean, and a young Dennis Hopper represented the male neurosis of this driving, searching for a self and a home through the frames of a mechanically rotating fifties, and attempting to find an image where the two might find some postwar balance. With the new waves of the sixties, the security of the road itself began to be washed away, and the relation with modern history became a crisis of images that never quite fit, marking the melancholic distance between a masculine self and his restless regeneration. Since the early seventies, this crisis of self has become the carnival of a male narcissism without subjectivity, where the vehicle seems to run according to its own culturally mechanized point of view, like Spielberg's driverless truck in *Duel* (1971). Indeed, the road to this road has historically wound its determined way from Joseph Strick's prophetic *Road Movie* (1974), along the roadsides of Godard's *Weekend* (1968) to George Miller's post-apocalyptic *Road Warrior* (1981): in all three, the contemporary world becomes a wasteland strewn with industrial junk and lost male souls whose vehicle has become a rusty collage of postmodern cultural debris. In today's historical place, the most concise and accurate image of the status of that once-dominant male ritual may be Travis's first gesture as he crosses "Devil's Graveyard" in Big Bend, Texas: he carefully caps an empty bottle before he tosses it away.

In the hysteria of this contemporary ritual, watching the drama of a vacated patriarchy, a viewer, of any gender possibly, may therefore be able to participate in it only as the ritual of repo men, hysterical and paralyzed cultists who can, at best, recycle the images of this genre as generic name brands and who, if lucky, might be released through the ascension of the vehicle into an outer space free of their historical burden. Today, as the many different readings of *Paris, Texas* might suggest, that predominantly male road movie invariably turns into, for its producers and its audiences, a sci-fi film that is historically incomprehensible.

I will conclude, though, on a slightly different road, found in a recent television commercial and suggestive, I believe, of the other roads that might be pursued in the futuristic space of the present. The setting for the commercial is a roadside, perhaps abandoned, gas station, set on some wide-open Western plain, perhaps Texas. A teenage couple tenderly and poignantly say good-bye, and the young man hops into an old red sportscar and zooms down the dusty road—

perhaps the beginning of another road movie. As the car heads into the sunset, the images suddenly rewind to the beginning of the scene; the frame pulls back and we realize that the young woman who has just said good-bye is reviewing the scene on a VCR. As she caresses the television screen and the recycled sequence ends, the logo queries, "Is it love or is it Memorex?" The answer may be that the difference is insignificant today. Or it may be that the answer, as the young woman watches the man drive off into space, is left to the woman with the remote control to determine herself: in that case, it would be a choice of *her* relation with her own roadside history.

In this other space, the debris of generic history now has the potential of becoming the generic cure. The departure of a male subjectivity under the burden of its hysterical relation with its own history may mean that other roads can now be mapped across the landscapes of contemporary culture (which certainly have more contours than a desert). As contemporary viewers, in short, we can select, across an expanded galaxy of images, other roads, other generic rituals, and other subjectivities with which to try to formulate different histories within other generic economies. Once the buddy movie has driven itself into outer space, other drivers might take the wheel. As movies such as Agnes Varda's *Vagabond* (1986), Chantel Akerman's *Meetings with Anna* (1979), or Percy Adlon's *Bagdad Cafe* (1987) have shown, the road might now explore other cultural and other gendered geographies. According to the rager on the bridge overlooking the road in *Paris, Texas,* "the safety zone has been eliminated" and we have been "extradited to the land of no return . . . flying blind to nowhere. And if you think that's going to be fun, you've got another thing coming." For those of us looking for other roads, it may indeed.

CHAPTER

SIX

INTERMINABLE TALES OF HEAVEN AND HELL

□□□

" 'You only had two characters, one of which was dead
on page two.'
'One guy killed the other guy.'
'It wasn't motivated!'
'Sure it was. One guy in a hat killed the other guy in
a hat.' "
— *THROW MAMA FROM THE TRAIN* (1988)

"Who's the dame? . . . Where's the body? . . . Who's
trying to swing you into this number?"
—MARLOW, *THE SINGING DETECTIVE*

Probably the most pervasive change in film narrative during the
last fifteen years concerns the attenuation of plot and the related
breakdown of character motivation. Whether one points to the most
popular and commercially shameless sequels, the steady stream of
gigantic spectacles, or even the more reflective of art films, plot has
played an increasingly slighter role in the action of contemporary
movies. Concomitantly, the complexities of character, which in the
past might often have successfully substituted for a weak story, have
been replaced these days, as the nostalgic are wont to claim, by the
most solid and unflinching displays of untrammeled personality and
pure image. If the Stallone films seem to have as few plot twists and
surprises as the *Friday the 13th* sequels (beginning 1980), it is
equally difficult to decide whether the Stallone hero has more psy-

chological depth or subtlety than the faceless Jason. This should not become, however, a wistful complaint about the loss of good Aristotelian cinema and of screenwriters who know how to tell stories (as often is the complaint). The conditions and terminology of film narrative have simply shifted their grounds beyond the boundaries that organized film stories for more than fifty years. As a part of these industrial, technological, and sociological shifts, movies no longer tell and audiences no longer look for the real story in the story.

As much as contemporary film addresses the rituals of genre, it engages the mythic formulas of Western narrative. Pervading these formulas has been the dominant Biblical narrative of the transformation of history through the progressive action of the individual imagination (Kearney), the multitude of its versions locating themselves in the action that temporally moves a character between a realized hell and a promised heaven: it is a wonderful life when an individual can redeem events in a life by finding transcendent motivations for those events. Contemporary narrative has, however, displaced this organizing myth by forsaking the demand to historically resurrect the quotidian through the vision of the individual character. According to Jameson, "narrative has not here been subverted or abandoned . . . but rather effectively neutralized, to the benefit of seeing or looking in the filmic present" ("On Magic Realism" 321). That filmic present now means an evasion of dominant narrative patterns by locating itself in a neutral moment which vacates its teleology of heaven and hell of its motivations and metaphysics—or, as is so common today, a moment that collapses the adult back into childhood. This purportedly neutral narrative moment thus frequently becomes a perspective that either seems to precede actions as a figurative but emptied heaven *or* to immerse itself in the unimaginable chaos of historical actions as a figurative but meaningless hell. If both classical and modern narrative involve the motivation and naturalization of the historical action between these poles, contemporary narrative frequently drifts into the impossible crisis of having to discuss the events of its history from a point of view or within a formal teleological logic that seems to blissfully precede or nightmarishly exceed a relation to those historical events.

Contemporary narratives thus frequently become allegories about the difficulty (or impossibility) of engaging a world whose story they are trying to tell, either because the character stands too much out of the world or the world is too much with the character. Failing to find human characters to adequately motivate stories, contemporary narratives find themselves in figurative hells or heavens where too much is happening or nothing ever happens. According to this postmodern myth (where the present is "after" a classical and modern history and thus aligned with a preclassical utopia), hell becomes the tense boredom of seeing too much and heaven the fascinating spectacle of remembering a time before anything occurred. If contemporary genre describes a compulsive need to reappropriate, repeatedly, the tale of contemporary history in spite of that history's refusal to be appropriated, contemporary narrative tries to remove itself from that tale because there is too much to tell and therefore, in the peculiar logic of the contemporary, nothing ever happens. Contemporary narrative, in short, often finds itself before the beginning and after the end of the road. If viewers frequently complain of being bored by these narratives (as opposed to the compulsive anticipation of genre movies), this, in a sense, may simply be an index of the paralysis felt before a history that refuses to be

Heavenly Narratives: Where Nothing Ever Happens (*Made in Heaven*, Lorimar, 1989. Manayunk Pictures)

motivated (as opposed to the excited need to watch genres be refused by history again and again).

As in Spielberg's *Indiana Jones* cycle (beginning 1981), hell in many of these films becomes an unrecuperable historical moment like the holocaust of World War II and heaven becomes the myth of an archeologist's prehistory.[1] Mediating the two and often replacing narrative logic itself is usually the spectacle of technology. Thus, the counterpart of Spielberg's transcending narratives is Claude Lanzmann's *Shoah* (1985), a searing epic of hell put in place by a fascist technological apparatus whose shattering of human subjectivity and motivation (in the name of a Christian teleology of heaven on earth) counterpoints Spielberg's technological heaven. Across its

Raiders and Its Sequels: Making Heavens out of Historical Hells (Paramount, 1981. Cinemabilia)

nine and a half hour narrative, *Shoah* is about the minutiae of time (train schedules and the mechanical details of how what happened when) that proceeds not so much like a story but like a long tracking shot. It is about the disappearance of bodies that—deprived of any motivations by the amnesia of history, by bureaucrats who knew nothing, by citizens who remember nothing—become lost in the detritus of a historical moment that cannot be organized as a narrative. It begins with the tale of Simon Srebnik, a boy who survived the concentration camps because of "his melodious voice." Now forty-seven, this boy singer sings of a prelapsarian time and place at the other end of narrative history: "A little white house/ lingers in my memory./ Of that little white house/ I dream every night." Discussing the "master plot" of this century, Peter Brooks has noted that "the interminable would be meaningless" (283). In the shadow of an interminable hell, so, in many instances of contemporary narrative, is the utopian.

Cartoon Narratives: Recycling and Remaking the Classical

The classical model, which contemporary narratives so notoriously recall, is well documented in its historical variations. Its principles would include plots that adhere to some logic of temporality and characters drawn to meet standards of psychological depth that in turn motivate events and actions in the story. A motivated ordering of time is the key here, since a narrative's ability to engage a spectator's interest in the provocations and expectations of a temporal history—formal or humanistic—is the classical mark of its achievement: Will a protoganist, such as the Yellow Man in *Broken Blossoms* (1919), have enough time to rescue the heroine? Will future actions or scenes explain earlier complexities, as happens in *Mildred Pierce* or most detective films? Will an establishing shot be followed by a more revealing close-up? Indeed, it is difficult to find a significant and widespread break with these patterns through the sixties, even in the auteurist and art cinema. At most, there is self-conscious and creative manipulation of the elements of classical narrative: Resnais's cinematic questionings of memory and historical time (or Fellini's in a different way) posit a crisis in the ordering of classical time and history, but not its presiding imperative; they rethink how we engage and fashion narrative, not our failure to do it. For most Western narrative films through the sixties, temporality remains motivated by human action or perspective. When the logic of the narrative is disturbed or deconstructed, it is for the most part only to remotivate that temporality through the still humanistic terms of ideology, gender, or certain semiotics.

In more recent movies, however, the central tendencies of film narrative have been, in a technical and cultural sense, to waste narrative time. Even with films outside the mainstream, narrative structures and expectations continue to adhere to a classical rather than an oppositional order, but those structures and expectations are now dispersed rather than coherently motivated across the barest of stories and a most fragmented collection of incidents. In terms of that classical paradigm, contemporary movies put in play an extraordinary exaggeration of narrative incident, character-images, and technical form to the extent that the excessive quality of these elements usurps any motivational significance. Dana Polan offers this example:

> In *1941,* the individual vignettes, the character motivations, the sheer interest of story, become so many elements in a broader process whose "sense" is more than any simple addition of the pieces. To be sure, the individual narrative bits add up to a narrative kernel, a signified: everything that happens in the film signifies that 7 December 1941 was a particularly confused and confusing night. But beyond that meaning, the narrative becomes a mere pretext for a more encompassing signification or intimation of confusion as a good show *for the spectator.* A scene where an out-of-control army tank goes crashing through vat after vat of paint with corresponding color changes might stand as a paradigm for the whole film, trading as it does narrative sense for kinetic visual display. There is in a film like *1941* a kind of leap from quantity of visual effect into a realm of different quality; the film exceeds story and becomes an explosion (literally so in the end credits) of sights and sounds. ("Above All Else" 59)

As recyclings of narrative elements now vacated of their traditional motivations and uses, these contemporary narratives appear made up of what once would have seemed the excrescences or by-products of narrative progressions. They quickly become an allegory of emptied forms, as when the pyrotechnics of a spaceship replaces any sense of its going somewhere. Like the narrative voice-over of Terrence Malick's *Days of Heaven*, the signs of narrative coherence are there but not the coherence (which is one way of distinguishing these narratives from Robin Wood's notion of "the incoherent text"). In that film, a young girl narrates her heavenly days in 1906, beginning as she escapes Chicago and the hellish industrial fires that start the twentieth century. With a vacant and disconnected rhetoric obsessed with the emptiness of death ("Sometimes I feel very old. Like my whole life's over. Like I'm not around anymore"), the narrative voice does not so much ironize but strangely brings into high relief images and characters whose vibrant autonomy stands at an extreme distance from the poetically fragmented and uncomprehending narrative voice. As the characters flee down the river at the film's conclusion, the child-narrator drifts across its flashing images: "And you could see people on the shore but it was far off and you couldn't see what they were doing. They were probably calling for help or something. Or they were trying to bury someone or something." Like many less self-conscious contemporary narratives, here the narrative discourse vacates and abstracts itself so extremely that it is as if a cartoon discourse—a discourse without a humanistically motivated relation with an imagistically stable world—were aiming to tell historical tales. The narratives of *Who Framed Roger Rabbit?* (1988), *Batman,* and *Dick Tracy* are also historical tales.

Three related institutional and commercial narrative strategies are perhaps the strongest indicators of this wasting and evacuation of contemporary narrative: the sequel, the series, and the remake. Speaking specifically about remakes, James Monaco has described the usual scapegoat for this modern tendency: "Film is an aging art. . . . Not having confidence in their own stories or the way they tell them (or not having any stories to tell), filmmakers in increasing numbers turn to the past for desperate inspiration. The straight remakes . . . are invariably lesser films than their ancient models" (280). Closer to the point, however, is the recognition that the proliferation of these three formulas is part and parcel with conglomerate take-overs, attributing "the trend not to an idea shortage but

to the desire to reduce financial risk" (Simonet 155). Or, as *Variety*
puts it: "Most original screenplays are difficult to describe or characterize, and the resulting films enter production (and unfortunately,
even theatrical release) with no publicity or advance interest. A remake or sequel is instant news" (Cohn 17).[2]

What these contemporary narrative tendencies have most evi-
dently in common with their predecessors in the B-film serials of the
thirties or even with the epic movie of the twenties is a temporally
extended and fragmented narrative form that, as Roger Hagedorn
has demonstrated about the history of the serial, aim fundamentally
to promote the consumption of the medium in which they appear
and through which they compete with other media. That the contemporary versions of these narrative forms (particularly the series or
mini-series movie) owe much of their success to a television format
suggests, however, some critical differences from their more traditional forerunners in matters of production and reception. Cross-
overs ("shareability," "amphibious productions") have become, as
I have indicated in the first chapter, much more the rule today than
territorial distinctions in medium: while the release of epic productions like the two *Godfathers* or *Dune* are geared to theaters first, a
television serialization is frequently anticipated; sequels to *Star Trek*
(beginning 1979) come from television and are meant to return there
eventually; many contemporary movies, such as the *Porky's* group
(beginning 1982), are recognizably shot and structured for the commercial breaks and close-ups of television. In the last twenty years
especially, the sequel and the series film have been industrial and
media cousins, the first being the theatrical descendant from the
television family of the second (which springs from the soap opera)
and both being extended versions of the repetitions inherent in the
remake. As Caryn James remarked about the endless incarnations
of *Friday the 13th* and *Nightmare on Elm Street* (1984), "These
tamed-down slasher films owe less to Hitchcock than to 'All My
Children'" (1). In the neutralization of the former competition between media that they once promoted, the sequel, remake, and series now can be commonly defined as the valorization of repetition
beyond narrative differences. What they now promote is the consumption of a technology and images that can reconcile the differentiating competition between television and movies.

Today the sequel, the series, and the remake thus presume and respond to that different kind of reception I detailed in Chapter 1, a distracted and interrupted viewing that, to put it simply, remembers moments and images but not motivations. Today their significance is not so much in their historical recycling and expansion of narrative, as one can claim about the cultural and historical revisions that inform Hitchcock's and Lang's remakes. It is in how that contemporary recycling can severely reduce or fully dismiss narrative motivations and naturalizations in favor of the self-sustaining action of and interest in the repetition of images across the contemporary bond of film and television. Indeed, in terms of contemporary reception, the purest examples of this technological abstraction of narrative repetition are the popular "teenpics" capable of being watched over and over again—*Heathers* (1989) being a fine parody of this postmodern ability of teenagers to recycle endlessly[3]—and the all-too-common ability of home audiences to slide through two, three, or even four movies in an evening. Compared to the expanded narrative epics of the twenties and thirties (De Mille's, for instance) where narrative progressions supercede repetitions, narrative repetitions as technological performance in itself becomes what most centrally defines the series, sequel, and remake as the contemporary epic.

In all three, narrative repetitions do not serve primarily to organize and anchor time but to make temporal repetition itself a technological distraction. If narratives once used repetition to anchor and highlight differences, repetition now supports distraction; and differentiations are now the homogenous ones of technology and the stylized image. Whereas the first admits the spectator's boredom as the foundation for contemporary narrative, the second aims to recuperate boredom as the fantasy of distraction.[4]

As this repetition simultaneously disperses narrative motivation and maintains itself as a technological distraction, contemporary narrative moves closer and closer to a cartoon discourse where the representationally reduced image of the characters replaces questions of motivation (any attempt to explain *why* Batman, Superman, or Roger Rabbit do what they do is clearly an imported afterthought), while the episodic logic (from day to day) follows the paralogical leaps of separated performative frames. With the better and lesser known examples of all three forms—from *Invasion of the Body Snatchers* (1978) and *Breathless* to the *Star Wars* and *Indiana*

The Human Cartoon of Contemporary Narrative (*Who Framed Roger Rabbit?*, Disney, 1988. Tokyo Stills)

Jones sequels, an original plot becomes a minimal background for figures of technological or stylistic extravagance, of image beyond what Gilles Deleuze calls "action-images." These figures in effect detach themselves from the path of character psychology and plot incident and become located instead as an imagistic or technological performance, which then moves from the margins to the center of the narrative logic.

Here, the remade character becomes the star-image who takes over the role rather than inhabits an original character. The star as image replaces character psychology as a narrative motivation, and does not so much address and narratively anchor its audience (as, say, the fictional complexities of Bogart and Bacall might gather up and complicate the loose ends of a story) but poses as a publicity display whose significance is in how it extends beyond this particular story. Like Luke Skywalker, Indiana Jones, or any Richard Gere vehicle, character becomes a flattened, cartoonish display whose chief action is to exhibit its exaggerated figuration (and certainly not comment on that exhibition as Belmondo does in the first *Breathless*). In *Raiders of the Lost Ark,* a theatrical and acrobatic, sword-swinging Arab threatens Jones who mugs for the camera and then shoots him, an incidental moment, which like the incidental logic of cartoon narratives is what the entire story primarily serves. The several avatars of James Bond become insertions into a exotic technological and political backdrop, their main skill and victory being not to initiate action but to "reappear" again and again in disarming, self-contained poses.[5]

Between technology and cartoons, this kind of character thus becomes assimilated by the special effects necessary to maintain and revitalize recycled narratives. To watch and enjoy these movies is not to watch for a story (which is already known or at least already available); it is to watch and participate in those "moments of special effect" that exceed an original story (the sequel and the remake) or that exceed narrative itself (the series). As many reviewers have remarked, the story of the 1986 version of *The Fly* is the technological wizardry that transforms a character who, until then, has only a series of the same outfits to wear again and again. Just as these remade narratives are literally removed from a historical context that supports a narrative significance (the original *The Fly,* for instance, being a story of social and scientific peril as much as a horror story), so too the narrative structure, as the reflection of a history, begins to literally absent itself from the focus of the film and is absorbed into an abstracted instant of isolated technological, imagistic, or audial display.

What the remake and the sequel and their extension into a series describe then is the tendency to release narrative from its motivations in time and character and to relocate the remnants of those elements in the technological repetitions and figurative abstractions. In this sense, they represent not the traditional movement of narrative to reflect an organized history or the modernist demand to reorganize that history but the more contemporary perspective of narrative as an unresolved plenitude where history fades into the starry images of an idyllic past or the technological nightmare of an inhuman future.

These narrative changes are, I think, stunningly apparent in the fable that describes the rebirth of *2001* (1968) as *2010* (1984).

Kubrick's original is, in its narrative elusiveness, a hypercritical commentary on the violent motivations that, through the force of technology, move human history forward or (more likely) back on itself, the history of the future being locked into the violent motivations of the past. In *2010,* however, the strenuous demands that the original made on the viewer's sense of a narrative logic and motivation are replaced by the luxury and wonder of technological effect, effect which far outshines its irrelevantly thin plot line and the moronically simple question that generates it (what did happen in *2001?*). Appropriately, the remade sequel replaces the human/inhuman ambiguity that oversees human history at the end of *2001* with the transcendent bliss of voices and figures whose sketchy lines and morality resembles a cartoon, a technological brilliance identified within some metaphysical heaven placidly removed from the turbulence of the earth.

The Music-Video Story: Technologies and the Unmotivated Body

The telling and retelling of many contemporary film narratives thus rely on a technology that moves the narration into a cartoon discourse with minimal narrative and historical motivation. Concomitantly, the spectacles of technology within these narratives become moments of sublime transcendence whereby technology and its representations become a heavenly or hellish remedy replacing the burden of historical engagement. These technological spectacles become performative instances within the narrative scheme, glaringly prominent in a movie like *School Daze* (1988), for example, and what they most consistently perform is some version of a shattering or transcendence of human subjectivity as historical identity. If barely differentiated narrative repetition generates an attenuated cartoon logic and representation, the supportive technology offers discontinuous moments of identification and unity with the technological spectacle of some unattainable other world (hence Spike Lee's utopian politics in that film and other films by him). This is the sublimity of spectatorial performance found most intensely in the condensed narratives of music videos.

In *The Postmodern Condition,* for instance, Jean-François Lyotard argues how contemporary scientific method, as an alternative to the anxious collapse of positivism, has merged with the strategies of postmodern narrative. Gradually liberating itself from the securities of the "grand narratives" of the nineteenth century, which were based in models of spiritual order and social emancipation, modern science has legitimated itself through the performance of certain "moves" (in accordance with the narratives of game theory). Previously, the justification and motivation for scientific narratives was a function of the efficiency with which they performed the human body and their ability to turn expenditure into surplus value. But the teleology and economics of this kind of narrative have since been replaced by what Lyotard calls the *paralogy of performance*, a shuffling of the logic and continuity of narrative performance, a performative logic in which the human body is dislocated and dispersed from its classical narrative center:

> Postmodern science—by concerning itself with such things as undecidables, the limits of precise control, conflicts characterized by incomplete information, "fracta," catastrophes, and pragmatic paradoxes—is theorizing its own evolution as discontinuous, catastrophic, nonrectifiable, and paradoxical. . . . It is producing not the known but the unknown. And it suggests a model of legitimation that has nothing to do with maximized performance, but has as its basis difference understood as paralogy. (60)

Now, "the best performativity cannot consist in obtaining additional information. . . . It comes rather from arranging the data in a new way, which is what constitutes a move properly speaking" (52).

Indeed, this conjunction of scientific technology and narrative motion is nowhere more clearly put into action than in contemporary movies where a postmodern narrative can be described as the spreading or attenuation of the classical through the work of a series of technological moves. Especially in contemporary movies, as I have been suggesting, the imagistic moves of technology suspend and neutralize the motivations of narrative, while at the same time focus this distraction in the performance of excessive spectacle. In this sense, a film like *Close Encounters of the Third Kind* (1977) might be seen as symptomatic of the state of postmodern history: most distinguished by its extremely weak narrative line (a number of different people feel drawn to a mountain) and the passive agency of the characters (why is this happening?), this is a narrative made up of a group of separate little narratives that are bound clumsily together by their need to perform the technological spectacle of Speilberg's grand Other, the spiritual technology of the extraterrestrial. Motivation of any kind is radically obscured and displaced into the promise of the technological visitation of the future. Finally, a disconnected past (the World War II pilots and other figures of a lost history who emerge from the space ship) shares the same place as an "inhuman" future, the historical continuities and discontinuities of both being absorbed in the heavenly space(ship) of technological performance.

That contemporary hybrid of music halls and opera, the music video is, however, the most essential instance of this contemporary narrative form—so much so that it has become the critical financial and narrative ingredient in the movies and television today, including *Miami Vice* (1985), *Top Gun, Dirty Dancing, To Live and Die in L.A.* (1985), *Batman,* and countless other contemporary films. Differing fundamentally from the traditional supportive music score, this dimension of a movie is frequently determined even before the narrative line is fully worked out, fully cashing in on what David James calls "the big story that describes the supplanting of cinema by music as the hegemonic cultural force in the post-war period."[6] Indeed, a movie like *Stop Making Sense* can be described as an extended and self-conscious, almost parodic, construction of itself—from an empty stage and boom box to the light show of an overflowing crowd of musicians—as the technological spectacle of a music video. In their original form (practiced increasingly by many commercial and semi-commercial filmmakers from John Landis to Nicholas Roeg), music videos represent an extreme condensation of many traditional narrative elements into a three-minute spectacle of almost pure technological consumption: while the glimmer of one or more character types frequently focus the quick sketch of a dramatic plot, the real subject of these stories is the ability of the technological image, coupled with music, to diminish the inevitable presence of narrative causality in favor of a performative relation with the image and characters within it. As a consequence of a quick collage structure and television conditions, which encourage a spectatorial repetition and omnipresence, viewers truly recuperate,

True Stories: Narration as Music Video (Warner Bros., 1986)

consume, and interpolate themselves into these images according to their own needs and desires (Kinder "Music Videos" 4–13). Aimed mostly at a young audience positioned at the edge of a social history, these condensed little narratives are about the pleasures of exceeding the narrative that threatens them and the inefficient body that restricts them.

Here I would argue that the explicit sadomasochistic motifs that occupy many of these videos, with their various versions of "disembodiment," could be described as provoking and supporting a psychologically and perceptually similar activity on the part of their viewer-consumer. Ann Kaplan and others have detailed the relation of these narratives to a consumer ideology through which the pleasure of the viewing is bound up with spending one's time and money on images and objects that must be rapidly changed and recirculated. This viewer-consumer temporally, psychologically, and financially expends his or her self in the constantly recycled arena of domestic distraction. When a music video calls attention to the technological and commercial mechanisms of its performance (as they so often do), it constructs the fascination of that expenditure as a paralogical series of extravagant moments whose power lies in the ephemeral and sublime technology of their self-construction: commonly these are collapsed narratives about the elaborate setups for a concert or for the production of the video itself, the convoluted re-creation of a memory of passionate love on film or through a view finder, or the story that inscribes the dull life of the fan into the escape of the rock star. In these cases, the technology of the event becomes identified with the extraordinary quality of the event (or vice-versa), and the domestically dislocated and distracted perspective of an audience finds its appropriate object in a technological performance that tends to overtake any musical (and humanistic) expression. The attention to the technology and mechanics of the video is an attention to and involvement in what is necessarily and ecstatically a waste of domestic time and money and the traditional reliance of both on narrative.[7]

Adrian Lyne's *9 1/2 Weeks* is one of the more controversial and unabashed transpositions of the structures of this music-video narrative into commercial narrative form. Its girl-meets-boy plot has no more than that as a starting premise before it focuses on its real story, the subjugation and absorption of Elizabeth, the art dealer, into the fantasies of John, the wealthy practicer of arbitrage, the purest form of spending and consuming. Like many other contemporary movies, it is best described as a series of music-video scenarios (featuring an eclectic variety from reggae to Billie Holiday and Joe Cocker), paralogical video games about the performance of (female) sexual ecstasy as the performance of self-abandonment. No wonder *Variety* makes the short-sightedly conventional but remarkably accurate complaint about this film that "the virtual absence of anything happening . . . leaves one great hole on the screen for two hours" (Halliwell 742).

9 1/2 Weeks: The Technological Ecstasy of Performance (MGM-UA, 1986. Cinemabilia)

Besides their definition by diegetic or nondiegetic rock music, the two salient characteristics of these often sadomasochistic encounters between John and Elizabeth are their aleatory logic and their high-tech gloss. Part of the sublimity of their lovemaking is absolutely dependent on unexpected and rapid movement from one exotic (sometimes gothically gritty) setting to another, from steely clean apartment to clocktower to Algonquin Hotel. Critical here is that this sadomasochistic play is absolutely sanitized (unlike, say, that in *Last Tango in Paris*). Like the early encounter when John casually puts new sheets on a bed and points out how isolated they are, the threats and danger are never realized in this film except through the visual suggestion of an immacuately high-tech Sadean theater.

Indeed, as a kind of distillation and denial of narrative motivation, Elizabeth's actions proceed, as full-blown narcissism, towards the negation and sublimation of her character in the material technology of images she desires. The very status of John's existence remains enough in doubt (none of her friends ever see or meet him) to describe the romance as exclusively her play with the images of her own narcissistic spectacle. At one point, Elizabeth reviews slides in a darkened room: against the track of the Eurythmic's "The City Never Sleeps" (with the refrain "It's only just a feeling"), the camera cuts faster and faster between her watching the slides and the cuts between the slides themselves. She becomes swept away in a masturbatory ecstasy provoked, it seems, as much by the graphics of the images and the "feeling" of the song as by any feeling for another human being. After the remote control switch slides under her body, the rapid cuts between the slide images respond to her orgasmic movements, acting out the quintessential music-video performance, the sublime technological narrative of self-consumption.

As she becomes increasingly consumed by this romance (or more exactly its images), Elizabeth becomes more and more distracted (forgetting appointments, etc.), expending herself more completely in the games and moves of a technologically sexual sublime. In the Hollywood ending, her failure to go on with this relationship is, to put it sarcastically, a sentimental flight from the posthumanism of music-video love. She retreats to the sense of history and story she finds only in the aging patriarch Farnsworth, an alienated modernist painter. That Lyne is also responsible for that more commercial version of this logic, *Fatal Attraction* (1987), suggests the scope of this narrative sensibility, as well as its reactionary direction (in at least these two films). As countershots of the same sadomasochistic scene, in this second film the ability of a woman to (sexually) distract a male viewer from a domestic scene and to disrupt its narrative logic with ecstatic and frightening temporal eruptions is quickly revealed as the most humanly dangerous and self-destructive of performances.[8]

If narratives without motivation become a dispersal of narrative incident and spectatorial interest, the music-video format of movies like *9 1/2 Weeks* is perhaps the predominant way that subsequent threat of narrative boredom is averted through the fascination with a technological sublime. The technological and mass-media descendant of the operatic aria, the music video thus appears as the commercial counterpart and industrial partner to contemporary epic narratives (just as VCRs complement blockbusters): the excessive reductions of the first reflect and frequently counterpoint the excessive displacements of the second. As they both work to suspend historical and narrative time, the two become the necessary matching of the extravagance of the minute with the extravagance of the interminable. Music-video narratives attempt the impossible creation of momentary heavens within a cartoon hell of a story built on few if any motivations—the impossible reconciliation demonstrated so successfully in *Batman* where archenemies hate and pursue each other because they are so much alike. While watching those stories over and over and over again elicits that anaesthetized distraction which is contemporary boredom, the spectacular technological and imagistic moves that violate that boredom become a sublime transcendence of narrative and human subjectivity itself. Within the conditions of contemporary viewing, this is the marriage of narrative heaven and hell.

Music from Heaven, Bodies in Hell:
The Singing Detective

If repetition through technology has structured hells as heavens that usurp contemporary motivation and human subjectivity, this narrative predicament has necessarily become, for many movies, a central part of their questioning the crisis of the body within time and history today. Reflecting the conditions of its distracted viewing, the postmodern narrative has created a kind of arrested body-character narratively suspended or dissipated across an evacuation of time. Here the possibilities of understanding human action as narrative action then becomes a question of perceiving that action as at odds with contemporary narrative formulas. In Jon Amiel's and Dennis

Potter's *The Singing Detective,* this becomes specifically a question of mobilizing the body *outside* narration rather than trying to motivate that character-body within the antagonistic terms of contemporary narrative. Whereas *Singin' in the Rain* used classical narration to naturalize and motivate the generic performances of the song, *The Singing Detective* aims to open contemporary narrative to a "denaturalized" world, which is motivated, if at all, only by the always-changing needs of different human and historical performances.

Inseparable from the narrative project of *The Singing Detective* has been the particularly mobile patterns of its reception, from its original programming on BBC television to its appearance on U.S. PBS stations in different time slots, and its later release in theaters like New York's Public Theater. Like other examples of this contemporary mobility, *Berlin Alexanderplatz, Shoah, Our Hitler* (1979), the television combination of *The Godfather I and II* (1989), and the re-released, restored, and lengthened version of *Lawrence of Arabia* (1989), for example, this has meant viewing the narrative either as discrete episodes through several months or all eight hours condensed into one or two or three days of epic screenings, an instability that both severely troubles a more traditional story and perfectly accommodates the viewing of contemporary narrative. With either the serial structure and the single epic screening of one of these postmodern epics like *The Singing Detective,* the narrative and its audience must literally make and remake characters and incidents whose definition is nonetheless constantly eroded by the expanse of time they inhabit. Whereas earlier long epics such as *Alexander Nevsky* (1938), *Napoléon* (1927), or *Intolerance* might be described as about the redemption of the burden of historical time (and their own running time) through the actions of a character or characters, more contemporary epics, in keeping with the structure of "viewing time" in today's media culture, describe either the failure of the narrative to fully organize its events through time (such as those that surround Hitler) or the inescapable dismantling and wasting of characters (from Michael Corleone to Franz Biberkopf) by that temporal action.

In *The Singing Detective,* the central character, Philip Marlow ("No 'e' on the end; what else could I do but write detective stories"), arrives in a hospital ward disfigured and crippled by an extraordinarily severe case of psoriasis. During the course of his treatment for his skin disease, three overlapping temporal discourses describe the action. Besides the present tense that he lives in the hospital, Marlow struggles with the childhood memories of his parents' rocky marriage during the last years of World War II and his own childhood betrayals (of his mother and a friend) during that time. Interwoven with these personal memories and story is Marlow's struggle to *retell* his already published detective novel *The Singing Detective*. In a remark that could apply to all three, as well as to the postmodern obsession with narrative forms, Marlow later observes: "The worst thing about a detective story is the plot. The best thing too. You have to work it all out in your head. That's what I've been trying to do like a rat in a maze."

The disjunctions among these three levels—most specifically associated with his repressed inability to come to grips with his mother's sexuality, her infidelity, and his guilt about her suicide— produce and reflect the disfiguration and paralysis of Marlow's body, caught up in his inability to motivate his life as a coherent narrative. Bound up with this excessively oedipal repression, moreover, is Marlow's childhood betrayal of Mark Binney: after defecating on the desk of a demonically patriotic schoolteacher (who daily marks the Allied victories on the schoolroom map), he successfully accuses Binney of the deed. This two-part violence and repression (phallic and anal, against the sexuality of a mother and the social vulnerability of an outcast) create a Marlow character who pursues murder mysteries as a way of confirming his sordid and moribund vision of the world, a vision that is psychologically and literally a rejection and repulsion of the material of the human body—most specifically the bodies of women and that of his own. Somewhere between sarcasm and confession, he screams from his hospital bed the call for a wasting that is likewise played out on his bodily skin: "I believe in Malthusianism, compulsory depopulation, genocide, AIDS . . . and most of all I believe in vomit." If *9 1/2 Weeks* performs its sadomasochistic spectacle across a patriarchal perspective, *The Singing Detective* unveils a patriarch who likewise self-destructs as part of that performance of self-loathing.

Surrounding this sadomasochistic performance of the disintegration of his physical body is explicitly the simultaneous search for clues and decipherment of them. For Marlow the narrator, this means moving across those several narrative discourses—the autobiographical, the historical, and the fictional—in an attempt to discover and thus create motivations for the events and characters that dart and hide on the edge of a narrative chaos. Here clues are questions looking for motivations, and what is so exceptional about this narrative and its reflections of its contemporary conditions is its assembly and dramatization of questions as actions without motivations. The child Marlow hides in the treetops (from which he spots his mother's illicit tryst) and cries out in anxiety, "I'll find out, I'll find out. . . ." This vague quest (which seems to reflect his relationship with his mother and all the women who would later substitute as objects of sexual loathing) merges in turn with the horrifying accusations of the schoolteacher whose desk someone has defecated on: "Who? Which one? Who did it?" The detective shouts, "I'll get you! Whoever you are, wherever you are. . . ." Asked by his ex-wife Nicola to "write about real things in a real way," Marlow erupts in what could be called a realist's defense of contemporary narrative indeterminancy: "Solutions! All solutions and no clues. That's what the dumbheads want . . . 'He said,' 'She said'; descriptions of the sky . . . All clues, no solutions, that's the way things really are."

As a figure in and the figurer of the detective narrative, Marlow becomes both the missing motivation and the agency of a desperate narrative structure struggling to hold itself together. In effect, there is only one story here, the missing one of Marlow's betrayal, and the other narratives that supplant that absent story contend for a lost coherence. As Jim Collins has pointed out about detective fiction in general, these narratives are by definition contending discourses. Emphasizing within them the unresolved plurality of voices outside a dominant legal structure, Collins argues that "detective fiction is, more often than not, a discourse which forces contradictions rather than compromises; that is disruptive rather than integrative, because 'justice' is characterized as provisional, incomplete, and virtually unenforceable by a state incapable of understanding its complexity" (34). In this case, the separate discourses contend for and work for some narrative coherence that would bring Marlow's physical figures, characters, voices, and points of view together in a relationship that would unify and mobilize them through the course of a narrative time. While traditional detective fictions might use the status of the detective as outside those contending discourses (such as Bogart's Marlowe) to orchestrate (rather than reconcile) them around his character, the crisis in *The Singing Detective* is that the character and body of the detective-narrator is, on one hand, itself divided and fragmented by the separate "little" narratives it attempts to decipher and, on the other, revealed as both the killer and victim (his repressed involvement in his mother's suicide being associated with his own immobility). Indeed, the psychologist who serves as an interlocutor for Marlow points directly at this narrative crisis where the searching for motivations does not lead to narrative solutions and resolutions but to making oneself part of a sadomasochistic performance: "I know that clues are supposed to point in the direction of the murderer but what if they also reveal the victim a little more clearly?"

The predominant marker of this sadomasochistic performance within the narrative is the body of the novelist Marlow stretched between a narrative heaven and hell. In one sense, Marlow's physically suspended and immobile body ironically refers to that timeless and imaginary heaven where nothing ever happens and where one dreams, like Marlow, of fictional cartoonish characters. Conversely, the physical deterioration of that body dramatizes the hellish wasting that occurs when the human figure fails to motivate events circling wildly around it. The two most prominent figures identified with this immobile narrator are the boy Marlow who sees the forest but not the trees from his detached, heavenly perch in the stationary treetops and the sad, stiff figure of his father who is the helpless victim of events he cannot control. (Paralleling both are the many dying and dead whose immobile bodies accumulate rapidly in the film: stabbed and shot spies, the naked, bloated female dragged from the Thames, and the series of patients who die grotesquely in the bed next to Marlow.) Marlow's body becomes, in short, the textual location of that central crisis within contemporary narrative, a human figure at once stripped of motivations and spread across the boredom of an immobile and interminable present. "Something about this place," Marlow says as he arrives in his hospital bed, "strips away all the unimportant things like love and hope . . . and skin."

World War II and the period immediately following it are the historical contexts through which Marlow tries to narrate and locate the crisis of his immobility and wasting. The events of Marlow's childhood are permeated with the atmosphere and talk of the final days of that war, the music and songs are all recordings from the forties, and even in the hospital ward a patient next to Marlow tells tales of sexual encounters while invading Germany. Just as this period describes, for many, the end of modernism and the laying of the foundations for postmodernism, in *The Singing Detective* it becomes a condensed point between a mythical historical heaven and a monstrous contemporary hell: on the one hand, there is that anticipated moment in the serial when the end of the war will announce a heavenly utopia ("The bells will be ringing! All the lights will go back on—lights, lights, everywhere!"); on the other there is the moment of his mother's infidelity and suicide, which triggers a chaos in which returning soldiers become physical and sexual threats and, concomitantly, a hellish grim-reaper scarecrow appears on the horizon to pursue Marlow. Between these two mythical points is Marlow's own childhood betrayal, the time and place when he accuses the child Mark Binney as punishment for the sexual crime of his mother and Binney's father and begins to participate himself in the collapse of his own domestic narrative. Again reinforcing the connection between that historical text and the physical-psychological one, Marlow explicitly superimposes this betrayal on the action along the Allied front, now implicating himself in the contradiction and contentions of that historical discourse: as part of his lie, the boy Marlow claims he caught Binney defecating on the desk when Marlow had come into the classroom to place another flag on the map of the Allied invasion of Germany; later Marlow would remember from the present how the rest of his classmates "came out to the front" and readily joined in the mob hysteria of the false accusation. For, like the many atrocities of that war, "any lie will result in corroboration if it results in public pain . . . and humiliation." Finally, the novel within the serial appropriately assumes its own place across this collapsed point by evolving its thin plot around the politically topsy-turvy espionage scheme of smuggling Nazi rocket scientists to the United States. The locus for the espionage scheme, introduced in the first scene, is, moreover, the nightclub "Skinskapes" where a narrative mystery is initiated and worked through—without solution—as a displacement of the narrative and skin crisis of the contemporary Marlow.

Throughout these overlapping narrative lines, the stiff and shedding body of Marlow thus becomes a kind of textual surface guiltily implicated with a variety of physically wrecked bodies of World War II (including the sexual bodies of women, from Russian spies to Lili Marlene, who betray lovers or nations). At one point, the patient Marlow listens with disgust while George, another patient, tells tales of sexually conquering German girls during the invasion; as George suddenly suffers a heart attack Marlow sarcastically baits the grotesquely jerking body with those exploits and lets him die while the narrative crosscuts to the boy Marlow's peeping perspective on his mother's secret affair. Here, as with his betrayal of Binney and his own mother, the *inaction* of Marlow is fully implicated in the passage from a historical heaven to a historical hell.

At the center of this narrative and historical space, Marlow displaces and mediates the heaven of his immobile body and the hell of its wasting as the singing detective, a kind of music-image cartoon with the exaggerated gestures and tautological cliches ("Am I right or am I right?") that support and dissipate contemporary narrative. This fictional counterpart of Marlow is a mobile narrator-detective from the forties, a hardened detective who doubles as a dashing "crooner" at the Laguna Dance Hall. Seeking out the hidden motivations in events, he frequently integrates that action into the performance of big-band tunes, yet, the result of these performances is neither a utopian suspension of narrative action nor a movement of that action (as, according to Richard Dyer, is often the function of musical numbers in more classical musicals) but instead a cartoonish transformation of the often unmotivated violence that permeates the narrative. Pursued by two incompetent and clownish British agents, for example, Marlow spots them while singing and dancing his way through a lavish version of "The Old Umbrella Man." Without missing a beat, he dances and ducks behind the umbrella props, as their gunfire kills the unlucky drummer. In this and other sequences like it, the stylization of the violence absorbs, through the technical choreography of the music and spinning umbrellas, the attacks on Marlow, reducing that action to incidental material for his performance. Where the body of the novelist-narrator Marlow is suspended, torn, and wasted by the impossibilities of his narrating his historical and childhood past ("desperate pastiche" in the words of the psychologist), the singing detective gathers up, like a music video, all threats and horror into the space of his musical performance and technique.

While the historical plot of Marlow's childhood memories and traumas employs a similar narrative structuring of the songs and performances, their transition into the contemporary world of the hospital ward marks, unlike most contemporary narratives, the grotesque cost of that narrative transcendence through performance. On whichever narrative level the songs appear, they are fabricated as a highly *technological* performance of previous recordings—the materially scratchy or echoey sound of a prerecorded Bing Crosby or Andrew Sisters tune, for instance. In all cases, musical expression as a technological and lip-synched performance removes human expression from the horror and miseries of the different narratives by abstracting and denaturalizing it. As Marlow's narrative voice-over explains, "There are songs to sing, thoughts to think, feelings to feel. I can sing the songs; I can think the thoughts; but you aren't going to catch me feeling the feelings." If the historical narrative within the film attempts (as in *Singin' in the Rain*) to naturalize those songs and the detective fiction aims to think clues through them, their transference into Marlow's contemporary hell reveals them within a surreal and dehumanized logic, their technological performance itself sharply distancing them from the human form and its feelings.

At one point, for instance, an often-repeated shot of the boy Marlow in a tree cuts from his reciting "The Lord's Prayer" through a recording on the soundtrack of the Andrews Sisters' "Don't Fence Me In"; the source for this transitional recording is a radio surrounded, in a tight shot, by the boy's mother and father and the father's parents. After the mother's angry accusation of the father's docility before his parents (the boy Marlow feeling responsible for the confrontation), two more musical scenes follow: cutting forward to the hospital, the old man dying in the bed next to Marlow lip-synchs Bing Cosby's "It Might as Well Be Spring"; flashing back to Marlow's youth, his father sings the same recording (as if in his own voice) before a local pub crowd. Throughout sequences like this, the recording technology of the musical numbers originates as a more historically and materially naturalized expression whose metaphorical irony attempts to recuperate and motivate the tensions and suppressed violences of the past scenes, in this case the helpless victim-father being reshaped and idealized as an active figure only in those moments when he croons on stage. Yet, in the transition from these musical performances into the crisis of Marlow's narrative present they become nightmarish *danse macabres* of singing corpses, spectacular instances of a narrative sublime becoming a historical grotesque.

Indeed, what is most grotesquely mocking of those sublimely romantic songs is the formal and stylistic overlay of their 1940s technique on the figures of wasted and crippled contemporaries. Shortly after Marlow arrives at the hospital, doctors and patients perform "Dry Bones" through elaborate Busby Berkeley camera and scene setups, nurses using skulls as percussion instruments; later, a bouncing rendition of "It's a Lovely Day Tomorrow" counterpoints a montage of writhing and dying patients. Put briefly, when Marlow asks his three-part question (which parallels the three narrative discourses in the film)—"Who's the dame? Where's the body? . . . Who's trying to swing you into this number?"—the single answer is precisely what keeps him from being able to answer any of those questions or from solving his narrative clues: namely, those characters and figures have been displaced by a technology that performs history, narrative, and the human body from a place outside of human motivation.

As the series progresses, this disturbing disjunction between performative technology and the human figure begins to trouble the material techniques of the narrative itself. Losing control of his contending narratives, Marlow's narration becomes more and more a technical performance in which the performative mechanics and technology of the narrative become identified with and act out physical destruction and sadomasochistic violence. A patient, Reginald, reads a dog-eared copy of *The Singing Detective* throughout the serial to distract him from his illness (his finishing the novel coinciding with his discharge). More dramatically, the paralytic Marlow begins to speak not only the story but its printing (". . . full stop . . . new paragraph"); and during the climactic conclusion, when his contemporary crisis over the fate of "The Singing Detective" screenplay folds into his fictionalized telling of the novel, his character-wife and character-rival begin to speak in the same materialized technology of print, announcing exclamation points, periods, and commas that foreshadow their violent ends. As Nicola's lover Mark Finney and she finish transcribing Marlow's script before sending it to Hollywood, Finney becomes edgy and notes how

Marlow's script changes the names of a character in the novel from Howes to Mark Binney: "In that script of his, he describes this apartment—where he's never been. . . . It's almost as if he made all *this* up." As the camera closes in on him, he begins to "speak the print," completing the take-over of character motivation and will by the performance of the discourse itself: "I have this awful. Dash. He stops himself. Comma. And almost shudders. Full stop." Nicola responds: "Darling, Dash. Question mark." They repeat their phrases, and Mark ends the troubled sentence: "Premonition." On the verge of three final narrative betrayals (these two will betray Marlow, Finney will give up Nicola for a Hollywood contract, and Nicola will stab Finney), the two character-figures are usurped, overwhelmed, and finally destroyed, like cartoons, by the exaggerated techniques and signs of their discourse. Finney's premonition at this climactic point may be the violent end of human characterization when technological performance replaces narrative motivation.

The premonition is fully realized in the next sequence when a gun battle in the hospital ward where characters and figures from each of the other narrative discourses have arrived. At the center of this battle are the two cartoonish spies who have trailed Marlow throughout the detective story. Shortly before this, the two have realized, like two Beckett figures, that they have been moving through the narrative without any legitimate motivation or human character (discovering they have no past nor even names, they are "bloody orphans" according to Marlow). As a central metaphor in the detective narrative, their search at this point crosscuts with the boy Marlow's rediscovery of his lost and passive father, the essential unmotivated figure in Marlow's psychological narrative, who wails beneath the boy high in a tree. This confrontation with characters now existing only as narrative techniques, choices, and figurations thus becomes the final showdown for the slowly recovering Marlow: his most important discovery here is his place within a logic of multiple conflicting narratives, none with motivated solutions and all contending for a performative legitimacy that requires a violence across the human figure to sustain itself. In the end, they naturally expose and destroy each other as they shatter bodies and characters around the ward, leaving Marlow no stories to tell but a body to leave with.

In these final sequences, as Marlow and his stories reveal themselves as ultimately about their own performance of a narrative vio-

The Detective in Search of Motivation (*The Singing Detective,* Lionheart Television, 1986)

lence, it becomes clear, I think, that this is more than the tale of confrontation with a repressed trauma that in turn leads to Marlow's physical cure. More in keeping with the "desperate pastiche" of its style and structure, *The Singing Detective* is about an accelerated conflict and overlapping of narrative performances (across their technological differences) and Marlow's decision to actively position himself within and against those narratives. As Marlow more fully articulates his memories and fictions for the hospital psychologist, these narratives start rapidly to blend into and conflict with each other, revealing themselves as a series of displaced and material narrative performances that even in their most entertaining musical form enact a sadomasochistic violence. The dead woman dragged from the river in his fictional narrative—first a Russian prostitute-spy, then his wife—finally appears as his mother, who apparently killed herself after the historical narrative shows Marlow the boy telling her of witnessing her infidelity. Characters from the hospital ward reappear in the detective narrative, a group of them watching from the bridge at one point as the female corpse is brought from the water; and his ex-wife's affair is acted out as a betrayal with Mark Finney (echoing the betrayed boy who is fictionalized in the *The Singing Detective* as the despicable British agent Mark Binney).

Pinpointing the demands of this crisis at the beginning of the fourth part of the serial, the psychologist formulates the postmodern question that haunts this narrative pastiche: are these events the result of fate or accident; can one reconcile inhumanly random events with some grand human narrative; or, following their remark at the close of that conversation, are these stories about metaphysics or music? After this query, the next cut shows Marlow now fully and actively involved in the present-tense plot of Mark Finney and Nicola's betrayal. He begins, through a series of images tied together by the song "You Always Hurt the One You Love," to recollect the images of prostitutes, a father unable to act, his confrontation with his mother about her infidelity (which is also the moment she and he first notice his psoriasis), and his false accusation of the boy Mark Binney. He, in short, begins to reposition himself *actively* outside the narratives that controlled his character and to realize the danger and responsibilities of creating narrative technologies: "For the first time in my life," he says as he begins to painfully learn to write again, "I'll have to think about the value of every word. . . . Words make me hold my breath." His implicit answer to the psychologist is therefore that these stories are about the technology of both metaphysics and music and that the truly human exists in carefully negotiating that fluctuating space between the fated heaven and the accidental hell that infuse contemporary narrative life.

From this series of final narrative conflagrations, Marlow steps out, not of his past, but out of his attempt to naturalize and motivate it as a narrative performance. Giving up the search for narrative motivations, he becomes a mobile body: killed in that apocalyptic shoot-out by his narrative embodiment, Marlow the patient is released from the paralysis of being performed by narrative technique;

that he is killed interceding for the chubby spy, a substitute for the betrayed boy Mark Binney, indicates that his release comes with a recognition that human action today must be compelled and enabled by something beyond narrative and its conscious or unconscious motivations. Retrieving the life of a Mark Binney, he also climbs down from the tree to join his father and walks away with his ex-wife, one of the many women who had been violently reduced and performed through his narrative chains. "Hold onto me," she says as they walk out of the hospital ward; "There's not many others around anymore." The narrative impulse remains of course unavoidable. At the conclusion, "We'll Meet Again Someday" accompanies close-ups of each of the characters singing the tune and a final shot of the boy Marlow in his tree saying "When I grow up I'm going to be a detective." But if, as this ending suggests, narrative will necessarily be repeated, one can choose to be reduced or enabled by an understanding of its technological negotiations of the myths of history.

The final twist of *The Singing Detective* is its meta-narrative move to reflect back on its own place within commercial media. Early in the series, Marlow's former wife Nicola visits him in the hospital to trick him into signing papers that would release to her and her new lover Mark Finney the rights to a screenplay version of *The Singing Detective*. Not unlike the Hollywood fate of Potter's original *Pennies from Heaven* (1979), this other *Singing Detective* is presumably a version somewhere between the out-of-print novel, the one that we are watching (which is somewhere between its BBC broadcast and its various other appearances, including the publication of the script by Faber and Faber and later by Random House), and the one that Marlow claims is "turning . . . into something else . . . in my head." As viewers we are thus made to confront how these narratives about narration can and will spread and differentiate themselves through a large, if not infinite, number of narrative technologies and receptions. In keeping with Marlow's own crisis and recognition, audiences of this film series face and participate in the multiple possibilities of narrative performance, none of which can claim to be an original story and all of which change with their material and technological conditions and reception. This ability to inhabit that shifting performative place within and outside different narrative conditions—an ability I have earlier associated with the contemporary condition of viewing—is finally what *The Singing Detective* provokes.

In this regard the serial format of *The Singing Detective* complements and parallels the structure of the plot, its anticipated transformation into a film, and its convoluted narrative address. With its fundamentally linear development and character-oriented plot, this format certainly suggests that classical movie structure which Marlow had so quickly ridiculed when he learned of Hollywood's interest in his screenplay (which he imagined would star Al Pacino). Yet, as a serial spread across and through larger periods of time and divided into three contending discourses, the narrative necessarily dissipates and interrupts any tightly linked chronological motivations and narrative unity. Its serial structure specifically assumes and must respond to repetition as its foundation and an audience that, unlike the focused and concentrated viewer of traditional theatrical narrative formulas, forgets and loses narrative motivations across the time of its viewing. Unlike even the standard serial film, here the promotion of a narrative of distraction supports an "unmotivated viewing" that finally does not surrender itself to the search for narrative sense and motivation but acts out its own mobile viewing as a continual awareness of its physical place spread through other time zones, across multiple social and aesthetic narratives. In one horrifying scene for Marlow, a Jesus group enters the hospital ward and begins singing a hymn whose refrain is "Be in Time." Ironically, this is the imperative that Marlow is asked to work his way back to and the imperative that constantly intercedes for the spectator in the viewing of this eight-hour narrative. This other "time" is, unlike the narrative of heaven and hell performed by the Christian singers, one where human actions must substitute for narcissistic motivations.

If heaven is a place where nothing ever happens and hell is a place where everything is remembered, then narrative boredom and the narrative bliss that momentarily relieves it represent a contemporary crisis in which the human subject tries to fit mind and body in that large interstice, called history, that separates the two. If human history is usually blurred across those interstices and the human figure violated by its technological performance, it should also be clear—through at least the one (but not only) example of *The Singing Detective*—that this crisis within contemporary narrative can also be the source for a more active spectatorial relation with the projects of narrative. If contemporary movie narratives tend to bore audiences, boredom can also provoke other responses, as Jameson has reminded us: "Boredom with a particular kind of work or style or content can always be used productively as a precious symptom of our own existential, ideological, and cultural limits, an index of what has to be refused" in the multiplicity of cultural history ("Reading without Interpretation" 203). Like the evacuation of auteurism of its authority or the hysterical fissures within contemporary genre, the heaven and hells of contemporary narrative can become a place where we are forced to come to terms with the politics of interpreting our distracted relationship with our historical present.

POLITICS AND CONTEMPORARY MOVIES

□□□

CHAPTER
SEVEN

SPINNING THE SPECTATOR
Fans and Terrorists in the Third Generation

□□

> "For to move from interpretation to its politics is in large measure to go from undoing to doing, and this, given the currently accepted divisions between criticism and art, is risking all the discomfort of a great unsettlement in ways of seeing and doing."
> —EDWARD W. SAID

> "We have a kind of domestic colonialism here because they don't allow us to run our own communities. . . . But how should we fight? That's what I want to know."
> —DANNY VICTORIA, *SAMMY AND ROSIE GET LAID*

Movie culture is hardly alone today in having difficulty addressing political questions or engaging audiences in politically motivating terms. Politics of any sort—and especially the American kind— have been so widely identified with media events that any position on the first can too easily be deflected and often dissipated into the slippery, entertaining gloss of the second. Indeed, one of the persistent debates and concerns within studies of postmodernism is the very possibility of a truly political position in a cultural landscape where the reception of ideology through opaque and shifting media surfaces seems to disallow thoughtful engagement, provocation, or social reading itself. The question becomes: if a political film operates with some notion of public effectiveness, how does a film become socially and politically effective when its meaning is always wrapped in its reception as a kind of private distraction or a mere public outing? This, of course, is the complaint of Baudrillard: it suggests that both casually "political" films from *Reds* (1981) to *Mississippi Burning* (1988) and more analytical, confrontational ones like *Our Hitler* share similar trouble in their attempts to address a contemporary audience in any kind of political discourse. Always subject to the cultural and technological conditions of their address and reception, they must either claim the avant-garde politics of exile and marginality or absolutely reduce what political engagement might mean today. This is not to say that film and other popular media cannot take on a legitimate political engagement with events but that their dissemination through contemporary media seems invariably to disengage its meanings in order to dramatically restructure them.

Here I would like to address this question of contemporary film politics across the generational logic with which I began this book and specifically as it manifests itself in the work of three films. Scorsese's *The King of Comedy* (1982), Fassbinder's *The Third Generation,* and Frear's *My Beautiful Laundrette* are each in their different strategies about the lost history of both a classical patriarchal ideology and the more radical subversive stances of the sons and daughters. That celebrated filmmakers are behind each of these films is significant only within the context of the institution of the postmodern auteur, which relates the controversies that frequently surround the filmmaker directly or indirectly to the ideological project of the films themselves. More importantly, each of the films locates itself within the recent history of a particular contemporary culture whose politics have regularly threatened to become its media images. Most importantly (for my argument), each addresses an audience as a *localized, emotional, and temporary position* where the fascinating power of ideology lies in its instability and where the politics of a public sphere plays itself out within the distracted arena of private games and personal feelings.

The contemporary cultures, which these films are part of, offer a plethora of examples of this distracted privatization of political life across a public sphere. In this environment, there are certainly a number of positive ramifications, such as local ecological and regionalist movements and the new political activism of groups in terms of an independent marginalism (Solidarity, AIDs task forces, African Union of Mineworkers, and abortion-rights platforms within conservative parties). The more dependent this privatizing of the public becomes on the way media moments valorize and communicate political significance, however, the more problematic is the localized and temporary value of those ideological moments. Habermas's dream of a universal consensus begins to fall before the distortions of media simulations where universal truths are now merely responses to the advertisement of partial and passing self-interests, locked in Baudrillard's "moebius-spiraling negativity" (*Simulations* 30–38). Since the authenticity of those public images have now become, more than ever, a function of private engagements with them, this allows the political spectator to both fully believe and commit to an event, action, or image and then, with remarkable quickness, adjust, reinterpret, or disbelieve the same media event or image. The response to the short, highly fictionalized, "docu-film" of the Reagan campaign, "A New Beginning," is indicative of this: responding to it as they would to an advertisement whose "truth" has nothing to do with the reality of its referent, voters were nonetheless willing to vote for Reagan, just as many of the decisions that negatively affected individual lives during his first term as president were easily forgotten or forgiven in the overwhelming presence of his television personality that led to his second term. The most dramatic image as metaphor, however, could be the celebrated fall of the Berlin wall: the frenzied need of individuals to claim their own piece of the event becomes a carnival media spectacle that rejoices about an impending social unification under the sign of political consumerism.

Within this cultural space, terrorism becomes the extreme extension of its political logic, equally available to any ideological position from the actions of the Vietcong to the actions of the American soldier in Vietnam. Far from being confrontational, it is, at worst, an absolute commitment to the basic principles and structures of contemporary political life: that political action is randomly and emotionally positioned, that the public sphere is fully subject to private intervention, that spatial boundaries are fluid and relocatable, and that its meaning is largely a function of its successful advertisement as a media spectacle. Its difference of course is that actual terrorism makes frighteningly explicit and concrete the violence implicit in more sanitized and legitimated versions of political power. Whereas once John Doe might battle the machinery of political spectacle, today his American grandsons and grandaughters, living after a Vietnam war in which they both invaded the enemy and were, in their living rooms, invaded by that enemy, realize that there is no political or social life outside that spectacle nor any way of marking the difference (even in terms of their own narcissism). As Laura Kipnis puts it, terrorism "is the postmodern critique of the Enlightenment; it is, in fact, a decentering" (163).

Defined primarily by its mobilization of contingencies, a politics of terrorism can describe a variety of political potentials. From the most dour of standpoints, all that it allows is some version of a parodic intervention (as so pathologically parodied in the "I'm not going to take it anymore" outburst of *Network*) whose aim is not to tear apart the fabric of ideological spectacle but to reveal its fabric as fully unmotivated by any ideas or aims and entirely inconsistent with any cohering logic. With a much less pessimistic perspective, however, Stanley Aronowitz notes that this postmodern ground for various terrorisms can also be the space for contemporary notions of radical democracy:

> The space of this politics could be situated in the intentional communities attempted by various countercultures. These are postmodern because they deny evolutionist ideology. They assume that the existing state of affairs may last indefinitely and, even if overturned, may not make room for freedom as long as the new society remains statist and ideologically committed to social hierarchy (as opposed to economic equality). Mass politics signifies for them the end of public discourse, in which there is face-to-face communication and decisions are arrived at by consciously applying the rules of evidence and argument. . . . Postmodern politics, then, takes as its objective the pragmatic willingness of ruling groups to accommodate the demands of organized movements that, in turn, frame their own politics entirely in terms set externally by the ruling class. This assessment provides the basis for the terrorist alternatives, but also for the countercultures. (54–55).

Following the darker path of this political logic (and reserving the brighter possibilities of Aronowitz for later), the paradigmatic story for contemporary politics and movie ideology may be John Hinckley and Ronald Reagan's. Witnessed from an arch distance, the plot fol-

Travis and the Secret Service: The Politics of Terrorism in *Taxi Driver* (Warner Bros., 1976. Museum of Modern Art/Film Stills Archive)

lows an inevitable logic through which each character, with little indication of a larger awareness or motivation, attempts to absorb the other into a specific fantasy-fiction aligned with stardom and the movies. Each of these fictions is localized and provisional, yet their interaction binds them to a common ideological effort to overcome their differences and any other differential resistances. Hinckley's infatuation is not so much with the actress Jodie Foster but with Iris, her character in *Taxi Driver;* that she must dismiss him as a crazed fan, far beyond her own purview, only inspires him further. His attempted assassination of Reagan is not about Reagan himself but an effort to co-opt the image of the presidency, an image that is appropriately the Hollywood grandfather-star. In a critical sense, Hinckley plays only the political game of images that Reagan has so successfully played (and in which Foster has so successfully played fictional victim), and, while Hinckley certainly wins his stardom, the stage for that stardom crosses too far over into public life, where he has yet to gain any power.[1]

In fact, power within contemporary politics is ultimately only a product of the scope of the contingent and frequently spontaneous emotional alliances that an image or figure can draw upon. Reagan, of course, realizes this by quickly staging his tragedy with a series of quips and cliches that elevate him above the personal and disassociate him from the political causes and motivations behind the event ("I'd rather be in Philadelphia" and "I forgot to duck"). For him, "Power can stage its own murder to rediscover a glimmer of existence and legitimacy" (*Simulations* 37). Hinckley, on the other hand, recognizes this truth of contemporary politics only later when from his institutional prison he reminds Reagan (quite accurately) that the assassination attempt was perhaps the crucial boost in a faltering presidency. As a central part of the formula for his political success with audiences around the world, Reagan has instinctually known that images are not power *except as they find and as they appropriate a fortuitous place in a network of social and aesthetic contingencies*, making Reagan, the movie, the disturbing paradigm for the successful invasion of the politics of the public sphere by the contingent and transient images of a private performance.

Hinckley, whose voyeurism becomes social action, describes conversely the ideological plight of one kind of postmodern spectator—absolutely immersed in the *mise-en-abyme* of ideology and images and able to comprehend the situation only *after* his moments of participation. For this postmodern spectator, political reflection (and possibly movement) cannot arrive within the narcissistic bind of viewing, but only after the fact and as a consequence of its unbearable frustrations: analogous to and very much dramatized in the cultish paraphernalia that surround the release of a movie, contemporary viewing desperately requires a version of that political spin through which "handlers" locate political images or action within the contingencies of a present situation. Unlike older fan hysteria where the mesmerizing image has priority, here the meaning of that image is usurped by its theatrical reenactment across the viewer's media-saturated imagination.

The revealing logic of the Hinckley-Reagan event is, of course, that it was inspired by a movie that uncannily anticipated it: a möbius twist in which the media fantasy creates the historical event and the subjective reaction to it carries over into the public arena. *Taxi Driver* is supposedly the film through which Hinckley's obsession with Jodie Foster moved to new extremes; it is also a movie about a partially psychopathic individual's self-characterization of himself as the savior of the Foster character, Iris, whom he seems, much like Hinckley, to substitute for his displaced passion for the female handler of a political candidate. Born of his frustration with a world that seems to have originated in the terror of the Vietnam war (though, this too could be a performance), a world which he is now able to enter only through the frames of his cab windows, Travis attempts in *Taxi Driver* what he believes is a bloody rescue of Iris, while in fact it is a hysterically narcissistic gesture erupting as the culmination of a series of unrelated postures and images (dressing himself as an Indian, Vietnam vet, and so forth). His violence is the frustrated consequence of not being allowed to or not wanting to enter, as an active participant, the constant flood of spectacles and mini-movies—from hookers to political campaigns—that New York forces him to witness. In the end, Travis (who certainly anticipates the Travis of *Paris, Texas*) simply takes his own movie to the streets and becomes simultaneously its viewer and performer. That the media hails his slaughter of the pimp as the action of a hero is all that is needed to confirm that decision as culturally and thus politically correct (even if it is largely confusing—or illegible—for most viewers of the film). As all politicians in the age of Reagan realize, media spin replaces political understanding. While Hinckley may have followed Travis through the frustrations of contemporary viewing, he stumbles within postmodern politics (like most citizens) by failing to spin the movie he makes of himself and his illegible act into some explanatory contingency.

The Contingent Politics of Being a Fan

As the next spin along this möbius strip of contemporary movies and politics, Scorsese's *The King of Comedy* becomes his most timely political film, exactly because of its place within the cycle from *Taxi Driver* through the Hinckley-Reagan showdown. It too concerns a terroristic gesture defined not primarily by its violence but by its ability to disrupt the ideological and media orchestration of contingencies by creating another spin-off show. More excruciatingly than any Scorsese film, this one follows the path of the spectator-fan, Rupert Pupkin, from a place described absolutely by the media and its central figure, Jerry Langford, through that fan's remarkable ascension as a media event himself. As Rupert joins the mob of fans waiting for Langford (a Johnny Carson clone) at the beginning of the film, he ironically remarks that this is "not my whole life" when in fact this media life is the only life for even the less eccentric characters in the film. Rupert seems to have never lived off the social stage where Paul of *After Hours* learns how to negotiate and perform his life in all its variations.

Here Rupert is Travis and Hinckley and Paul at once but with all distracting connections with traditional social and ethical behavior contingencies jettisoned, so that the essential point is unmistakable: terroristic and revolutionary actions (the overthrow of a king, a president, or a father) occur entirely through a media logic that proceeds primarily according to the relentless turning of contingencies that appear in its path. Exactly because there are no signs of overt political life, *The King of Comedy* becomes one of the most ideologically lucid movies within the contemporary film scene. As Scorsese himself has admitted, this is not really a comedy (*Scorsese on Scorsese*): it is, rather, the generic comedy inherent in a contemporary political life where, regardless of the violence and human trauma during the transition of a political aristocracy, the media never suffers a crisis.

In a very important sense, Rupert is no different from other Scorsese obsessives: he is a person in search of a home, stretched and contradicted by his need for a domestic place and the violence implicit in its narcissistic appropriations. From *Taxi Driver* through *Goodfellas* (1990), this tension appears as a disturbing reflection of the position of their own audiences, acted out, for instance, in the public media's acceptance of Travis Bickle's grotesque slaughter in the name of Iris's family or Henry Hill's amicable pleading, to the explicitly acknowledged audience of *Goodfellas,* of gangland brutality as a part of a happily active home life. Travis, Henry, Rupert, and a variety of other Scorsese characters are able, in short, to reconcile—horribly and happily—a domestic utopia and its terrible violence only through the eyes of the public media.[2]

The tension in that reconciliation is the tension of the fan whose desire for stardom is always maintained and inhibited by the knowledge that the reconciliation cannot be achieved or can be achieved only as a kind of false relic (such as Travis's photo in the newspaper). Whereas the desire of the traditional fan has always been maintained and postponed by the social and physical barrier of the cinematic screen and the cinematic institution, Rupert however inhabits a cinema without walls and barriers—not unlike that of the preclassical spectator who supposedly could mistake and approach the cinematic image as if it were an inhabitable world. Every night he is able to appropriate Jerry within his private domestic space; he quite literally creates a cult of media images within the basement clubhouse of his utopian fantasy.

At the start of the movie, Rupert is no more than one of many extremely passionate fans of Jerry Langford, seeking the cultish material of an autograph to place in his book, which features the signatures of Marilyn Monroe, Ernie Kovacs, a host of other celebrities—and his own. When he manages to intercede between Langford and the increasingly violent mob, he is allowed to ride briefly with the star and receive a perfunctory—and clearly meaningless— invitation to audition for Jerry's show. When that invitation is regularly and politely denied by Langford's slick network handlers, Rupert remains absolutely consistent as a cultist in pursuit of the objects, people, and environments that will allow him to define himself in terms of the starry images of the media: he kidnaps the star in order to ransom him for an appearance on the show. However violent and terroristic this action is in one sense, in another it becomes just another interpolation of himself into the imagistic material that *is* media identity and media power for Rupert. Like his need to collect famous names or his furtive theft of Langford's monogrammed handkerchief, he has merely collected the real person as an image.

For Rupert, the gunpoint abduction is all part of his stand-up performance; here all social realities are also performative realities. As a passionate fan, Rupert can easily usurp the place of the performer since from the beginning that performer is no more than an imagistic extension of the fan's private space. Jerry Langford, in his brooding and minimalist isolation, appears as the remnant of the modernist artist as aristocracy, still maintaining hierarchical notions of boundaries and differences (yet still needing to walk the streets as if they were a stage where he responds to admiring fans). For the gawdy Rupert, however, any place is his stage, and the charm and horror of his character is that he never recognizes a public space beyond his private, performative control. He blithely occupies the Langford business offices calmly insisting he will wait there until Jerry can listen to his act; he transforms a public telephone near Times Square into his "business office" while waiting for Langford to return his call. Frequently, the film switches, with no traditional cinematic punctuation to mark the move, to Rupert's fantasies which Rupert then lives out as realities: an encounter with a former high-school classmate after sixteen years leads to an immediate marriage proposal; and a daydream invitation leads Rupert to the door of Langford's summer house.

As a performer, not an artist, he orchestrates all contingencies on his own stage, like the comedian who creates a sketch from a line tossed from the audience. Just as he and Masha physically take Jerry off the streets as part of a comic masquerade (silly hats and dark glasses), the comic monologue that Rupert finally performs on the show is apparently a painfully comic reassembling of the ugly or tragic realities of his real past (jokes about his alcoholic parents, their rejection of him; "I see the awful terrible things in my life and turn them into something funny," he observes blandly). The culminating moment of the comic monologue (viewed by 87 million television fans) is the seamless spinning of the kidnapping itself into the stand-up performance: he jokes how "the only way I could break into show business was by hijacking Jerry. . . . He's tied up in a chair somewhere." This line, of course, gets the biggest laugh from the audience, and leads quickly and logically to a conclusion in which Rupert receives a one-million-dollar advance to write his memoirs in jail (*King for a Night*) and, following his release from jail, does indeed become a late-night celebrity, inhabiting his own utopia.

In this performative take-over of the public sphere by the individual, the notion of the individual here is paradoxically redefined by complete incapacity to differentiate an internal and external reality, or to put it another way, by a total evacuation of an internal subjectivity and a reconstitution of it as absolute narcissism. Instead, the surface of a mass-media logic and images fully replace any more traditional figures of psychological crisis (family, parents). Rupert's life is a basement stage with cardboard replicas of Liza Minnelli and Langford recreating the setting of a late-night talk show; occasionally the voice of his mother intrudes from above, only to be quickly dismissed or smoothly integrated into the fantasy. Rupert easily accommodates himself to this scene because he is bothered by no more internal or subjective depth than these cartoon cutouts. When Langford is held at gunpoint in the townhouse of Masha (Rupert's equally obsessed friend), his capture is a strange domestic opportunity to fit him with a red sweater she had knitted for the television personality: "This is the look I like to see him in. . . . I'm so glad I went with the red. It looks great on him." Perhaps the strangest feature of this fitting is how Langford's actual physical presence in the room seems *not* to trouble his status as a media presence (an immobile television image that basically doesn't talk back), which these terrorist-fans can move and address as if he were entirely subject to their personal desires and manipulations within that domestic place.[3] In the bizarre candle-lit seduction sequence that follows, Masha positions the bound-and-gagged Langford (wrapped from head to toe in tape) at an elegantly set dinner table and performs her passion through a series of entertainment stereotypes: she wants "to be black" like Tina Turner; does a torch-song version of "Come Rain or Come Shine"; and face-to-face with the media figure, which is her only unconscious, she fully unleashes that unconscious, "I feel completely impulsive, anything could happen. . . . I want to tell you everything about myself."

For the viewer, the overriding effect of this uncomfortable twisting of comedy is a kind of continuous embarrassment, an embarrassment that parallels the very real violence that seems to fade into the background of the narrative performances.[4] Rupert is, of course, the "constant embarrassment" (in Masha's words), but the violence implicit in that embarrassment erupts even in Langford, who responds to his embarrassment (of being held captive by a toy gun) by smashing Masha in the face. In general, embarrassment can be described as both a psychological and social recognition of and a response to the "inappropriate" claims of the individual or private group on accepted cultural and public regulations and boundaries. Unlike public shame or social shock (especially of the avant-garde kind), embarrassments, for oneself or for others, suggest the emotional pain or awkwardness of not knowing about a socially hidden part of oneself or about some unknown public truth or mores. In his essay, "Embarrassment and Social Organization," Erving Goffman notes that embarrassment "clearly shows itself to be located not in the individual but in the social system wherein he has his several selves." Thus, for viewers identifying with the embarrassing party, it becomes a kind of social invasion and contagion: "Having no settled and legitimate object on which to play out their own unity, the others find themselves unfixed and discomfited. This is why embarrassment seems to be contagious, spreading, once started, in ever widening circles of discomfiture" (108, 106). As embarrassments make clear that there is no socially essential morality or truth, they enact another version of Baudrillard's sense of "obscenity": embarrassments are most disturbing and threatening because they indicate that basic lack of clarity between the public and private realms and how easily any one at any time can be victimized by an inappropriate appropriation of a public place. The potential for anyone to embarrass or be embarrassed is one of the slightest yet ubiquitous measures of terrorist dynamics in everyday life, of emotional violence that easily erupts as social violence when the private acts itself out as its own public spectacle.

Of the relentlessly embarrassing moments in the film, surely the most acute is the sequence in which Rupert fabricates and then acts on an imagined invitation to Langford's estate, the most extreme of

Rupert Performs a Home: Invading the Langford Estate (*The King of Comedy*, 20th Century-Fox, 1982)

many instances when Rupert appropriates social space for the performance of his imaginary space. In part to impress Rita, a woman from his miserable high-school years, he arrives at the celebrity's palatial home, nonchalantly forces his way in by announcing to a domestic manservant that he has arrived to spend the weekend with Jerry, and then makes himself comfortably at home, explaining many of the objects and photos that he has come to know by watching his now real host as a television host within Rupert's own home. As the ruse becomes exposed (through telephone calls to the golfing Langford and then his outraged appearance at the home), the social horror grows more and more clumsy and violent as it evolves around the excrutiatingly embarrassed Rita. After Rupert tries to spin Langford's insults into jokes ("We could set up a story when you invite all your friends here and throw them into jail"), he finally returns to the original invitation to call, which Rupert mistook as truth. When Langford screams, "I told you to call to get rid of you," Rupert replies, "So, I made a mistake," and Langford shoots back, "So did Hitler." Flippant as the connection may be in Langford's mouth, the mistake that Rupert and Hitler share is the critically political one of violating the accepted ratio of private and public life. Even within the stupidity of a social embarrassment as a "misappropriation," there lurks a politics of violence and horror.

Perhaps the most disconcerting maneuver of *The King of Comedy* is how dexterously it inscribes its own audience in the embarrassing pleasure of that politics of misappropriation. During the scene in Langford's home, Rupert's date Rita becomes more and more intoxicated by finding herself in this media home, and, in a peculiar close-up at the end of the sequence, she snatches a small souvenir from a table. She willingly engages, in short, in the same appropriative violence that just humiliated her as a spectator. Similarly, the audience of the film finds itself spun in the very web that describes its discomfort. At one point, for instance, Rupert rehearses in his basement before a larger-than-life photograph of a laughing audience; as the camera tracks away down an empty hall, the soundtrack creates the audience laughter that Rupert hears, fittingly "canned" laughter which technologically and commercially aims to invade the space of an audience outside the edge of a film or television image. In other places, as in the seduction sequence, the extraordinary performances of Bernhardt and De Niro dominate and almost naturalize the absurdity of the various situations they invade. It is as if the panache of the performance fully distracts the viewer from the violence that these characters do to the surrounding contingencies. If from the very beginning Rupert is just one of many fans and private performers like him, the technological and performative extensions of the narrative gather our perspective as contemporary spectators, not innocently, within the same cultish community of private performers, terroristic fans, and the politics of embarrassment. As Ed Sikov describes this domestic cinema without walls and the embarrassing scandals it adumbrates (including that of John Hinckley):

> In revealing Rupert's disturbance as being connected to the effects of representations, and in treating the information being contained in every image as being highly manipulative and yet beyond control, Scorsese turns a scandal back on itself. Not a sociological battle between nuts and celebrities, Scorsese's conflict is played out on the screen, any screen, right in anyone's own home. (21)

The final embarrassment is thus ultimately our own capacity to be fans and the need to create Ruperts for and of ourselves. In the closing sequence, the film completes the *mise-en-abyme* logic that it has been pursuing by locating the perspective of the movie audience alongside the live television audience that thunderously applauds Rupert as the new king of comedy, inventor of his own utopia. Where the film opens with the familiar media stage of a late-night show, it concludes with a similar stage for Rupert's appearance as the new king of comedy. With this second stage, however, the audience is clearly visible and the camera angle makes our point of view a part of that audience. Rupert stands complacently smiling at center stage and an announcer's voice, which grows louder and louder on the soundtrack, repeats over and over "Rupert Pupkin, ladies and gentlemen. Let's hear it for Rupert Pupkin." Most audiences of this film undoubtedly feel at this point the embarrassed discomfort of seeing how easily the media and an audience's complicity with that media can replace a familiar public image with another, less stable and more violent, one. Yet, in this final scene there is an imagistic and audial insistence, coupled with Rupert's complacency, that suggests that, within the politics of this culture, we absolutely need and demand this aristocracy in order to distract us from the emotional embarrassments of our public lives and their political realities.

The Terror of Embarrassment: *The Third Generation*

In West Germany in the 1970s, a very uncomical terrorism was practiced by the Red Brigade. For them, terrorism was (they argued) the only available recourse when historical shame and guilt have been successfully blocked by consumer and media culture. For them, terrorism is often a political strategy used to embarrass and violate an explicit political and historical trajectory which, in a German postwar politics of exclusion, has maintained the illusion of progress by presenting that history according to the intensities of a generational logic. This generational logic allows a cultural identity to perform and spin itself according to different economically and socially evolving contingencies, to position itself as a series of discontinuous and different generations, while in fact maintaining absolute, familial continuity. To expose the political embarrassments of that logic—such as the continuing presence of former Nazi officials, like Hans-Martin Schleyer, within the industrial power structure of the economic miracle—is also to terroristically invade and temporarily disturb the comedic stage of the public sphere. Thus, those hilarious and horrific continuities of *The King of Comedy* parallel the more historical ones that Thomas Elsaesser describes behind Fassbinder's account of terrorism in *The Third Generation:* here, as in other films, Fassbinder establishes "above all a continuity within discontinuity, and thus an acknowledgment of collusion of the present with the past on the basis not so much of a hunger for experience but a hunger for images" (*New German Cinema* 269). In making that *unheimlich* of history, fascism, become a contemporary *heimlich*, Fassbinder makes history itself embarrassingly familiar. Unfortunately, according to Fassbinder, the violent embarrassments of terrorism are as easily accommodated by the networks they aim to expose as Rupert's attack is assimilated into stardom or Hinckley's assassination attempt is made to bolster the presidency.[5]

Most specifically, *The Third Generation* describes, through another outrageous kidnapping, the symbiotic relation between terrorism in Germany and international business. Made in 1979, it follows the simultaneously ludicrous and tragic exploits of a terrorist cell in West Berlin. The leader of the group is August, who is later revealed to be working for both the police chief, Gerhard Gast, and the head of a computer corporation, P. J. Lurz, who funds the terrorists in order to sustain a continual state of social emergency.

This state of emergency in turn generates more police protection for the corporation and supposedly sells more computers to monitor the shifting network of dangerous social relations: as Gast offers early in the film, "I once had a dream that capital invented terrorism in order to force the state to protect it better." Acting as the sexual bridge (a quintessentially Fassbinder link of the subjective and social spheres) between business and terrorism, Susanne joins her husband Edgar in the terrorist cell, works as Lurz's secretary, and performs as the lover of Gast, who is also her father-in-law.

The title has two references. The first indicates a third phase of terrorism in West Germany, which, for Fassbinder, had completely lost both the oppositional and intellectual idealism of the first generation represented by Meinhof, Baader, and Ensslin and the second generation's commitment to making those ideals part of a public debate, "those who understood the motives of the first generation and would often become their lawyers" (Fassbinder 69–70). One way of reading this first reference is, I think, across that great divide between modernism and postmodernism whereby any oppositional position can seem to get absorbed into the ubiquitous network of narcissistic spectacles, in Fassbinder's words, "the ecstasy of adventure experienced in the absence of ulterior motives" (71).

The second reference in the title is to the political drama that unites corporate finance and terrorism as it manifests itself in different forms through three different familial generations: Edgar the terrorist, his father Gerhard who is the police chief, and grandfather and grandmother Gast. The three generations live in the same home, and the second sequence of the film features the former-Nazi grandfather expatiating on the way war gives life meaning, just as the son and daughter-in-law prepare to leave for a terrorist meeting—each generation finding new forms of intensity in new forms of political violence. The three generations in the film cover the patriarchs of fascist Germany, their entrepreneurial sons and daughters who spawned the economic miracle, and the terrorists whose anarchistic attacks on that miracle are meant to call attention to empty social values and repressive ideological mechanisms. In this film, however, the generations do not evolve from a far political right to a far political left but from a commitment to the grand public spectacle of a national mass to the spectacle of narcissistic violations of that public space: the nightmare of nineteenth-century idealism that fascism acted out becomes the cultish code of terrorists who identify themselves in *The Third Generation* by invoking Schopenhauer's title *The World As Will and Idea*. From Nazism to terrorism, what serves as the middle phase in this generational evolution is the democratic law of the state where the public spectacle of individual choice and freedom is built on and maintained by private violence, power, and greed. Like Scorsese's many families, the generational image of this family survives violent differences.

In *The Third Generation,* each generation enacts a version of the same intensity, the same image of a narcissistic self-sacrifice to a public sphere. For Fassbinder, all that has really changed from fascism through terrorism are the social contingencies or conditions according to which that image is acted out and the efficiency of public technology to control that image. The key metaphor for this logic becomes a perpetual-motion toy (a string of steel balls that propel each other back and forth) that serves as another "code" identifying the home and apartments of each of the terrorists: like the generation-replacement logic that binds fan to star in *The King of Comedy,* the perpetual circulation of private spectacles of violence unites grandfather, father, and son as they wait their turn in history (a police investigator describes the toy, with unwitting insight, as a "patience game"). In the first section of the narrative, Gast tells Susanne after a sexual tryst, "I've only got the hots for you because you're married to my son"; laughing, Susanne responds, "I despise myself." These generations are perpetually bound together by a narcissism that consumes them as it consumes their public progeny.

Despite the dangerously concrete reality of political terrorism in Europe, these politics are as much a media game as those in Scorsese's film, which in many ways is all that distinguishes Fassbinder's third generation from the other two generations. Anticipating all the television screens and films that form the background of the movie (including one with Nazi war footage), the film opens with Susanne watching a videotape of the suicide—a nihilistic political gesture—that concludes Robert Bresson's *The Devil Probably* (1977) and which belongs to a politics of film before this generation. Shortly after, Gast and Lurz discuss a view from the window which is "exactly like this one" in Tarkovsky's *Solaris* (1971). Then Lurz, who like a media head controls the terrorist plot through his computer offices, remarks on this simulated filmic reality that he has in part helped to create from this powerful office: "In film there is false-hood twenty-four times a second. And since everything's a lie, it's also truth. And that this truth is also an untruth is revealed in every film. It's only that in film ideas disguise the lie and explain it as truth. And for me that's the tiny and only utopia." The politics of film have clearly changed since Godard could claim, "Film is truth twenty-four times a second."

The terrorist cell likewise simulate a play with utopian moments through their disguises, fictional names, and monopoly boards; each terrorist flirts, sadomasochistically, with the idea or image of uto-pian death or subjugation—like Hilde who practices her French by listening again and again to a tape of a young French girl who later kills herself, like Ilse's heroin addiction. For most of the characters in this film, the public sphere is merely a larger media event through which to explode personal identity through theatrical image. Like Rupert's culture, the world here becomes an easily terrorized stage for the theatrical wills and ideas of individuals whose utopian nar-cissism blinds them to the embarrassment of death. Searching the terrorist apartment towards the end of the film, Gast, the police chief, notes "the obligatory videorecorder."

The spin master within this movie politic is August, the leader of the terrorist cell, a master of disguises, and the orchestrater of con-tingencies. Rupert Pupkin with a real gun, he plays the game for the sake of the game itself, creating situations and scenarios that best fit the contingencies of his own situation. He both arranges for Paul, the professional killer, to join the group, and then, dressed as a woman, he conspires with Lurz to have Paul killed in a carefully staged scene in a Japanese restaurant. Having created the first real crisis in the terrorists' petty lives, he announces "Operation Monop-oly." As August disappears from the scene, they all remake their images and identities, and plot a carnivalesque series of attacks on the public: they decide to rob the bank managed by the husband of one of the terrorists and for "something exciting" to blow up the town hall. Finally, they decide to kidnap Lurz "for release of politi-cal prisoners because "that's the way it's done. . . . It's customary."

Amidst all these spinning theatrics, August, even more so than Rupert, survives through a cynically clear sense of how localized, temporary, and emotionally exploitative terroristic action is. Not unlike Rupert's marginal centrality, August's powerful position is

The Third Generation: The Carnival of Contemporary Politics (1979. Museum of Modern Art/Film Stills Archive)

rarely at the center of the image; he spies and lurks on the edges of the many frames within the Fassbinder mise-en-scène as a way of manipulating those images. For him, the private invades and usurps the public only as part of the constant rotation of public images, and his actions are accordingly constantly shifting, reflecting changing allegiances according to changing contingencies. His final meeting with Lurz takes place at the same Japanese restaurant where he had arranged Paul's death: when Lurz notes that "to meet here is very cynical," August responds "or sensible," implying that whereas the conventional public has marked the place in terms of one kind of terroristic violation only he is sensibly cynical enough to reappropriate and spin it again.

In the end, Lurz, the corporate extension of August, and perhaps the public itself, is capable of the same "sensible cynicism." His kidnapping, which concludes the film, is played out by both Lurz and the terrorists as a silly carnival stunt, a theatrical kidnapping that parallels the one that concludes *The King of Comedy.* Here the terrorists wear pig noses and clown outfits, Lurz and bystanders in the street laugh amidst the gunfire. In the next scene, the terrorists prepare to videotape Lurz delivering a ransom appeal, and as the terrorist crew works on the camera, the mise-en-scène, and the script, Lurz on the monitor in the foreground smiles calmly and repeats his lines in take after take. The videotape image that begins the film returns here not as an image watched but as one made for narcissistic recirculation. In this film too, both sides of the camera seem reconciled to the terroristic politics of private performance.

In *The Third Generation,* as a result of the insular focus of the film and the seeming absolute domination of the public sphere by various private interventions, embarrassment rarely disturbs the game. Only in the climactic fifth section, through the character of the benign outsider Bernhard, do the violations of the social sphere suddenly reveal themselves as incomprehensible social embarrassment on the brink of hysteria. After witnessing the violent slaughter of his friend Franz, Bernhard discovers that Gast and a police crew have broken into the apartment and are inspecting objects for clues. When Gast inadvertently mentions that he is Edgar's father, Bernhard is unable to comprehend and assimilate the violent continuities within the appearance of historical discontinuities that supposedly balance the public and private realms. Shocked and confused by this violation, he begins screamingly to repeat Gast's bureaucratic dictations to a stenographer of objects found: "Arrest the blinds, the ashtray, the hat. . . . Arrest the fruitcake!" In Bernhard's not inaccurate vision of these politics of space and objects, nothing can escape the appropriating assault of social theatrics.

During the opening images, *The Third Generation* announces itself as "a comedy in six parts about parlor games of cruelty and madness, similar to fairy tales told to children to help them bear their lives unto death." Recalling Godard's *Tout va bien* (1972), the bitter irony in this self-characterization is that the subject of the fairy tale is the unmistakable political violence that pervades especially West Germany but also much of the rest of the contemporary Western world. Whereas the trajectory that links the fantastic logic of *The King of Comedy* with an actual political arena is as oblique and contingent as that arena itself, in *The Third Generation* the fairy tale of images is searingly—and very emotionally—close to the political realities of terrorism, media participation, and a conservative backlash in West Germany, and thus can only appear as a grotesque distortion. *The Third Generation* is above all else a response to the political crisis surrounding the Mogadishu airline hijacking, the Schleyer kidnapping and killing, and the suspicious deaths of Baader and Meinhoff. Before the beginning of section one, the movie quotes Helmut Schmidt's statement in *Der Spiegel,* thanking the jurists for ignoring questions of constitutionality in investigating those actions. Referred to explicitly in the opening credits, these events are the same that propelled *Germany in Autumn* (1978), the collective effort meant not so much to document the events or the subsequent social panic in Germany but to engage and counter the controlled spin that the conservative government was giving those events. With *The Third Generation,* however, the possibility of even this kind of alternative perspective on political events has been cynically absorbed into the generational logic that has made both terrorism and oppositional politics merely a media event. All that remains is to spin the spin, like Bernhard, in even more offensive, delirious, and basically self-defeating turns.[6]

This film, therefore, does not so much implicate its audience in the politics of embarrassment but becomes an embarrassment itself, a grotesque emotional affront and political insult to its own audience. A cynically fantastic and self-defeating fairy tale, it collapses the cultural and aesthetic divisions that have usually allowed those same social actualities to be acted out by a spectator through a safer and more appropriative logic on a variety of other cultural screens. In this action, *The Third Generation* becomes a formal, social, and emotional assault: it takes from its audience and then returns the utopian look of a generational logic and narcissistic appropriation as an incoherent, suicidal carnival. The formal confrontation—where the audial and visual layering rarely allows a coherent point of view across the many overlapping soundtracks and multiple internal frames—becomes, as Anton Kaes describes it, "an assault; its deafening aggressive soundtrack (constant radio announcements are layered over dialogue) and its disorienting cuts (which serve to erase distinctions between terrorists and victims, pursuers and pursued) frustrate the viewer in the extreme" (101). The assault of these formal constructions reflect, then, the dizzying spin of variously unacceptable ideological alignments in the film, which offend, socially and emotionally, a political spectrum from the far left to the far right, from reactionary heterosexuals to gay activists. As with its continual, winding tracking through the apartment and the reversing of foreground and background focus, no political or formal position finds a stable or acceptable place in relation to this film. Here Sylvere Lotringer's description Baudrillard's practice may suggest an ideological attack more appropriate to Fassbinder: "You send them spinning away from you like tops. You wholly embrace the movement that animates them, you amplify their concepts to the maximum, pulling them into the vortex of your own dizziness. You draw them into an endless spiral which, like the treatment of myth in Levi-Strauss, leads them bit by bit to their own exhaustion" (132).[7] Like the textual and formal assaults within the film, this social figuration affronts an audience to the point of exhaustion.

Making historical discontinuities into continuities, terrorists into entrepreneurs, political actualities into carnival performances, and cinematic space into an impenetrable image, *The Third Generation* offends by refusing those viewers that *The King of Comedy* embarrassed by inscribing. If both films demarcate a generational logic within the narcissistic performance of contemporary politics, Fassbinder's film returns those positions to social and historical mean streets, while aggressively evacuating them of any subjectivity and stability. Spectators as performers remain the main players on the contemporary political stage but that stage is now the spinning slaughterhouse of the public sphere where to invade it is to be sooner or later reduced by it to nothing but an exhausted exterior. Watching the film (and many other Fassbinder films), an audience, figuratively and literally, *plays itself out,* exteriorizes its own private utopia as a masochistic, public fairy tale. Our social embarrassment about Rupert becomes our social humiliation as Bernhard.

Spin Cycles: *My Beautiful Laundrette*

That the narcissistic terrorism of *The King of Comedy* and *The Third Generation* proceeds from and perhaps only exaggerates the media carnival of contemporary politics does not, however, foreclose other political paths across that terrain. If, to return to Aronowitz, "mass politics signifies . . . the end of public discourse," and postmodern politics (like those of Lurz) then take "as [their] objective the pragmatic willingness of ruling groups to accommodate the demands of organized movements, . . . [t]his assessment provides the basis for the terrorist alternatives, but also for the countercultures." Thus, the utopian spin of contingencies, shared across much of the contemporary political spectrum, can offer alternatives beyond despair and cynicism:

> Even if utopian thought seeks to transform the present by articulating an alternative future, its power lies in its lack of respect for politics as the art of the possible, in its insistence that realism consists in the demand for the impossible. Utopianism is discursive terrorism to the degree that it challenges the prevailing historical and instrumental rationality of bourgeois culture. (54–55)

Within these other utopias, "new social movements speak in postmodern voices; they enter the national and international arena speaking a language of localism and regionalism," addressing rather than subverting power (61). Here Fassbinder's sadomasochistic carnival might approach the kind of political potential, with its contending heterogeneous voices and players, that Bakhtin once saw for it.

In Stephen Frears's *My Beautiful Laundrette*, the clash of political ideologies and utopias across the terrain of generations thus appears neither subversive nor cynical, while yet remaining more socially complicated than either of the two previous films. Here the generations are marked off not only by their chronological periods but in their different crosscultural alignments. Johnny is a young working-class British punk with earlier ties to the right-wing National Front, and Omar is a second-generation Pakistani, decidedly unpolitical. Their otherwise fairly straightforward love story (admittedly without the complexities of *Sammy and Rosie*) develops around and against Omar's left-wing Papa, whose political activity has forced him to leave his homeland for London, Omar's uncle Nasser, a successful businessman in England, and Omar's drug-dealing cousin Salim. At first glance, the dividing lines between these and other figures in the film seem fairly schematic: the traditional Pakistani culture of Nasser's wife; the radically left second generation of Papa, committed to ideas of utopian change; and the materialistic third generation of Nasser and Salim, committed only to profit and comfort.

Yet, these neat generational distinctions quickly get absorbed into the shifting pastiche that describes living in contemporary England, unable to maintain even that logic of continuity within discontinuity. Here changing social and political positions are not so much contradictions but adjustments to the contingencies within a Thatcher regime of "chronic instability" and "alien parentage" (Richard Rose 380, 57). Nasser, who characterizes himself and Salim as professional businessmen, not "professional Pakistani," describes England as "a country which we hate and love," where "you can get anything you want" if "you know how to squeeze the tits of the system." He has an attractive, intelligent mistress, Rachel, who asks for and receives sensitivity and independence, yet the demands of his daughter, Tania, for independence are gruffly rebuffed within the traditional mores and accoutrements of his home. His wife meanwhile is ultimately forced to concoct an ancient potion with which she places an effective spell on Rachel. Paralleling and counterpointing Nasser, the radical Papa admits that "the working class has been a great disappointment to me," and his hopes for Omar are the very conservative ones of a good education and a good wife. After leaving both the National Front and his punk pals behind, Johnny the squatter becomes, with little hesitation, Johnny the landlord.

This is, as one character observes, a community of "in-betweens" without homes or traditional historical places, whose lives are always contingent responses to their present yet who realize, in the words of one of Johnny's punk pals, "Everyone has to belong" somewhere. Within a much more sympathetic context, these are the postmodern relatives of Rupert and Fassbinder's terrorist cell, both suspended and mobilized across generational and social continuities, producing and performing themselves atop historically layered and socially shifting surfaces, all of them attempting to reassemble out of contingencies at least the temporary image of a home. Indeed, perhaps the most acute argument here is that, at least within this segment of contemporary culture, there are only mobile margins, which in the absence of a dominant center, become themselves a transient series of centers.

For *My Beautiful Laundrette,* the most important center among this culture of only margins is the relation between Omar and Johnny, which turns on the realization that contingent—and often temporary—alliances (financial and emotional) are what make the contemporary world turn round. Breaking with his father, Omar realizes that money and its spectacles are the formula for success, not ideas. Or, in the more suggestive terms of the film's title, happiness lies in attracting and laundering money through the personal conjunction of theatrical aesthetics and business, a media "Ritz among laundrettes."

At the Laundrette: The Utopia of Spin Cycles (*My Beautiful Laundrette*, Orion Pictures, 1985. Museum of Modern Art/Film Stills Archive)

That this mutual business venture provides the excuse and context for re-igniting a love affair between the two men emphasizes once more the contingency of even one's emotional life within a public sphere. Making both one's public and private way through a social landscape in which the old is continually collapsing and being recycled through the new, in which transcultural yuppies rehab the shells of traditional houses, requires especially a spin cycle whereby the material of a rapidly deteriorating culture can be reappropriated for the needs of private individuals—or, in the case of Johnny and Omar for the needs of a local and no doubt temporary relationship. Whether it is their socially unacceptable homosexual relationship or their theft of Salim's drug money (heroin becoming "powders"), Omar and Johnny survive through the ability to absorb, launder, represent, and perform the complications of social and historical life according to more desirable contingencies and as an image that their audience can applaud. (In a sense, I think, this same political necessity of performing according to social and economic contingencies might help mitigate the charge that Frears and his screenwriter Hanif Kureishi merely fantasize this relationship as a heterosexual romance.)

As with *The King of Comedy* and *The Third Generation,* the conflicts and negotiations in this film take place in spatial and territorial terms. (It is thus no coincidence that the laundrette is next to a "Turf Accountant," which, for the British at least, combines an economic denotation and a spatial connotation.) The first sequence of the film shows Salim and a black henchman forceably evicting Johnny and a another squatter from an abandoned tenement, and, from that point on, the reality and metaphor of "squatting" invades the narrative as a way of describing all the characters' marginal and temporary relations to the places where they live. Although most of these characters are haunted by the feeling or illusion that "people should make up their minds where they are," space and place are never more than shifting locations that one inhabits and cultivates as always foreign and moveable ground. (Unlike more romantic modernist films, here "home" does not even function as a lost reality or future dream except perhaps for the second-generation Papa who moans that "this country has done us in . . . we should be there, home"; for the majority, home is simply a temporary convenience.) Tania wants to be anywhere but with her family and is willing to leave with either

Omar or Johnny as a lover. Her familial home is itself a mass of cultural and sexual dislocations, and, in the end, Papa and Nasser watch from a window as a medium shot shows Tania, on her way to another home, visually swept off the platform by a series of trains that rush across the screen.

As in *Sammy and Rosie Get Laid* (1987), the violence that pervades *My Beautiful Laundrette* is terroristic especially in its refusal to adhere to any ideological lines or goals: the right and left find its invasive tactics equally useful. From the eviction of the squatters or Salim's almost casual running-down of a punk with his car to the curse of a skin disease (which Nasser's wife puts on Rachel), violence has little to do with a personal relation with a person or object; instead, it subsists on the anonymity and randomness of its agency, or, more accurately, it acts fundamentally as a sign that people and places have nothing but contingent security or stability. When Salim discovers Omar's theft of his drugs, he threatens violence if the money is not repaid but later offhandedly refuses the money as unimportant, claiming the threat was simply a "test." Thus, one reviewer's reservation about the movie that "some of the violence seems gratuitous" understates what is precisely the point about how even the less physical politics of terrorism throughout the film reflect contemporary culture (Quart 38).

Like all terroristic violence, that in *My Beautiful Laundrette* is about "style" as a utopian intervention: an indication that no reality or place is safe from a spin through an alien representation, threatening to make reality itself merely a conglomerate of competing styles invaded and unsettled by the contending images of entrepreneurial forces. Style is an appropriation like Rupert's or the terrorists', a smooth, theatrical and imagistic negotiation of difference, but especially in this film, the more political and social sense of stylistic appropriation as a very real violence comes to the foreground. When the punks attack Salim—an act of vengeance directed first at his faceless car—his subsequent beating seems almost choreographed as a media image similar to the riots in *Sammy and Rosie* or the social violence in *Dangerous Liaisons:* the first part of the attack is shot entirely from inside the laundrette so that the violence is presented silently through the window in the background, as if it was taking place on a television screen.

In the film, consequently, an exaggerated style and the overdetermined allegory of the plot that goes with it stand out as a kind of dominating surface over the grisly, almost documentary, landscapes of south London, with the laundrette itself being the grand spectacle of style within this landscape. Similar to some Fassbinder films, there is a hyperrealistic quality to various images and scenes: colors have an excessively bright or resonant look as in the blues and golds (the colors of the British presidential flag of Pakistan) that suffuse the scene when the punks first approach Salim's car early in the film; the framing and staging of particular sequences stand out as self-consciously theatrical. Paralleling the fairy-tale allegory of the plot, style, in short, works to appropriate the streets, its actions, and its meanings, but unlike the streets of Fassbinder's public sphere, that narcissistic carnival of style never entirely succeeds: social actualities and realistic surfaces contend too powerfully, and characters, precisely because they are at the intersection of so many contending generational and social theatrics, are capable of distinguishing their fluid subjectivity from its stylistic locations. Style and the film's allegory of style map, I think, shifting spaces not so much about personal triumph but about the temporary triumphs of utopian allegories of style.

During Salim's beating, therefore, Johnny's intervention on behalf of his enemy becomes a surprising twist of a politics of sensible cynicism one slight but politically critical degree. At first, this action seems simply one more illogical or self-serving betrayal of his old alliances. Yet, without much narrative explanation, there also appears to be a wry, oblique loyalty at work here: perhaps partly out of guilt for his past National Front activities, partly out of his love for Omar, and partly out of sympathy for Salim, Johnny leaves the laundrette to defend Salim, Omar's distant and unfriendly relative. Reacting to and mobilizing contingencies in this case now suggests the possibility of extending the narcissism of contemporary life to include the situational plight of another, of making temporary and superficial alliances based on the emotional illogic of compassion and a sense of one's own history. Indeed, the ideology of this gesture seems largely accidental, mostly thoughtless, and entirely localized. Yet, it is one of those rare instances within the territory of postmodern culture where its usually violent, unforgiving conditions allow something other than cynicism. Perhaps because of its transitory significance, outside of a generational logic and seemingly unmotivated, it offers a small but convincing space within the theatrics of contemporary political life, a space where some ethical sense of a shared human community briefly figures itself, in a kind of transitory cult, as an emotional bond beyond the violence of a familial logic.

That Johnny's intervention here is unexpected and to a certain extent illogical focuses a politics of surprise that informs the entire film. Earlier in the narrative, Omar sits with a gathering of Pakistani men at Nasser's home, when suddenly in the glass doors behind the group Tania appears baring her breasts. Omar's amused surprise is of course a product Tania's exhibitionistic disruption of this cult of patriarchs and boys (the daughter of the chief patriarch no less) and her unabashedly trying to seduce Omar across that space. Like Johnny's rescue of Salim and the editing of much of the film, it disconcerts and "surprises" its characters and its viewers by destabilizing different mise-en-scènes or crossing those spaces with "inappropriate" figures and actions. In this, these actions unexpectedly foreground what Jameson calls new visibilities ("Class and Allegory" 724), formerly placed on the margins or in the backgrounds of exhausted traditional spaces. Like the visual politics of embarrassment and humiliation, surprise here describes a way of destabilizing or terrorizing a world by defining it as always subject to contingencies and cycles of reappropriation. With surprise, however, that destabilization and those contingencies respond to an active or empowered agent: if the politics of those other two emotions describe a subject who is either evacuated of any subjectivity at all or excluded from any self-determining subjectivity, the politics of surprise imply a social subject who can act and can choose to act, even if that subjectivity always changes itself as it changes its structure. To be surprised or to surprise someone means, unlike even the implied paralysis of Benjamin's "shock," to be literally opened to new potentials, to be made aware of your ability to have a place in a space full of unconsidered potential. Tania, after all, is an empowered and enabled player in this scene, even if she is constantly changing the terms of her subjectivity (she is willing, as a version of Micki in *Choose Me*, to propose to both Omar and Johnny if it will enable her to escape her confining home). The politics of emotional surprise frees a spectator to imagine ways one *could* cross all those contending spaces and productively form cults of shared interests.

Far more than those earlier figures of embarrassment and humiliation, this is a *power* of emotion.

In the final sequence of the film, a medium close-up shows Omar cleaning up Johnny and their playfully splashing water on each other. What this water launders finally is a fragile affection, attempting to maintain and extend itself against the weight of the generations that surround it and the destructive pull of the streets. It is a small but utopian spin, like the laundrette itself, where locals otherwise unknown to each other occasionally share a room to recycle their clothes. Located in the backrooms and background of culture, this private community of two vastly different gay men in the back of the laundrette is refigured by the film to move to the foreground of social space. As Jameson puts it, if "the locus of our new reality, and the cultural politics by which it must be confronted, is that of space," then the narcissistic theatrics of postmodern politics and their private utopias can be refigured "onto at least two levels: the practical matter of this place, this terrain, and these resistances; and then above and beyond that, the cultural vision of Utopian space of which this particular enclave is but a specific figure" (Stephansen, "Regarding Postmodernism" 15). This refiguring is the utopian enclave that *My Beautiful Laundrette* provides for its various viewers, a glimpse of a small, semi-private community of two gay guys whose public significance may be, as one writer put it, that England "may yet be changed by innovation" (Kopkind 560).[8]

As with many of the films in this study, it is most appropriate that, as Pam Cook notes, *My Beautiful Laundrette* is "quintessentially a TV product, even down to built-in natural breaks" (332). Made as part of a "Film On Four" series, this Frears's film addresses very specific local issues through the domestic utopia of home viewing. Within this context, there are mildly terroristic disruptions and disturbances that inform its address: the confrontations of race and class, urban decay and unemployment, sexual love outside the heterosexual family. But, like the thematics of its plot and style, the invasion of the home by these images becomes appropriately presented as a highly mobile and contingent background that quickly moves to a social foreground, that is, like the media background within the local domestic spaces that have become the central arena for contemporary politics. In responding to the structure of this reception, *My Beautiful Laundrette* addresses its viewers across the distracted glance of those domestic spectacles, which is the only place perhaps where that glance and that narcissism can be refigured as communities with shared needs.

The politics of contemporary films are fashioned, therefore, across a variety of potential social positions, even as these audiences share a profoundly contemporary view of movie images. *The King of Comedy* embarrasses its audience by enlisting them in the violence of their spinning their own performative spaces in ever-tighter circles. *The Third Generation* assaults and humiliates any sense of power and integrity in inhabiting those spaces within a public sphere. *My Beautiful Laundrette* aims to empower those same viewers by offering the utopian possibility of refiguring, in sometimes surprising ways, that space of distraction and appropriation according to the shared needs and wishes of shifting social alliances and subjectivities. Finally, it is as part of this same contemporary predicament, I believe, that a film like *Do the Right Thing* (1989) and the many kinds of outrage it has provoked make sense, in W.J.T. Mitchell's words, as a "utopian venture," as "a monument of resistance, of 'intelligent violence,' a ready-made assemblage of images that reconfigures a local space—literally, the space of the black ghetto, figuratively, the space of the public images of race in the American public sphere" (898).

In those terroristic utopias that we now make of the movies, in short, there are many practical politics to be played out. If many of the old social securities and frameworks are no longer available to contemporary movie spectators, those viewers now have the option to activate and be activated by what they watch in a variety of ways across those violent and emotional social spaces connecting private and public life. Recognizing the options within those spaces may be all that differentiates a violent fan from a political innovator.

AFTERWORD
Mobile Homes

Outside the walls of the cinema, viewers are of course still subject to institutional and social determinants. Yet if the contemporary cinema offers audiences more than a way to pass time, it is the sense and feeling that those determinants are also mobile images that can be inhabited in many different ways. Outside those walls, vacancies can become potentials; viewers emptied of subjectivity by the homogeneous address of a blockbuster industry can become mobile viewers across heterogeneous identities. Outside, the many nostalgias that characterize contemporary culture can become, like so many narratives, from *Heaven's Gate* to *Blade Runner* to *Born in Flames* (1983), memories of different futures. In the streets as well as their homes, viewers can re-invent those images after or instead of merely appropriating them. This is why, as movies have become less and less central in our lives, the way we watch them has become more and more important culturally.

The contemporary predicament through which movies address their audiences may mean that we often find only illegible and cultish configurations, which make traditional categories for understanding and responding to the movies a disturbing and difficult fit: auteurs are too much part of commercial circulation, generic roads lead to outer space, and narratives have dissipated into cartoon performances. Because of this, watching the multitude of television and movie images today requires, it seems to me, an unusual mobility across the interminable digressions and distractions that condition those viewings. Viewing now means continually reinventing oneself and one's spatial and social location, appropriating and inhabiting, sometimes simultaneously, the most disparate of images, from cartoons to documentaries, from commercials to epics. If movie and television images are the backgrounds that viewers perpetually glance at, they can function both as narcissistic performances and as reimaginings of that narcissism in rapidly and widely changing forms. Whether that film is *Platoon* or *Full Metal Jacket,* we are able, because of their address and our position before it, to project ourselves into that particular history, battle and resist it, appropriate different moments, characters, or images, and ultimately mobilize that movie across our specific historical position in many different ways as part of many different social configurations and historical meanings.

"Against the Gaze," Norman Bryson has argued about paintings in the nineteenth century, "the Glance proposes desire, proposes the body, in the *durée* of its practical activity" (122). More so than many of us might always be conscious of, glancing at the movies means we can *practically* act out and socially reassemble different movies, pieces of movies, and a variety of other cultural media as part of a social and often critically active relation with those images. These practical performances can be as seemingly trivial and quotidian as conversations, fashions, and social decisions about the movies or as weighty as the way videotape has allowed local groups to re-imagine their relationship with their culture (from Asian students mimicking Western icons to South American Indian tribes videotaping and circulating tribal ceremonies).[1] A cultural shift, however, is quite apparent: if movies and other images suffuse cultural life, viewers in their daily variety, not the medium, have become the message.

In Paul Schrader's *Patty Hearst* (1988), a spoiled heiress from the sixties turned terrorist in the seventies serves as a parable for this viewer, a figure of unbound narcissism whose identity and subjectivity are violently crushed and refashioned when she is kidnapped from her home. A media fantasy, she becomes the quintessential postmodern subject, feared and fascinating because "No one wants to accept their mental state as so fragile, to be turned into a totally different person." In a final, mostly monologic address directed at her publisher father, however, she looks directly into the camera and breaks with his authority, announcing that she has chosen a new lawyer ("He's not rich or famous, but he's mine"). Then, sounding (according to the father) like her nineteenth-century grandfather, she claims the media as her vehicle rather than her victimizer: "We're going to change the climate, change people's minds about me. . . . The press is a tool; we'll use it. . . . People fantasized about me for so long, they thought they knew me. When I finally surfaced—a real person, a real story—I was inconvenient. But I'm here and I'll let them know it." Schrader's Hearst becomes here the audience of her own image and in that capacity she is determined to reinvent herself socially. She becomes, perhaps, a paradigm for the potential of the contemporary viewer to turn the loss of subjectivity and a centered self-image into inventions and interventions within contemporary social institutions. For the Hearst character and the contemporary viewer, in John Tagg's words about postmodern cultural practice in general, "Cultural practices always involve the mobilization of determinate means and relations of representation. . . . There is no meaning outside this framework but it is not monolithic. The institutions which compose it offer multiple points of entry and spaces for contestation—and not just on the margins" (5–7).

Inventing different historical logics within that space guarantees nothing of course. This is why viewers and their liaisons are so dangerous within contemporary film culture and why there is so much personal and social anxiety connected with postmodern culture. Finally these conditions require that we decide for ourselves how and what we will invent in our lives, in which images we will choose to make our home, and how those images will impact on our lives, for whatever length of time we decide. The very transitory nature of those inventions, however, may assure those actions the modest protection of a "holding zone" (James "Poetry" 176) where its power as a cultural and historical intervention is in simply "putting an arbitrary stop to this revolving causality" so "that a principle of political reality can be saved" (Baudrillard *Simulations* 31).

If with a movie classic like *Casablanca* a kiss is just a kiss and with a cultish postmodern film like *Choose Me* a kiss becomes part of an obsessive narcissistic performance, Frears's *Sammy and Rosie Get Laid* offers another kind of kiss. Rosie first kisses her husband

Sammy in front of his father Rafi (an older generation who, as a politician in Pakistan, apparently practiced his fascism as terrorism): "That is one kind of kiss," she says. She then crosses over to Victoria, the black semi-militant squatter who has befriended Rafi. While the embarrassed father and son look on, she passion-

Sammy and Rosie Get Laid: The Political Configuring of a Kiss (Warner Bros., 1989)

ately kisses Victoria: "Now that is a very different kind of kiss, with a different social, political meaning," she remarks.

This small, potentially narcissistic gesture, performing the fragmentation and instability of its own subjectivity, is a glancing moment within a narrative that is constantly spinning in a wide variety of "distracting" directions. It seems both to contrast and complement the blockbuster scale of the spectacular riots that fill the streets outside Sammy and Rosie's flat and the multiple private sexual infidelities that cross the narrative. Within the privacy of their living room, however, it reminds its three viewers, by momentarily invading and refiguring their attention, that even the most private and localized action can and should be socially configured and reinvented. Like Rosie's social work, the American journalist's fashion photographs of the riots, or the lesbian couple's personal "fact-finding" investigation of Rafi's political past, this temporary refiguring of attention represents the diversely active relations between a heterogeneous subject as an active viewer and the decentered images of her culture. It dramatizes, finally, that utopian vision which aligns a glance at a kiss inside a room with the conflicts in the streets beyond its walls, where individuals are continually inventing temporary wall-less communities.

NOTES

▫▫▫

Chapter 1: Glancing at the Past

1. There have, of course, been more than a few other examples of gross financial and artistic excess, most studios having produced their version of *Heaven's Gate:* Spielberg's *1941* (1979) and Coppola's *One from the Heart* (1982), for instance, were similar examples of greed and confusion. Moreover, the shuffling corporate maneuvering of the studio hierarchy is now entirely emblematic of the appropriative instability of the contemporary movie industry. In 1972, Alan Ladd, Jr., left Twentieth Century-Fox to form the Ladd Company. In 1984, the powers at Gulf and Western forced Barry Diller and Michael Eisner out of their executive positions at Paramount, despite the former's achievements with quality films and the latter's with popular hits such as *Flashdance* (1983); Diller resurfaced at Fox, Eisner at Disney. By the end of 1983, Coca-Cola had chosen to restrict Frank Price's cautious, though eminently profitable, leadership of Columbia; he subsequently moved to Universal.

2. Pamela Falkenberg formulates this point as how "the art cinema itself is transformed: the art cinema as self-opposition, the art cinema as the critique of the art cinema. . . . The remake of Jean-Luc Godard's *À bout de souffle* (1959, released March 1960) by Jim McBride's *Breathless* . . . might be characterized as . . . the hyperrealism of the remodeling of a model" (50–51).

3. That this situation has altered even since 1988 is one indication of the volatility of contemporary culture. The video market, which acted as the support and safety net for most of these small films, may have peaked. Research by Vidmark Communications shows a twenty-three percent drop in 1988 for orders by retailers for low-budget films, while movies like *Who Framed Roger Rabbit?* and *Batman*

continue to organize those blockbuster audiences. At the same time, independent investors have started to recognize that even sensational profits on a small-budget film are not the same as modest profits on a blockbuster release. By 1989, Lorimar, Tri-Star, New World, Atlantic, Vestron, and Island Pictures had gone bankrupt or been reorganized. (Some of this can be attributed to new tax laws, which have undone the attraction of investing in these companies.) Yet, despite all this, new talent and producers always seem in the wings, and the only clear direction at this point seems to be new alignments to form other semi-independent channels as the conglomerate studios absorb established money and talent.

4. The number of tickets sold has remained fairly steady at 1.1 billion for the last twenty-five years; the MPAA calculates that the number of so-called adults has increased thirty-nine percent since 1984.

5. With similar concerns but a larger historical scope, Barbara Klinger has described the bond between film commerce and reception where the glances of the spectator can be characterized as the "digressions" of the social viewer—digressions which she limits to the mini-narratives and promotional images that surround a movie and thus create "economies of viewing that *fragment* rather than assemble the text" (10).

6. Robin Wood's *Hollywood from Vietnam to Reagan* is one of several other recent accounts that uses that war as a focal point for recent film history. I would also recommend Michael Anderegg's collection *Inventing Vietnam: Film and Television Constructions of the U.S.-Vietnam War.*

7. Jameson goes so far as to locate the foundation for a contemporary logic of generations in the sixties: "The reemergence in the 1960s of the concept or category of the 'generation' as a way of narrativizing our lived experience and our broadest visions of recent history itself is a very significant symptom indeed" ("On Magic Realism" 310).

8. This historical privileging of contemporary music within the media excess of contemporary culture is described by David James: "What is significant about music is not just that its appeal is aural and that for some arbitrary or transcendental reason hearing has become a fashionable sense, but rather that the fact of its aural functioning made it an uniquely pliable medium in a period of expanding leisure time and the penetration of all life processes by the media industries" ("Poetry" 185).

9. Concentrating on the function of rock and roll in these Vietnam films, James writes: "The movies have authority in neither the experience of Vietnam nor representations of it, neither practically nor textually. In both they have been replaced by rock and roll, which will solve the awkwardness of Vietnam and make it possible for people to 'want to hear about it'" ("Rock and Roll" 83).

10. A common reading of these Vietnam movies is as repressive strategies. It should be clear that this is not what I believe is primarily going on. Different from Richard Slotkin's "regeneration through violence," the logic of regeneration that I

have been arguing is, at best, a retrieval of lost humanity and subjectivity, often disguised or displaced as preposterous machismo (Chuck Norris, Sylvester Stallone, and so forth). Like the characters that figure in so many of these films, the problem is that humanity has been so emptied out that there is nothing to repress.

Chapter 2: Illegible Films

1. Besides Bordwell's summary of the tradition of reading as interpretation in film criticism, I would recommend Tom Conley's "Reading Ordinary Viewing." Most sustained arguments about the problematics and dominance of reading practices are found, naturally, in literary studies, such as E. D. Hirsch's *The Aims of Interpretation* or Paisley Livingston's *Literary Knowledge: Humanistic Inquiry and the Philosophy of Science*.

2. The most cogent statement of this position is perhaps Umberto Eco's *The Role of the Reader*. The plurality of Roland Barthes's readers in *S/Z* takes it in a slightly different direction, but it remains committed to ideational patterns.

3. Besides those readings based in one or another model of realism, this reading formation would involve historical analysis that contextualizes cultural investigations, such as those of national cinemas, and cross-cultural readings that denaturalize cultural and historical place.

4. Barthes's argument is for a "third meaning" or obtuse sense in the photographic or cinematic image, beyond an informational or symbolic sense: it is "evident, erratic, obstinate" (*Image–Music–Text* 53). There are, additionally, many less semiotic versions of film's resistance to reading. More generally, Jean-François Lyotard argues how "figuration" in itself resists semiotic inscription (*Discours, Figure*).

5. See Michael Chanan's *The Dream That Kicks: The Prehistory and Early Years of Cinema in Britain*, Miriam Hansen's *Babel and Babylon: Readings in American Silent Film*, John Fell's (ed.) *Film before Griffith*, and Tom Gunning's "Early Film, Its Spectators, and the Avant-Garde."

6. See Hansen's *Babel and Babylon*.

7. This summary is admittedly a specific use of Benjamin's wide-ranging positions and a detour around much of what he inherited from Kracauer. See Miriam Hansen's "Benjamin, Cinema and Experience" and Kracauer's "Cult of Distraction." My interest is less in the complexities of Benjamin or the sources of these terms than in their contemporary relevance in a historically different sense.

8. See Maureen Quilligan, *The Language of Allegory* and Craig Owens, "The Allegorical Impulse," where he discusses "allegories of illegibility," which simultaneously promise and refuse meaning.

9. Responding to the violence against women in the film and the women's apparent complicity in that violence, Brunette and Wills are less accommodating to

the necessity of intervention when they argue that "the call for a singular reading is not so much a form of oppositional resistance as an abdication of strategical possibilities, at worst a form of critical masochism" (149n). See also Lynd Bundtzer's discussion of Dorothy as "a wild image of maternal joy . . . outside Lynch's narrative frame" (200).

10. These are from *Nation* 243.12 (1986): 383, *Time* 128.12 (1986): 86, *National Review* 38.21 (1986): 54.

11. Despite its apparently trans-historical claims, David Bordwell's recent call for film critics "not to read a film" is, from this point of view, not so much a revelation for but a reflection of a contemporary historical predicament; his historical poetics, as an alternative to reading a film, makes sense as a perspective for only those films outside the confusion of the present and its failure to offer a traditional scientific distance (*Making Meaning* 248–272).

Chapter 3: Film and the Culture of Cult

1. Bruce Austin's sociological, quantitative study comes to the same conclusion: "Cult films are not *made* (as, for example, a producer sets out to *make* a musical or Western) as much as they *happen* or *become*. It is doubtful that a filmmaker *could* consciously contrive to make a cult film; it is the audience that turns a film into a cult film. This implies that cult films are not genre-bound" (*Immediate Seatings* 83).

2. See Dick Hebdige's *Subculture: The Meaning of Style* for the best general discussion of cult style; J. Hoberman's and Jonathan Rosenbaum's *Midnight Movies* is the standard, mainly thematic, introduction to cult movies.

3. A wonderful alternative ending for the film had the statue in which Paul has been encased break open to reveal nothing inside.

4. Scorsese's self-parody as the "Man with the Lights" in Club Berlin, randomly flashing characters with his spotlight, seems to correlate with this description of a narrative without traditional authoritative control.

Chapter 4: The Commerce of Auteurism

1. A collection of the major documents and debates about auteurism can be found in *Theories of Authorship* edited by John Caughie. See also Robert Sklar, *Movie-Made America: A Cultural History of American Movies* (292–294).

2. See Peter Wollen, *Signs and Meaning in the Cinema;* Michel Foucault, "What Is an Author?" in *Language, Counter-Memory, Practice* (113–138); Stephen Heath, "Comment on 'The Idea of Authorship,'" (86–91).

3. The single most useful source for this position is Brecht's *Le Procès de*

quat'sous: experience sociologique (148–221). See also Ben Brewster, "Brecht and the Film Industry" (16–33).

4. A very direct and oversimplified example of this position, which responds to the special status of the auteur but fails to reflect on its larger cultural and critical implications, is Jospeh Gelmis, *The Film Director as Superstar.* "Over half the movie tickets sold today," he notes, "are bought by moviegoers between the ages of sixteen and twenty-five. They know what a director is, what he does and what he's done" (xvii).

5. Steven Bach's *Final Cut* is one particularly significant account of the contemporary auteur as self-promoting superstar. A much more sophisticated analysis of that tendency is Sheila Johnston's "A Star is Born."

6. One of the most sensational examples of how the production process of an auteur can usurp the film in several senses is Les Blank's film *Burden of Dreams* (1981/2), which documents Herzog's making of *Fitzcarraldo.*

7. See Timothy Corrigan, "Producing Herzog: From a Body of Images," in *The Films of Werner Herzog: Between Mirage and History,* ed. Timothy Corrigan (3–19).

8. In *Narration in the Fiction Film* David Bordwell recognizes this fragmentation of the auteur but sees it as a mere variation on the traditional auteur-narrator: "The popularity of R. W. Fassbinder in recent years may owe something to his ability to change narrational personae from film to film so that there is a 'realist' Fassbinder, a 'literary' Fassbinder, a 'pastiche' Fassbinder, and so on" (210). Obviously I believe that mobilizing these different agencies within an auteurist category has larger implications.

9. Not surprisingly, the ambivalent identification of the artistic self within the commerce of auteurism and its promise of the great spectacle of self becomes fraught with all the liturgical guilt of sin and self-sacrifice: "I am more interested in technology than I am in content. This, in some circles, is the same as admitting that one is a child molester and likes it. The truth is that I am interested in a content I can't get at. I yearn to be able to move into a world where story and content is available to me; where my ideas connect into a pattern that could be identified as a story. But I truly cannot get there" (Coppola "The Director on Content").

10. See also Thomas Elsaesser, *New German Cinema.*

11. Kluge remarks: "We are not postmodernists. I believe in the avant-garde. But that is not where the distinction lies. There are two different approaches: dominating the materials and respecting the materials. The first would take materials to realize intentions. The opposed attitude would be to accept the autonomy of these materials, which are living" (Liebman 57).

12. For additional examples of these moves within Kluge's artistic practice and biography, see Thomas Bohm-Christl, ed., *Alexander Kluge.*

13. Alexander Kluge, *Die Patriotin: Texte/Bilder 1–6* and *Die Macht der Gefühle.*

14. See also Michael Chanan (ed.), *Chilean Cinema*.

15. The most pertinent work of Schefer's in this context is his *L'homme ordinaire du cinéma*.

16. One is tempted to compare this exchange from the 1971 *Nobody Said Anything:*

"You remember the letter she sent me?"

"You mean the one about committing suicide?"

"No, no, the other one. . . ."

Chapter 5: Genre, Gender, and Hysteria

1. These specific historical and cultural variations on this connection between gender and genre have only recently started to get adequate attention. The issue is introduced in large terms in Neale (56–61). More focused are Mary Ann Doane's *The Desire to Desire* and Dana Polan's *Power and Paranoia*.

2. Barry Grant's *Film Genre Reader* is a recent anthology of a wide variety of these models and positions. Tom Schatz's *Hollywood Genres* is the standard introduction.

3. For a more extensive and both clinically and theoretically more detailed discussion, see Monique David-Menard, *Hysteria from Freud to Lacan*.

4. Despite the usual emphasis on the female hysteric, male hysteria has of course always been implicit in the model. Besides Kirby's study, there is also "Medusa's Head" by Neil Hertz, which discusses male hysteria in the context of the French Revolution. See also Jacqueline Rose's discussion of female hysteria in George Eliot's novels in *Sexuality in the Field of Vision* (117–122).

5. Indicative is the bizarre public reversal by *Time* magazine of its evaluation of *Bonnie and Clyde*. After trashing the film in the summer of 1967 (25 August), it hailed the film as its cover story on 9 December of that year.

6. See Dominique Laporte's discussion of debris and waste as part of the semiotics of postmodern culture.

7. For an alternative reading of photographic reality in this film, see Kearney's discussion in *The Wake of Imagination*.

Chapter 6: Interminable Tales of Heaven and Hell

1. This deferral towards a heavenly space that transcends narrative can be found more subtly in a wide variety of contemporary narratives from Wenders's *Wings of Desire* (1989) to Rudolph's *Made in Heaven* (1989), Diane Keaton's *Heaven,* and a variety of slightly less transparent examples such as Bertolucci's *1900* (1976) and *The Last Emperor* (1989). Robert Burgoyne has described what I would

call this utopian place in Bertolucci's films as "the analysis and narrative ordering of historical occurrences not as an immutable order of events but rather as if they were episodes in an 'unfinished plot' whose meaning is not fixed" (57).

2. This is not to say that these industry tactics are a more prevalent part of the movie scene today than they were thirty years ago; they are not. Numbers, however, have little to do with my argument as will be seen. Using a strict definition, there of course were more sequels and remakes available in the forties and fifties than there are today. See Simonet (158–159).

3. Compare Thomas Dougherty's discussion of teenpics in the 1950s, *Teenagers and Teenpics*.

4. On the issue of boredom specifically, compare Jameson's position in "Reading without Interpretation" as a more particular detour around history: "Even taken in the narrower realm of cultural reception, boredom with a particular kind of work or style or content can always be used productively as a precious symptom of our own existential, ideological, and cultural limits, an index of what has to be refused in the way of other people's cultural practices and their threat to our own rationalizations about the nature and value of art" (203).

5. See Tony Bennett's and Janet Woollacott's *Bond and Beyond* (158–164).

6. James connects this shift to various marketing and commodity moves during this period (such as the rapid spread of home stereo units), until by 1974 the $2 billion per year music industry had overtaken the movies ("Poetry" 166).

7. This, I believe, begins to describe the difficult bind of a political rock video where the common slide is from the theatrics of politics (with the Talking Heads, for instance) to the theatrics of theatrics.

8. Compare this with a narrative like Chantel Akerman's *Jeanne Dielman* (1975), which might be subtitled *3 1/2 Days*. Here the boredom of repetitions aspire to what Julia Kristeva has called "anterior temporal modalities" (17), a disturbing reconciliation of a woman's placid heaven within the only narrative terms allowed her, terms which look unbearable according to subjective (patriarchal) motivations.

Chapter 7: Spinning the Spectator

1. In her interview with *Esquire* afterwards, Jodie Foster adds her spin, explaining that her initial reaction was to laugh hysterically.

2. This self-reflexive guilt is interestingly carried over into the videotape version of *Taxi Driver*, which is frequently introduced by a disclaimer that the film does not condone Travis's concluding victory. Here too, there is the fear that there may be too many Ruperts in the home audience waiting to spin this movie.

3. Ed Sikov has pointed out that, while Johnny Carson turned down the part of Jerry Langford because he was nervous about how easily the fan can confuse live

action and entertainment, the substitution of Jerry Lewis into that figure is barely noticeable: "Instead of just having Carson play Carson, an image made in its own image, Scorsese then had the opportunity to play one image against another while also playing it against itself" (18).

4. This politics of embarrassment is found throughout contemporary film culture, most consistently and noticeably in films by the various members of the Monty Python groups: for instance, the vomiting scene in the posh restaurant in *The Meaning of Life* (1983) or Otto's excruciating baiting of the stuttering Michael Palin in *A Fish Called Wanda* (1988).

5. As I suggest in the "Afterword," the link between *The King of Comedy* and *The Third Generation* might be the later *Patty Hearst* (directed by Paul Schrader, the author of *Taxi Driver*). There the main character is the terrorist as media fantasy, the individual locked in a private room and stripped of any subjectivity.

6. For a more extended discussion of how identity in Fassbinder's films remains "irreducibly exterior" (57), see Kaja Silverman's "Fassbinder and Lacan: A Reconsideration of Gaze, Look, and Image."

7. An equally important institutional affront that this film activates is through Fassbinder's image as an auteur. Placed between commercially successful and far more accessible projects like *The Marriage of Maria Braun* (1978) and *Lili Marlene* (1980), *The Third Generation* anticipates his refusal to remain a dependably coherent auteur, which soon after is taken even further in *Querelle*. See chapter 4.

8. One way of conceiving what is refigured here is according to Ian Connell's term "structures of feeling," which Ann Gray makes use of in "Reading the Audience."

Afterword

1. While the first could refer to the 1989 Chinese student demonstrations in Tiananmen Square, a specific example of the second is provided by Terence Turner's "Visual Media, Cultural Politics, and Anthropological Practice: Some Implications of Recent Uses of Film and Video Among the Kayapo of Brazil."

WORKS CITED

Adair, Gilbert. "The Rubicon and the Rubik Cube: Exile, Paradox and Raul Ruiz." *Sight & Sound* 51.1 (Winter 1981/1982): 40–44.

Altman, Rick (ed.). *Genre: The Musical*. London: Routledge & Kegan Paul, 1981.

———. "A Semantic/Syntactic Approach to Film Genre." In *Film Genre Reader*. Ed. Keith Barry Grant. Austin: University of Texas Press, 1986.

Anderegg, Michael. *Inventing Vietnam: Film and Television Constructions of the U.S.–Vietnam War*. Ann Arbor: University of Michigan Press, 1990.

Arac, Jonathan (ed.). *Postmodernism and Politics*. Minneapolis: University of Minnesota Press, 1986.

Aronowitz, Stanley. "Postmodernism and Politics." In *Universal Abandon?: The Politics of Postmodernism*. Ed. Andrew Ross. Minneapolis: University of Minnesota Press, 1988. 46–62.

Austin, Bruce A. *Immediate Seatings: A Look at Movie Audiences*, Belmont, Ca.: Wadsworth, 1989.

Bach, Steven. *Final Cut: Dreams and Disaster in the Making of "Heaven's Gate."* New York: William Morrow, 1985.

Bakhtin, M. M. *The Dialogic Imagination*. Austin: University of Texas Press, 1981.

Balio, Tino. *United Artists: The Company That Changed the Film Industry*. Madison: University of Wisconsin Press, 1989.

Barthes, Roland. *Camera Lucida: Reflections on Photography*. Trans. Richard Howard. New York: Hill and Wang, 1981.

———. *Image–Music–Text*. Trans. Stephen Heath. New York: Hill and Wang, 1977.

———. *Roland Barthes*. New York: Hill and Wang, 1977.

———. *S/Z*. Trans. Richard Miller. New York: Hill and Wang, 1974.

Baudrillard, Jean. "The Ecstasy of Communication." In *The Anti-Aesthetic: Essays on Postmodern Culture*. Ed. Hal Foster. Seattle: Bay Press, 1983. 126–134.

———. "The Implosion of Meaning in the Media and the Implosion of the Social in the Masses." In *Myths of Information: Technology and Post-Industrial Culture*. Ed. Kathleen Woodward. Madison, Coda Press, 1980. 137–148.

———. *The Mirror of Production*. St. Louis: Telos, 1975.

———. *Simulations*. New York: Semiotext(e), 1983.

Belloni, Gabria and Lorenzo Codelli. "Conversation avec Francis Ford Coppola." *Positif* 161 (1974): 47–54.

Bellour, Raymond. "The Unattainable Text." *Screen* 16 (Autumn 1975): 19–27.

Benjamin, Walter. "The Author as Producer." In *Reflections: Essays, Aphorisms, Autobiographical Writings*. Ed. Peter Demetz. Trans. Edmund Jephcott. New York: Harcourt Brace Jovanovich, 1978. 220–238.

———. *Charles Baudelaire: A Lyric Poet in the Era of Late Capitalism*. London: Harry Zohn, 1973.

———. *The Origin of German Tragic Drama*. Trans. J. Osborne. London: New Left Books, 1977.

———. "The Work of Art in the Age of Mechanical Reproduction." In *Illuminations*. Ed. Hannah Arendt. Trans. Harry Zohn. New York: Schocken, 1969. 217–252.

Bennett, Tony and Janet Woollacott. *Bond and Beyond: The Political Career of a Popular Hero*. New York: Methuen, 1987.

Bird, Elizabeth et al. "On Postmodernism and Articulation: An Interview with Stuart Hall." *Journal of Communication Inquiry* 10 (Summer 86): 41–56.

Bohm-Christl, Thomas (ed.). *Alexander Kluge*. Frankfurt: Suhrkamp, 1983.

Bordwell, David. *Making Meaning: Inference and Rhetoric in the Interpretation of Cinema*. Cambridge: Harvard University Press, 1989.

———. *Narration in the Fiction Film*. Madison: University of Wisconsin Press, 1985.

Bordwell, David, Kristin Thompson, and Janet Staiger. *Classical Hollywood Cinema: Film Style & Mode of Production to 1960*. New York: Columbia University Press, 1985.

Bouzereau, Laurent. "An Interview with David Lynch." *Cinéaste* 15.3 (1987): 38–40.

Braudy, Leo. "The Sacraments of Genre: Coppola, De Palma, Scorsese." *Film Quarterly* 39.3 (Spring 1986): 17–31.

Brecht, Bertolt. *Le Proces de quat'sous: experience sociologique*. Paris: Editions de l'Arche, 1970.

Brewster, Ben. "Brecht and the Film Industry." *Screen* 16.4 (Winter 1976/1977): 16–33.

Brooks, Peter. "Freud's Masterplot." *Yale French Studies* 55/56 (1977): 280–300.

Browne, Nick. "The Spectator-in-the-Text: The Rhetoric of *Stagecoach*." In

Movies and Methods. Vol. 2. Ed. Bill Nichols. Berkeley and Los Angeles: University of California Press, 1985. 458–475.

Brunette, Peter and David Wills. *Screen/Play: Derrida and Film Theory.* Princeton: Princeton University Press, 1989.

Bryson, Norman. *Vision and Painting: The Logic of the Gaze.* New Haven: Yale University Press, 1983.

Buci-Glucksmann, Christine and Fabrice Revault D'Allonnes. *Raoul Ruiz.* Paris: Dis Voir, 1987.

Bundtzer, Lynd K. "Don't Look at Me! Woman's Body, Woman's Voice in *Blue Velvet.*" *Western Humanities Review* 42.3 (Autumn 1988): 187–203.

Burgoyne, Robert. "Temporality as Historical Argument in Bertolucci's *1900.*" *Cinema Journal* 28.3 (1989): 57–68.

Bygrave, Mike. "Hollywood 1985." *Sight & Sound* 54.2 (Spring 1985): 84–88.

Canby, Vincent. "Confessions of a VCR Recruit." *The New York Times* 24 November 1985: C.20, 26.

———. "The VCR's Are Causing Something Momentous." *The New York Times* 1 December 1985: C.19, 28.

Caughie, John (ed.). *Theories of Authorship: A Reader.* London: Routledge & Kegan Paul, 1981.

Cavell, Stanley. *The World Viewed: Reflections on the Ontology of Film.* Cambridge: Harvard University Press, 1979.

Chanan, Michael. *Chilean Cinema.* London: BFI, 1976.

———. *The Dream That Kicks: The Prehistory and Early Years of Cinema in Britain.* London: Routledge & Kegan Paul, 1980.

Cherchi-Usai, Paolo. "The Unfortunate Spectator." *Sight & Sound* 56.3 (Summer 1987): 170–174.

Chown, Jeffrey. *Hollywood Auteur: Francis Coppola.* New York: UMI Research Press, 1981.

Christie, Ian. "Exile and Cunning: Raul Ruiz." *Monthly Film Bulletin* 51 (Dec. 1984): 71–127.

Clark, Michael. "Vietnam: Representations of the Self and War." *Wide Angle* 7.4 (1985): 4–12.

Clément, Catherine. "Le rire de Demeter." *Critique* 323 (April 1974): 306–325.

———. *Opera, Or the Undoing of Women.* Trans. Betsy Wing. Minneapolis: University of Minnesota Press, 1988.

Cohn, Lawrence. "Hollywood More Original Than Supposed: Lucrative Re-do Wave Still Minor." *Variety* 7 December 1985: sec. 2, p. 17.

Collins, Jim. *Uncommon Cultures: Popular Culture and Postmodernism.* New York and London: Routledge, Chapman and Hall, 1989.

———. "Watching Ourselves Watch Television, or Who's Your Agent?" *Critical Studies* 3.3 (Oct. 1989): 261–281.

Conley, Tom. "Reading Ordinary Viewing." *Diacritics* 15.3 (Spring 1985): 4–14.

Cook, Pam, "My Beautiful Laundrette." *Monthly Film Bulletin* 52 (1985): 332–333.

Coppola, Francis. "The Director on Content versus Technology." *Washington Post* 29 August 1982: 3D.

Corrigan, Timothy (ed.). *The Films of Werner Herzog: Between Mirage and History.* London and New York: Methuen, 1986.

———. "Werner Schroeter's Operatic Cinema." *Discourse* 3 (Spring 1981): 46–59.

Cott, Jonathan. "Francis Coppola." *Rolling Stone* 18 March 1982: 20–24, 76.

David-Menard, Monique. *Hysteria from Freud to Lacan.* Ithaca: Cornell University Press, 1989.

Debord, Guy. *Society of the Spectacle.* Detroit: Black & Red, 1983. (Paris, 1967.)

Deleuze, Gilles. *Cinema 1: The Movement-Image.* Trans. Hugh Tomlinson and Barbara Hammerjam. Minneapolis: University of Minnesota Press, 1986.

———. *Cinema 2: The Time-Image.* Trans. Hugh Tomlinson and Robert Galeta. Minneapolis: University of Minnesota Press, 1989.

Denzin, Norman. "*Blue Velvet:* Postmodern Contradictions." *Theory, Culture and Society* 5.2–3 (1987): 461–473.

Derrida, Jacques. "The Law of Genre." In *On Narrative.* Ed. W. J. T. Mitchell. Chicago: University of Chicago Press, 1981. 51–79.

Doane, Mary Ann. *The Desire to Desire: The Woman's Film of the 1940s.* Bloomington: Indiana University Press, 1987.

Docherty, David, David Morrison, and Michael Tracey. "Who Goes to the Cinema?" *Sight & Sound* 55.2 (1986): 81–85.

Dougherty, Thomas. *Teenagers and Teenpics.* Boston: Unwin Hyman, 1989.

Dyer, Richard. "Entertainment and Utopia." In *Genre: The Musical.* Ed. Rick Altman. London: Routledge & Kegan Paul, 1981. 176–189.

———. *Stars.* London: BFI,.1979.

Eco, Umberto. *The Role of the Reader: Explorations in the Semiotics of Texts.* Bloomington: Indiana University Press, 1979.

———. *Travels in Hyperreality.* New York: Harcourt, Brace, Jovanovich, 1986.

Ehrenstein, David. "Raoul Ruiz at the Holiday Inn." *Film Quarterly* 40.1 (Fall 1986): 2–7.

Eidsvik, Charles. "Machines of the Invisible: Changes in Film Technology in the Age of Video." *Film Quarterly* 42.2 (Winter 1988/1989): 18–23.

Eisenstein, Sergei. *The Film Sense.* New York: Harcourt, Brace, & World, 1942.

Ellis, John. *Visible Fictions. Cinema: Television: Video.* London: Routledge & Kegan Paul, 1982.

Elsaesser, Thomas. *New German Cinema: A History.* New Brunswick: Rutgers University Press, 1989.

———. "Two Decades in Another Country: Hollywood and the Cinéphiles." In *Superculture: American Popular Culture and Europe.* Ed. C. W. E. Bigsby. London: Paul Elek, 1975. 199–216.

Falkenberg, Pamela. " 'Hollywood' and the 'Art Cinema' as a Bipolar Modeling System." *Wide Angle* 7.3 (1985): 44–53.

Fassbinder, Rainer Werner. *Filme befreien den Kopf: Essays und Arbeitsnotizen.* Ed. Michael Toteberg. Frankfurt am Main: Fischer Taschenbuch, 1984.

Fell, John L. (ed.). *Film before Griffith.* Berkeley: University of California Press, 1983.

Feuer, Jane. *The Hollywood Musical.* Bloomington: Indiana University Press, 1982.

Foucault, Michel. "What Is an Author." In *Language, Counter-Memory, Practice.* Ithaca: Cornell University Press, 1977. 113–138.

Gelmis, Joseph. *The Film Director as Superstar.* Garden City, N.Y.: Doubleday, 1970.

Giddens, Anthony. *Central Problems in Social Theory: Action, Structure, and Contrast in Social Analysis.* Berkeley: University of California Press, 1983.

Goffman, Erving. "Embarrassment and Social Organization." In *Interaction Ritual: Essays on Face-to-Face Behavior.* Garden City, N.Y.: Anchor, 1967. 97–112.

Grant, Barry Keith (ed.). *Film Genre Reader.* Austin: University of Texas Press, 1986.

Gray, Ann. "Reading the Audience." *Screen* 28.3 (Summer 1987): 24–35.

Gundersen, Edna. "Cult Films." *USA Today* 21 October 1985: 3E.

Gunning, Tom. "Early Film, Its Spectators, and the Avant-Garde." *Wide Angle* 8.3/4 (1986): 63–70.

Habermas, Jürgen. *Communication and the Evolution of Society.* Boston: Beacon, 1979.

Hagedorn, Roger. "Technology and Economic Exploitation: The Serial as a Form of Narrative Presentation." *Wide Angle* 10.4 (1988): 4–12.

Halliwell, Leslie. *Film Guide.* 6th Edition. New York: Scribners, 1987.

Hansen, Miriam. *Babel and Babylon: Readings in American Silent Film.* Cambridge: Harvard University Press, 1991.

———. "Benjamin, Cinema and Experience." *New German Critique* 40 (1987): 179–224.

———. "Cooperative Auteur Cinema and Oppositional Public Sphere: Alexander Kluge's Contribution to Germany in Autumn." *New German Critique* 24–25 (Fall/Winter 1981–1982): 36–56.

Heath, Stephen. "Comment on 'The Idea of Authorship.' " *Screen* 14.3 (Autumn 1973): 86–91.

———. *Questions of Cinema.* Bloomington: Indiana University Press, 1981.

Hebdige, Dick. *Subculture: The Meaning of Style.* London: Methuen, 1979.

Hertz, Neil. "Medusa's Head: Male Hysteria under Political Pressure." *Representations* 4 (Fall 1983): 27–54.

Hirsch, E. D., Jr. *The Aims of Interpretation.* Chicago: University of Chicago Press, 1976.

Hoberman, J., and Jonathan Rosenbaum. *Midnight Movies*. New York: Harper & Row, 1983.

Hutcheon, Linda. "The Politics of Postmodernism: Parody and History." *Cultural Critique* 5 (1986/1987): 179–207.

James, Caryn. "Yech! It's Jason, Dripping Soap." *The New York Times* 24 July 1988: sec. 2, pp. 1, 21.

James, David E. "Poetry/Punk/Production: Some Recent Writing in LA." In *Postmodernism and Its Discontents: Theories, Practices*. Ed. E. Ann Kaplan. London and New York: Verso, 1988. 163–186.

———. "Rock and Roll in Representations of the Invasion of Vietnam." *Representations* 29 (Winter 1990): 78–98.

Jameson, Fredric. "Class and Allegory in Contemporary Mass Culture: *Dog Day Afternoon* as a Political Film." In *Movies and Methods*. Vol. 2. Ed. Bill Nichols. Berkeley: University of California Press, 1985. 715–733.

———. "Nostalgia for the Present." *South Atlantic Quarterly* 88.2 (Spring 1989): 53–64.

———. "On Magic Realism in Film." *Critical Inquiry* 12.1 (Winter 1986): 301–325.

———. "Periodizing the 60's." In *The Sixties without Apology*. Ed. Sohnya Sayres, et al. Minneapolis: University of Minnesota Press, 1984.

———. "Postmodernism, or the Cultural Logic of Late Capitalism." *New Left Review* 146 (1984): 53–92.

———. "Reading without Interpretation: Postmodernism and the Video-text." In *The Linguistics of Writing: Arguments between Language and Literature*. Ed. Nigel Fabb, et al. Manchester: Manchester University Press, 1987. 199–223.

———. "Reification and Utopia in Mass Culture." In *Social Text* 1 (1979): 130–148.

Jauss, Hans Robert. *Toward an Aesthetic of Reception*. Trans. Timothy Bahti. Minneapolis: University of Minnesota Press, 1982.

Jencks, Charles. *What Is Post-Modernism?* London: Academy Editions, 1986.

Johnston, Sheila. "A Star Is Born: Fassbinder and the New German Cinema." *New German Critique* 24–25 (Fall/Winter 1981–1982): 57–72.

Kaes, Anton. *From Hitler to Heimat: The Return of History as Film*. Cambridge: Harvard University Press, 1989.

Kaplan, E. Ann (ed.) *Postmodernism and Its Discontents: Theories, Practices*. London: Verso, 1988.

———. *Rocking Around the Clock: Music, Television, Postmodernism, & Consumer Culture*. London and New York: Methuen, 1987.

Kearney, Richard. *The Wake of Imagination: Toward a Postmodern Culture*. Minneapolis: University of Minnesota Press, 1988.

Kinder, Marsha. "Back to the Future in the 80s with Fathers and Sons, Supermen & Peewees, Gorillas & Toons." *Film Quarterly* 42.4 (Summer 1989): 2–11.

————. "Music Videos and the Spectator." *Film Quarterly* 38.1 (1984): 2–15.

Kipnis, Laura. "Feminism: The Political Conscience of Postmodernism?" In *Universal Abandon?: The Politics of Postmodernism*. Ed. Andrew Ross. Minneapolis: University of Minnesota Press, 1988. 148–165.

Kirby, Lynne. "Male Hysteria and Early Cinema." *Camera Obscura* 17 (May 1988): 113–132.

Klinger, Barbara. "Digressions at the Cinema: Reception and Mass Culture." *Cinema Journal* 28.4 (Summer 1989): 3–19.

Kluge, Alexander. *Alexander Kluge and the Occasional Work of a Female Slave*. Ed. Jan Dawson. Perth: A Perth Film Festival Publication, 1975.

————. *Die Macht der Gefühle*. Frankfurt am Main: Zweitausendeins, 1984.

————. "On Film and the Public Sphere." Trans. Thomas Levin and Miriam Hansen. *New German Critique* 24–25 (Fall/Winter 1981–1982): 206–220.

————. *Die Patriotin: Texte/Bilder 1–6*. Frankfurt am Main: Zweitausendeins, 1979.

Kopkind, Andrew. "Films." *The Nation* 242 (1986): 560.

Kracauer, Siegfried. "Cult of Distraction: On Berlin's Picture Palaces." *New German Critique* 40 (1987): 91–96.

Kristeva, Julia. "Women's Time." Trans. Alice Jardine and Harry Blake. *Signs: Journal of Women in Culture and Society* 7.1 (1981): 17.

Laporte, Dominique. *Histoire de la merde*. Paris: Christian Bourgeois, 1978.

de Lauretis, Teresa. *Alice Doesn't: Feminism, Semiotics, Film*. Bloomington: Indiana University Press, 1984.

————. *Technologies of Gender: Essays on Theory, Film, and Fiction*. Bloomington: Indiana University Press, 1987.

Liebman, Stuart. "On German Cinema, Art, Englightenment, and the Public Sphere: An Interview with Alexander Kluge." *October* 46 (Fall 1988): 23–59.

Lindsey, Robert. "Francis Ford Coppola: Promises to Keep." *New York Times Magazine* 24 July 1988: sec. 6, pp. 23–27.

Livingston, Paisley. *Literary Knowledge: Humanistic Inquiry and the Philosophy of Science*. Ithaca: Cornell University Press, 1988.

Lopez, Bob. "Scorsese Speaks." *City Paper* 18 October 1985: 16, 18–19.

Lotringer, Sylvere. "Forget Baudrillard: An Interview with Sylvere Lotringer." In *Forget Baudrillard*. Trans. Nicola Dufresne. New York: Semiotext(e), 1987. 128–140.

Lyotard, Jean-François. *Discours, Figure*. Paris: Editions Klincksieck, 1985.

————. *The Postmodern Condition: A Report on Knowledge*. Trans. Geoff Bennington and Brian Massumi. Minneapolis: University of Minnesota Press, 1984.

Macherey, Pierre. *A Theory of Literary Production*. London: Routledge & Kegan Paul, 1978.

Macksey, Richard. " 'The Glitter of the Infernal Stream': The Splendors and Miseries of Francis Coppola." *Bennington Review* 15 (1983): 2–16.

Malraux, André. *The Voices of Silence.* Princeton: Princeton University Press, 1978.

Marcus, Greil. "Journey Up the River: An Interview with Francis Coppola." *Rolling Stone* 1 November 1979: 51–57.

Mayne, Judith. *Private Novels, Public Films.* Athens, Ga.: University of Georgia Press, 1988.

McBride, Joseph. *Orson Welles.* New York: Viking, 1972.

Merritt, Russell. "Nickelodeon Theaters, 1905–1914: Building an Audience for the Movies." In *The American Film Industry.* Ed. Tino Balio. Madison: University of Wisconsin Press, 1976. 59–79.

Metz, Christian. *Le significant imaginaire.* Paris: 10/18, 1977.

Miller, Mark Crispin. "Hollywood: The Ad." *The Atlantic* 265.4 (April 1990): 41–54.

Milne, Tom (ed.). *Godard on Godard.* New York: Viking, 1972.

Mitchell, W. J. T. "The Violence of Public Art: *Do the Right Thing.*" *Critical Inquiry* 16.4 (Summer 1990): 880–889.

Monaco, James. *American Film Now.* New York: New American Library, 1979.

Morris, Meaghan. "Tooth and Claw: Tales of Survival and Crocodile Dundee." In *Universal Abandon?: The Politics of Postmodernism.* Ed. Andrew Ross. Minneapolis: University of Minnesota Press, 1988. 105–127.

Mulvey, Laura. *Visual and Other Pleasures.* Bloomington: Indiana University Press, 1989.

Murray, William. "*Playboy* Interview: Francis Ford Coppola." *Playboy* 22 (1975): 53–68, 184–185.

Neale, Stephen. *Genre.* London: BFI, 1980.

Owens, Craig. "The Allegorical Impulse: Toward a Theory of Postmodernism, Part I." *October* 12 (Spring 1980): 67–86.

———. "The Allegorical Impulse: Toward a Theory of Postmodernism, Part II." *October* 13 (Summer 1980): 59–80.

Pick, Zusanna M. "Chilean Cinema in Exile." *Framework* 34 (1987): 39–57.

Polan, Dana. " 'Above All Else To Make You See': Cinema and the Ideology of Spectacle." In *Postmodernism and Politics.* Ed. Jonathan Arac. Minneapolis: University of Minnesota Press, 1986. 55–69.

———. "Brief Encounters: Mass Culture and the Evacuation of Sense." In *Studies in Entertainment: Critical Approaches to Mass Culture.* Ed. Tania Modleski. Bloomington: University of Indiana Press, 1986. 167–187.

———. *Power and Paranoia: History, Narrative, and the American Cinema.* New York: Columbia University Press, 1986.

Quart, Leonard. "*Blue Velvet.*" *Cinéaste* 13 (1986): 38.

Quilligan, Maureen. *The Language of Allegory.* Ithaca: Cornell University Press, 1979.

Rainer, Yvonne and Ernest Larsen. "'We Are Demolition Artists': An Interview with Alexander Kluge." *The Independent* June 1989: 18–25.

Rentschler, Eric. *West German Film in the Course of Time.* Bedford Hills, N.Y.: Redgrave, 1984.

Rodowick, D. N. *The Crisis of Political Modernism: Criticism and Ideology in Contemporary Film Theory.* Urbana: University of Illinois Press, 1988.

Rose, Jacqueline. *Sexuality in the Field of Vision.* London: Verso, 1986.

Rose, Richard. *Politics in England: Persistence and Change.* London: Faber and Faber, 1985.

Ross, Andrew (ed.). *Universal Abandon?: The Politics of Postmodernism.* Minneapolis: University of Minnesota Press, 1988.

Ruiz, Raoul. "Entretien avec Raoul Ruiz." With Serge Daney. *Cahiers du Cinéma* (special issue) (Autumn 1981): 41–43.

———. "D'Une Institution L'Autre: Entretien avec Raoul Ruiz." *Cahiers du Cinéma* 287 (April 1978): 18–23.

———. "Interviews with Raoul Ruiz." *Cahiers du Cinéma* 345 (March 1983): 7, 74–82.

———. "Les Relations d'Objects au Cinéma." *Cahiers du Cinéma* 287 (April 1978): 24–32.

Ruiz, Raoul and Jean Louis Schefer. "L'Images, La Mort, La Memoire." *Ça, Cinéma* (special issue) 2 (1980): 3–73.

Said, Edward W. "Opponents, Audiences, Constituencies and Community." In *The Anti-Aesthetic: Essays on Postmodern Culture.* Ed. Hal Foster. Seattle: Bay Press, 1983. 135–159.

Sarris, Andrew. "O Hollywood! O Mores!" *Village Voice* 5 March 1985: 5.

Sarris, Andrew. "Stranded in Soho's Mean Streets." *The Village Voice* 17 September 1985: 54.

Schatz, Thomas. *Hollywood Genres: Formulas, Filmmaking and the Studio System.* New York: Random House, 1987.

Schefer, J. L. *L'homme ordinaire du cinéma.* Paris: Gallimard, 1980.

Scorsese, Martin and David Thompson. *Scorsese on Scorsese.* London: Faber and Faber, 1989.

Siegel, Joel. "Alan Rudolph's Urban Fables." *L.A. Weekly* 14–20 March 1986: 38.

Sikov, Ed. *"The King of Comedy." Film Quarterly* 36.4 (Summer 1983): 17–21.

Silverman, Kaja. "Fassbinder and Lacan: A Reconsideration of Gaze, Look, and Image." *Camera Obscura* 19 (January 1989): 54–85.

Simonet, Thomas. "Conglomerates and Content: Remakes, Sequels, and Series in the New Hollywood." In *Current Research in Film: Audience, Economics and Law.* Vol. 3. Ed. Bruce A. Austin. Norwood, N.J.: Ablex, 1987. 152–164.

Sklar, Robert. "Homevideo." *Cinéaste* 14.4 (1987): 60, 29.

————. *Movie-Made America: A Cultural History of American Movies*. New York: Vintage, 1975.

Slotkin, Richard. *Regeneration Through Violence: The Mythology of the American Frontier, 1600–1860*. Middletown, Ct.: Wesleyan University Press, 1973.

Sontag, Susan. *Against Interpretation*. New York: Dell, 1961.

Spivak, Gayatri. "In Praise of *Sammy and Rosie Get Laid.*" *Critical Quarterly* 31.2 (Summer 1989): 80–88.

Stephansen, Anders. "Regarding Postmodernism—A Conversation with Fredric Jameson." In *Universal Abandon?: The Politics of Postmodernism*. Ed. Andrew Ross. Minneapolis: University of Minnesota Press, 1988.

Stewart, Susan. *On Longing: Narratives of the Miniature, the Gigantic, the Souvenir, the Collection*. Baltimore: Johns Hopkins University Press, 1983.

Studlar, Gaylin. "Midnight S/excess: Cult Configurations of Feminity and the Perverse." *Journal of Popular Films and Television* 17.1 (1989): 2–14.

Studlar, Gaylin and David Desser. "Never Having to Say You're Sorry: *Rambo's* Rewriting of the Vietnam War." *Film Quarterly* 42.1 (Fall 1988): 9–16.

Tagg, John. "Postmodernism and the Born-Again Avant-Garde." *Block* (1985/1986): 3–7.

Tambling, Jeremy. *Opera, Ideology and Film*. New York: St. Martin's Press, 1987.

Taylor, Charles. *Human Agency and Language: Philosophical Papers*. Cambridge: Cambridge University Press, 1985.

Theweleit, Klaus. *Male Fantasies*. Two Volumes. Minneapolis: University of Minnesota Press, 1987 and 1989.

Thompson, Kristin. *Eisenstein's "Ivan the Terrible": A Neoformalist Approach*. Princeton: Princeton University Press, 1981.

Thomson, David. *Overexposures: The Crisis in American Filmmaking*. New York: Morrow, 1981.

Turner, Terence. "Visual Media, Cultural Politics, and Anthropological Practice: Some Implications of Recent Uses of Film and Video Among the Kayapo of Brazil." *CVA Review* (Spring 1990): 8–13.

Ulmer, Gregory L. "The Object of Post-Criticism." In *The Anti-Aesthetic: Essays on Postmodern Culture*. Ed. Hal Foster. Seattle: Bay Press, 1983. 83–110.

Walker, Beverly, and Leonard Klady. "Cinema Sanctuaries." *Film Comment* 22.3 (May–June 1986): 61–66.

Wollen, Peter. *Signs and Meaning in the Cinema*. Bloomington: Indiana University Press, 1972.

Wood, Robin. *Hollywood from Vietnam to Reagan*. New York: Columbia University Press, 1986.

Wyatt, Justin and R. L. Rutsky. "High Concept: Abstracting the Postmodern." *Wide Angle* 10.4 (1988): 42–49.

INDEX